The Real North Korea

The Real North Korea

Life and Politics in the Failed

Stalinist Utopia

FULLY UPDATED AND REVISED

ANDREI LANKOV

OXFORD
UNIVERSITY PRESS

OXFORD
UNIVERSITY PRESS

Oxford University Press is a department of the
University of Oxford. It furthers the University's objective
of excellence in research, scholarship, and education
by publishing worldwide.

Oxford   New York
Auckland   Cape Town   Dar es Salaam   Hong Kong   Karachi
Kuala Lumpur   Madrid   Melbourne   Mexico City   Nairobi
New Delhi   Shanghai   Taipei   Toronto

With offices in
Argentina   Austria   Brazil   Chile   Czech Republic   France   Greece
Guatemala   Hungary   Italy   Japan   Poland   Portugal   Singapore
South Korea   Switzerland   Thailand   Turkey   Ukraine   Vietnam

Oxford is a registered trade mark of Oxford University Press
in the UK and certain other countries.

Published in the United States of America by
Oxford University Press
198 Madison Avenue, New York, NY 10016

Library of Congress Cataloging-in-Publication Data
Lankov, A. N. (Andrei Nikolaevich)
The real North Korea : life and politics in the failed Stalinist utopia / Andrei Lankov.
    pages   cm.
"Fully updated and revised."
ISBN 978-0-19-939003-8 (paperback)
1. Korea (North)—Politics and government—1994–2011.
2. Korea (North)—Politics and government—2011–
3. Korea (North)—Foreign relations.   I. Title.
DS935.774.L36   2015
951.9305—dc23   2014013874

9 8 7 6 5 4 3 2 1

Printed in the United States of America
on acid-free paper

CONTENTS

CHAPTER 3 The Logic of Survival (Domestically) 111

CHAPTER 4 The Supreme Leader and His Era 139

CHAPTER 5 Survival Diplomacy 179

INTERLUDE The Contours of a Future: What Might Happen to North Korea in the Next Two Decades 221

CHAPTER 6 What to Do about the North? 231

TRANSCRIPTION

The transcription of Korean personal names has always been a challenge. The book generally follows the McCune-Reischauer system, but in the case of people whose names are frequently spelled differently in the mass media, the established spelling is used instead (this being the case with Kim Il Sung, Kim Jong Il, Kim Jong Un, Kim Jong Nam, and other members of North Korea's top leadership).

ACKNOWLEDGMENTS

The present book would have been impossible without the support and encouragement of many individuals with whom I have discussed the numerous issues dealt with in the book. Among many others, I would like to mention Rüdiger Frank, Scott Snyder, John Park, Stephen Haggard, Nicolas Eberstadt, Marcus Noland, Fyodor Tertitsky, Tatiana Gabroussenko, Kim Yŏng-Il, Kim Sŏk-hyang, Yu Ho-yŏl, Nam Song-uk, Yu Kil-chae, Kim Byŏng-yŏn, and Zhu Feng.

I am especially grateful to Peter Ward, who typed most of the manuscript while correcting my less than perfect English and also providing me with advice on both style and subject matter, as well as with valuable critiques of my ideas and arguments. His involvement with this revised and updated edition was both extensive and vital. I also would like to express my gratitude to Peter Sylvester, who proofread the manuscript for the second revised edition.

When it deals with issues of the recent social and economic developments, the book draws on the results of research supported by a grant from the National Research Foundation of Korea (NRF-2010-330-B00187). I also would like to express my deep gratitude to "Moravius," who allowed me to use some photos from his extensive collection.

The hardcover edition of this book was published in April 2013 and was basically completed the year before. As many readers will no doubt be aware, North Korea has been in the news a lot in the last year, and many changes have occurred there. A new era has begun in earnest inside the country.

This warranted a thorough revision of the book. This paperback edition is thus different from the hardcover in many regards. A chapter on Kim Jong Un has been added, and the rest of the book has been heavily revised.

Therefore, it is hoped that this edition will introduce not only earlier events, but also will acquaint readers with the background to recent and dramatic events that have occurred on the Korean peninsula.

I hope the book will also help readers understand what may happen in the future of this very troubled nation.

INTRODUCTION: NORTH KOREA, THE SURPRISINGLY SANE PLACE

What does the average Westerner think of North Korea? If the person has any experience with the media coverage of this country, he or she will probably think of a number of sound bites. It is "a mad country," "the world's last Stalinist regime," "a nation of nuclear blackmailers," and other similar clichés. Above all, North Korea is "irrational." This country run by a "pigmy" is said to defy common sense and sometimes even the laws of physics.

But there is one problem with these clichés: they are largely untrue. North Korea's leadership is quite rational, and nothing shows this better than its continuing survival against the odds. North Korea is the political equivalent of a living fossil, a relic of a bygone era that few miss. Other similar regimes have long since either changed beyond all recognition or disappeared entirely. Most people remember such regimes with disdain, if at all. How many people in Europe today have ever heard of Antonín Novotný or Mátyás Rákosi?

Yet the Kim dynasty in Pyongyang remain masters of their country. In defying the "political laws of gravity," North Korea today faces an almost universally hostile world. It is a small country with few resources and a moribund economy. In spite of all this, however, it has managed to survive and exploit divisions between the world's major powers to maximum effect. You simply cannot achieve this by being irrational. The North Korean leaders know perfectly well what they are doing. They are neither lunatics nor ideological zealots; rather, they have shown themselves to be remarkably efficient and cold-minded calculators, perhaps the most ruthless and Machiavellian leaders in the world today.

North Korea's leaders are notorious for their gruesome and blood-curdling threats. Many bemused residents of Austin, Texas, were made aware of this when they learned that North Korea had declared its intention to nuke their city in the event of a war between the two Koreas. It is understandable that such things make many question the sanity of those in charge in Pyongyang. However, it is precisely this sort of macabre rhetoric, occasional armed provocation, and the nuclear weapons program that ensure the North Korean government's survival. While Pyongyang's extreme risk-taking may appear near suicidal at times, so far North Korea's leaders have shown that they know where to stop. Indeed, they have employed saber rattling for decades as part of a shrewd (and highly rational) strategy that has succeeded—in most cases, at least—at manipulating other countries into paying a hefty ransom.

This book is, first, about the inner logic of North Korean behavior. This logic is defined by the peculiarities of North Korean society—and the strangeness of the North is not new. I have written this book in order to explain how North Korea has become a hot international issue, and also to elucidate why North Korea's leadership prefers, indeed *needs*, to be an international issue.

The book starts with a short sketch of North Korean history. This is because a familiarity with the history of the North is vital for anyone who wants to understand the country's current predicament. The Kim regime began as a bold experiment in social engineering. This experiment was led by a revolutionary elite, whose efforts were much encouraged—and often directed—by Stalin's USSR. Much of what the government in Pyongyang did initially also enjoyed considerable and active support from the North Korean people themselves.

However, the original rosy expectations and popular enthusiasm were sadly misplaced. Soon North Korea found itself saddled with an inefficient and unsustainable economic model that was dependent on constant infusions of foreign aid. To make matters worse, the North Korean elite became hereditary and almost impossible to challenge or change. As time passed, and with no apparent way out of the predicament, North Korea's economy went from slow decline to disaster zone.

In this regard North Korea differs little from many other countries in the Third World. Bad governance, authoritarian politics, and chronic aid dependency are major problems in several corners of this planet. Yet few places resort to the kind of tactics that have made Pyongyang infamous. The staggering economic success of Korea's other state—the Republic of Korea (ROK), or South Korea, as it is commonly known—is what has made North Korea so very unique, and simultaneously explains many of the extraordinary and tragic choices made by North Korea's leaders.

Even though it was impossible to know back in 1945, South Korea took a path that, at the end of the day, proved to be far more efficient and promising than the choices made by (or partially forced on) North Korea. The existence of the highly successful South Korea has created nearly insurmountable problems for the North Korean elite.

As things deteriorated rapidly from around 1990, the North Korean elite decided not to reform their country. They did this in order to stay in control of their country and people. At the same time, they chose to use diplomacy (backed, when necessary, by a bit of nuclear blackmail) to extract foreign aid, vital for their survival. The decision to not reform ultimately led to a massive famine, not to mention the perpetuation of the country's horrendous prison camp system. Tragically, however, it has worked out well so far for the country's elite: unlike other Communist regimes, the North Korean state has survived against seemingly impossible odds.

As we shall see, the North Korean elite are neither zealous ideologues nor sadistic killers—even though they occasionally look like (and indeed want to look like) both of these. In fact, some of these people might be quite nice human beings who, from time to time, feel sorry about the suffering that their policies have inflicted upon their people. However, given the present situation, they see all alternatives as near suicidal. Indeed, as I will argue, there may be no alternative to current policy if survival is what the North Korean elite wants.

Many suggest that Chinese-style, market-oriented reforms are the solution to the North Korean problem. Some people believe that North Korean decision makers can be lured or blackmailed into starting reforms, while others hope that they will finally come to their senses and do the right thing for their people. However, as we shall see, there is a sound logic behind the stubborn unwillingness among the North's decision makers to follow the Chinese way. Their fears might be exaggerated, to be sure, but they are by no means unfounded.

This book might appear to be rather pessimistic. Even though I contend that there are ways to mitigate the problems and control the damage, it seems that there is no panacea to the North Korean problem.

At the time of writing, a new leadership has begun to emerge in North Korea. As one might expect, the emergence of this new leadership has been accompanied by hopes for a better future for North Korea. As we will see, however, the country's past gives little ground for optimism. Nonetheless, it is of course not completely impossible that the plump and jolly-looking young Kim may well seek to break with the past and reform the country. There is the possibility that he might not agree with the logic of its survival strategy and that he will attempt to improve the lives of the North Korean people. Such attempts might even succeed, but it is far more likely that the old guard is right, and that tampering with the system will ultimately lead to implosion of the regime.

At any rate, we might be on the brink of some serious changes, or even a transformation, in North Korea. Nevertheless, given the earlier experiences and sad present of this country, one should not expect a miracle. On the contrary, if past precedent is anything to go by, changes are likely to be painful and dangerous.

Indeed, it might be that the worst is still yet to come—for both the North Koreans and for outsiders. Hungarians are known to say, "What is worse than Communism? The things that come after it." It is not impossible that one day, North Koreans will recycle this joke, saying, "What is worse than the Kim dynasty? The things that come after it."

We do not know what is going to happen yet, but the eventual transformation of North Korea is unlikely to be easy. At the end of the book, I discuss how North Korea might change, and readers will see that some of the solutions to the current impasse might be more palatable. However, all are deeply flawed.

The North Korean regime might be a source of danger and irritation for the outside world, but its major victims are the North Koreans themselves, the vast majority of the some twenty-four million people who inhabit this unlucky country. They are the primary victims of the regime, but also victims of history. North Korean rulers do what they are doing not because they are "evil" or driven by some quasi-religious fanaticism, but rather because they sincerely believe that they have no alternative. To most of them it seems that any other policy will bring them (and their families) ruin. Unfortunately, their fears might be well founded. The concerns of the "top ten thousand people" (as well as a million or two of their henchmen, big and small) are understandable. This is, of course, of little comfort to the vast majority of the North Korean population whose lives have been—and continue to be—ruined by the regime.

The Real North Korea

CHAPTER 1

The Society Kim Il Sung Built and How He Did It

One cannot understand modern North Korea without having a look at its past. North Korea has never gone through a process of "reform," but this does not mean that it has not changed. The North Korea of Kim Jong Il's era was dramatically different from the North Korea of 1953 to 1994. Nonetheless, the legacy of the Kim Il Sung era hangs heavily over contemporary North Korea.

The North Korea of the Kim Il Sung era was a very peculiar place indeed—arguably, one of the most idiosyncratic places in the entire world. It was established as a Soviet client state, but with a great deal of support, enthusiasm, and hope from below. Soon, it evolved into the archetypal National Stalinist regime, and in this form it managed to survive all outside challenges and exist without much change until the early 1990s. This was the time when the Kim dynastic regime grew and matured, and it was also the time when it learned how to survive and even thrive amidst an utterly hostile external environment.

CAPTAIN KIM RETURNS HOME

On an autumn day in 1945 (the exact date is still in dispute, but it seems to be the 19th of September) a group of men, Asian yet clad in Soviet military uniforms, disembarked from the Soviet steamer *Pugachev* at the Korean port city of Wonsan. The port had recently been taken over by

Soviet forces. Among the arrivals was a slightly stout man in his early thirties, wearing the insignia of a Soviet Army captain. To his comrades he
was known as Kim Il Sung, the commander of the 1st (Korean) battalion
of the 88th independent brigade of the Soviet Army.

This young Soviet captain, soon to become the supreme leader of the
emerging North Korean state, was returning home after almost two decades spent beyond the borders of Korea. In the 1930s Kim Il Sung was a
guerrilla field commander in Northeast China, and by the early 1940s had
become a battalion commander in the 88th Brigade of the Soviet Army.
Nonetheless, he was a native of the city of Pyongyang, which in late August
became the headquarters of the Soviet forces in Korea.[1]

By late August 1945, after a short, intense, and successful military campaign, the Soviet Army found itself in full control of the northern half of
the Korean peninsula. If the Soviet command had wished, it could have in
all likelihood taken the southern half as well, but at that stage Moscow was
still inclined to respect agreements made with Washington. One such
agreement envisioned a provisional division of the Korean peninsula into
two zones of occupation. It took half an hour of deliberation by two US
colonels (one of whom eventually became US secretary of state) to draw
what they saw as a fair provisional demarcation line between the Soviet
and US military zones of operations. Neatly divided by the 38th parallel,
the two zones were almost equal in area, but vastly different in population
size and industrial potential. The southern zone had twice as many people,
but its industry was seriously underdeveloped since before independence,
southern Korea was an agricultural backwater.[2]

The Soviets found themselves in control of northern Korea. And yet,
they had only a dim understanding of the country, politically and socially.
Suffice to say that when Soviet troops entered Korea in August 1945, they
had no Korean-speaking interpreters because they were fighting the Japanese
Army and thus employed only Japanese interpreters. Only in late August
did the first Korean-speaking officers (almost exclusively Soviet citizens of
Korean extraction) arrive in the country.

Newly declassified Soviet documents seem to indicate that until early
1946, Moscow had no clear-cut plans for the future of Korea. However, the

wartime alliance between the United States and Soviet Union proved to be short-lived as the Cold War set in. This new era of hostile relations between the superpowers saw neither side willing to compromise. As a result, by early 1946 the Soviet Union was increasingly inclined to establish a friendly regime in its own zone of occupation (arguably, the United States had similar plans with regard to the southern part of the peninsula). Under such circumstances it was all too natural that the regime established in the North would be Communist, but there was one problem: there were no (well, almost no) Communists inside North Korea.

A native Korean Communist movement had emerged in the early 1920s, and Marxism was much in vogue among Korean intellectuals of the colonial era. Nonetheless, due to the harshness of Japanese colonial rule, a majority of prominent Korean Communists by 1945 had been operating outside the country, while those few Communists who in 1945 could be found in Korea proper were overwhelmingly in Seoul and thus outside the Soviet zone. Therefore, from late 1945 Soviet military headquarters began to import Communist activists into North Korea from elsewhere. Some of them were Soviet officials and technical experts of Korean extraction who were dispatched to North Korea by Moscow; others came from China, where a large number of ethnic Koreans were active in the Chinese Communist Party. A third group consisted of Communist activists who fled the US-controlled South, where between 1945 and 1946 the Communist movement experienced a short-lived boom, only to be driven underground and subsequently suppressed. But we should also not forget those who returned with Kim Il Sung, the former guerrillas who spent the war years in the Soviet Union after having fought a ragtag guerrilla war with the Japanese in the 1930s in Northeast China.[3]

It was the last of these groups that was destined to have by far the greatest impact on Korea's future, but initially it appeared to be the least significant. These former guerrillas were the survivors of a heroic but small-scale and ultimately futile armed resistance to the Japanese occupation of Manchuria in the 1930s. After resistance collapsed around 1940, the survivors fled to the Soviet Union, where they were enlisted into the Soviet Army and retrained for a future war against Japan. Ironically, the victory against Japan was so swift that this band could not participate in the last, decisive battle with the Japanese Empire. Nonetheless, even after the sudden end of hostilities, the Soviet military authorities found good use for these men and women. Ex-guerrillas were repatriated on the assumption that they would be useful advisers to and intermediaries for the Soviet occupation forces.

Kim Il Sung was one of these former guerrillas. The triumph of North Korea's propaganda apparatus and the power of hindsight have combined to ensure hagiographic exaggeration of his political significance in the years prior to 1945. Nonetheless, by the time of Korea's liberation, Kim Il Sung probably was already seen as an important leader—in spite of his young age and, admittedly, somewhat unheroic looks. A participant in the events of 1945 described to me his first impression of the would-be Sun of the Nation and Ever-Victorious Generalissimo in less than flattering terms: "He reminded me of a fat delivery boy from a neighborhood Chinese food stall."

The events of 1945–46 are rather convoluted, but to simplify a bit we can say that Kim Il Sung was finally selected by the Soviet military as their man in Pyongyang. The reasons behind this decision may never be fully known, but Kim Il Sung seemingly had the right combination of biography and personality to be chosen. After all, he was a reasonably good speaker of Russian, and his military exploits, though grossly exaggerated by propaganda in later years, were nonetheless real and known to many Koreans. It also helped that Kim was a native of North Korea and had no connection to the crowd of Comintern professional revolutionaries and ideologues whom Stalin despised and distrusted.

Kim Il Sung was born in 1912 (on the day the *Titanic* sank, April 15th) under the name Kim Sŏng-ju—he adopted the nom de guerre Kim Il Sung much later, in the 1930s. In their attempts to create a befitting hagiography for the Ever-Victorious Generalissimo, North Korean official historians prudently glossed over some inconvenient facts about his family background to present him as the son of poor Korean farmers. This is not really true: like the majority of first-generation Communist leaders of East Asia (including, for instance, Mao Zedong), the future North Korean dictator was born into a moderately affluent family with above-average income as well as access to modern education. Kim's father, a graduate of a Protestant school, made a modest living through teaching and practicing herbal medicine while remaining a prominent Christian activist.

Kim Il Sung himself graduated from high school—an impressive achievement for a Korean of his generation (only a few percent of the population could afford to take their education that far). Most of his childhood was spent in Northeast China, where his family moved in 1920.

With his above-average education, Kim Il Sung could have probably opted for a conventional career and become a well-paid clerk, businessman, or educator. However, he made another choice: in the early 1930s he joined the Communist guerrilla movement that was resisting the Japanese invasion of Manchuria.

The North Korean narrative always plays down the Great Leader's foreign connections, so it remains silent on his decade-long membership in the *Chinese* Communist Party and his position as a junior officer in what was, essentially, a Chinese guerrilla force. Instead, the official narrative insists that the Great Leader created a Korean guerrilla army at the age of twenty (we should not be surprised, for, if this narrative is to be believed, he became the supreme leader of all Korean Communists at the tender age of fourteen). Actually, until 1945, Kim Il Sung's military career was spent first under Chinese and then Soviet command, albeit usually in ethnic Korean units.[4]

What made young Kim Sŏng-ju choose the arduous and harsh life of a guerrilla, and what kept him in this dangerous pastime for more than a decade? Obviously, he was an idealist, a fighter for (and believer in) a Great Cause—in his case, Communism. However, one should keep in mind how the ideology of Communism was understood in East Asia. While aspiring European Communists were motivated, above all, by the desire to ameliorate social injustice, the East Asian version of Communism had both social and nationalist dimensions. In the 1920s and 1930s, when Kim Il Sung, Mao Zedong, and Ho Chi Minh were young idealists, Communism in East Asia was widely seen as a shortcut to national revival and modernity, a way not only to create a more equitable society but also as a means to put a quick end to backwardness and colonial dependency. In the last years of his life, Kim Il Sung would confess that he was both a Communist and a nationalist. Frankly, the same could be said about the majority of the East Asian Communists of his generation.

Even though initially installed in power by the Soviet military, Kim Il Sung had no desire to be Moscow's puppet—or, for that matter, anyone else's. In the 1940s the young ex-guerrilla probably still sincerely believed in the cause of international Communism, but he, as well as a majority of his supporters, did not want to sacrifice Korea's national interest in the name of other countries, however progressive or revolutionary these countries asserted themselves to be. From a Soviet perspective, Kim Il Sung was a poor choice, as they ended up promoting a cunning man who could not be easily manipulated. In due course this made him a serious thorn in the side of Moscow (and, for that matter, Beijing). However, given Korea's situation in the late 1940s, had Soviet officials chosen someone else, the eventual outcome would have probably been quite similar. Subsequent events demonstrated that Korean Communist leaders (and, for that matter, other Communist leaders of East Asia) made bad puppets—not least because of their deeply ingrained nationalist convictions. Surprisingly, these leaders' stubborn adherence to the spirit of national independence was not always good news for their subjects. In the late 1950s nationalist East Asian Communist leaders rejected post-Stalinist Soviet Communism—which ironically was also much softer than what had come before.

However, such issues became obvious only later. Whatever Kim Il Sung's private thoughts, in the years between 1945 and 1948 the nascent North Korean regime operated under the complete control of its Soviet sponsors. Soviet advisers drafted the 1946 Land Reform Law, and Stalin himself edited the draft of the 1948 North Korean Constitution. The Soviet military police arrested all major opponents of the emerging Communist regime. These "enemies of the people" were then sent to prison camps in Siberia, there being no North Korean penitentiary system at that time.

Even relatively mundane operational decisions by the North Korean government at this stage needed approval from Moscow. Important speeches delivered by North Korean leaders had to first be approved by the Soviet Embassy. Key decisions required approval from further up. The Soviet Politburo, the supreme decision-making body of the Soviet Communist Party and thus the USSR, approved the agenda of the North Korean rubber-stamp parliament and even formally "gave permission" to hold a military parade in February 1948 when the establishment of a North Korean army was formally announced.[5]

My favorite story in this regard occurred in December 1946, when the first elections in the North were being prepared. On December 15, General Terentii Shtykov, then responsible for political operations in Korea, discussed the future composition of the North Korean proto-parliament with two other Soviet generals. These men (not a single Korean was present) decided that the Assembly would consist of 231 members. They also decided the exact distribution of seats among the parties, the number of women members, and, more broadly, the precise social composition of the legislature. If we have a look at the actual composition of the Assembly, we can see that these instructions were followed to the letter with all but the smallest deviation.[6]

Guided and assisted by Soviet advisers, between 1946 and 1950 North Korea quickly went through a chain of reforms that were standard for nascent Communist regimes of the era. In spring of 1946 the aforementioned radical land reform led to a redistribution of land among the peasantry, while also sending a majority of former landlords fleeing southward. Around the same time, all major industry was nationalized, though small independent handicrafts were tolerated until the late 1950s. In politics, the local incarnation of the Leninist Party, known as the Korean Worker's Party (KWP), began to exercise increasingly thorough control over society.

In spite of his Christian family background, Kim Il Sung and many other Communist leaders persecuted Christians with great ferocity. Following the landlords, many former entrepreneurs and Christian activists chose to flee southward across the poorly guarded demarcation line. Nobody bothered to collect exact statistics, but the number of North Koreans who fled South between 1945 and 1951 is estimated to be approximately 1.0 to 1.4 million people, or some 10 to 15 percent of the entire North Korean population. Among other things, this exodus meant that at least some of the potential opposition exiled itself, inadvertently making the emerging regime more stable.

At first glance, the North Korean state of the late 1940s appeared to be a near perfect specimen of what cold warriors once described as a "Soviet satellite," but such a view is incomplete. North Korea might have been a puppet state, but this does not necessarily mean that the new regime was unpopular and lacked support from below.

In the 1980s a Marxist- and semi-Marxist-oriented left re-emerged in South Korea as a political and intellectual force, and soon afterward the nature of the early North Korean regime became a topic of hot (and largely ideologically driven) debate in Seoul's intellectual and academic circles. Left-leaning historians and journalists usually present the events of 1945–1950 as a homegrown popular revolution that might have been opportunely assisted by the Soviet presence, but generally developed spontaneously and independently. It is not surprising that South Korean leftist historians have demonstrated such a remarkable ability to ignore newly published documentary evidence that revealed the true extent of Soviet control, as it undermines such cherished fantasies.

At the same time, the South Korean right remains strangely obsessed with the desire to prove that Syngman Rhee's regime in South Korea was the "sole legitimate government of the entire Korean peninsula." Therefore, right-leaning historians are generally unwilling to acknowledge the ample evidence of the genuine popularity enjoyed by Kim Il Sung's government in its early days.[7]

Such arguments, being ideological in nature, are likely to continue for years, if not decades, to come. Nonetheless, both sides seem to rely on a false dichotomy: the events of the late 1940s were *both* a foreign occupation and a popular revolution. The Soviet authorities and the then-accepted Communist orthodoxy to a very large extent determined the shape of the emerging North Korean society and its institutions. Nonetheless, the promise of the Communist project generally coincided with what many North Koreans sincerely wanted at the time. The dream of universal equality and affluence, enforced by a watchful but benevolent state, was difficult to resist. We should also remember that the blueprint for such a society was presented in the "modern" and "scientific" jargon of Marxism-Leninism and supported by the seemingly impressive success of the Soviet Union.

After all, in those days, everybody knew that the USSR made good fighter jets and had the world's best ballet, while almost nobody knew that a few million Soviet farmers had starved to death in the 1930s. As a result, government initiatives, even though imposed by Soviet advisers, often met with an enthusiastic response from below.

THE WAR AND WHAT CAME AFTER

By late 1946 the division of the country had become a fact of life. In 1948 two Korean states formally came into being: on August 15, the Republic of Korea (ROK) was proclaimed in Seoul, and on September 9, the Democratic People's Republic of Korea (DPRK) was declared in Pyongyang. Neither state recognized the other; each government claimed itself to be the only legitimate authority on the entire Korean peninsula. This still remains technically the case now, more than six decades later.

At times, both sides went to slightly comical extremes to emphasize their fictional control over Korea in its entirety. For example, until 1972, Seoul (not Pyongyang!) was constitutionally the capital of the DPRK. Concurrently, the ROK government still appoints governors to the provinces of North Korea. Incidentally, the joint offices of these five governors are located not far from the university where this book is being written—and these offices are bustling with bureaucratic activity every time this author visits.

Both Korean states claimed—and still claim—that national unification is their foremost political goal. Nowadays, as we will see later, such claims ring increasingly hollow and are rather disingenuous, but back in the late 1940s, both Pyongyang and Seoul meant what they said.

Both left and right were willing to use force for unification. The government in Seoul, headed by Syngman Rhee, engaged in much bellicose rhetoric without doing anything substantive to prepare for attack. Meanwhile, the North Korean leadership kept petitioning Moscow for permission to invade the South and "liberate" its allegedly oppressed population from the yoke of the US imperialists and their puppets. Kim Il Sung—and, for that matter, other Korean Communist leaders—assured Stalin that victory would be quick, with America having neither the time nor the will to intervene. Kim Il Sung cited the reports of South Korean Communists, who insisted that the entire people of South Korea would rise up against the hated pro-American clique of Syngman Rhee at the first sight of North Korean tanks rolling across the border.[8]

Stalin was initially unenthusiastic about the aggressiveness of his Korean appointees: he didn't want to get dragged into a full-scale confrontation with the United States—then the world's sole nuclear power—by the excessive nationalist zeal of some third-rate client state. However, by late 1949 things had changed: in August, the Soviet Union successfully tested its first nuclear device, and soon afterward, in October, Communists swept into power in China. Soviet intelligence reports also seemingly confirmed that the United States did not see Korea as a vital strategic interest. In this new situation, the Korean gamble looked less risky.

Consequently, in early 1950, Stalin gave in. On January 30, Ambassador Shtykov met Kim Il Sung and told him that Stalin had at long last given permission to invade. As the ambassador's cable to Stalin says: "Kim Il Sung received my report with great satisfaction.... Kim Il Sung, apparently wishing once more to reassure himself, asked me if this means that it is possible to meet with Comrade Stalin on this question." Indeed, it was possible, and in April 1950 Kim rushed to Moscow, where he spent a few weeks discussing operational war plans. He repeated his assurances of a painless victory, for in the words of a Soviet memo, Stalin was told: "The attack will be swift and the war will be won in three days: the guerrilla movement in the South has grown stronger and a major uprising is expected." Senior Soviet officers were dispatched to Pyongyang to draw up detailed plans for war, and by June 1950 everything was ready for the "liberation" of the South.

The war began on June 25, 1950. Initially, everything went according to the starry-eyed expectations of Pyongyang's leaders. Although the anticipated mass uprising in the South never materialized, by early August 1950, the North controlled some 95 percent of the Korean peninsula. Soon, however, the United States decided to join the war, and this decision turned the tide.

A massive American intervention began in September 1950. Within a couple of weeks, North Korean forces were all but annihilated, and the

North Korean leadership had to flee to the Chinese border. In turn, China decided to intercede and in late November staged a massive counterstrike that became probably the most successful large-scale operation in China's recent military history.

After much fighting and bloodshed, the front line stabilized by spring 1951, although trench warfare and intensive bombing campaigns continued for another two years. The final front line stabilized more or less where the initial demarcation was drawn in 1945. In 1953 the Armistice Treaty was signed, and the front line became known as the Demilitarized Zone or DMZ, the de facto border between the two Korean states. Millions died, but the war ended in a near complete stalemate.

Ironically, the Korean War greatly strengthened Kim Il Sung's personal power. Before the war he was one of many North Korean Communist leaders, merely a primus inter pares in Pyongyang, whose slightly special standing was largely—or maybe even exclusively—derived from Soviet support. After the war, Kim emerged as the undisputed leader of the country; people who joined the Korean Worker's Party during the war and who remained the core of the North Korean bureaucracy for decades to come were joining the Party of Kim Il Sung as he was the only leader they knew. Understandably, he also used this opportunity to promote his guerrilla friends to positions of power.

The Soviet decision not to get involved in land warfare in Korea was also of great help to Kim Il Sung. From that time on, the influence of the Chinese could be relied on to counter the influence of the Soviets—more so since relations between Beijing and Moscow were never as good as official rhetoric implied. The two Communist great powers began to drift toward open hostility in the late 1950s, and this shift gave North Korean leaders ample opportunity to exploit the contradictions between its two major sponsors. Indeed, from 1953, Soviet control, so omnipresent in the late 1940s, greatly weakened, and Kim Il Sung began to take the first cautious steps toward reducing the ability of the "great Soviet Union" to meddle in North Korea's internal affairs. Several prominent pro-Soviet officials were ousted from their positions, and the leader of the pro-Moscow group was first demoted and then found dead in his house (officially it was a suicide, even though foul play was widely suspected).[9]

However, at that stage the purges largely targeted "domestic" Communists—those who had been involved with the Communist underground of the colonial era. Between 1953 and 1955 a majority of these Communist zealots were purged, with some prominent leaders subjected to show trials and others shot or imprisoned without much attention to legal niceties. The accusations were de rigueur for Stalinist regimes: the founders of the Korean Communist movement were accused of being spies and saboteurs on the payroll of the Americans and Japanese (as usual, the accusations were often comically inconsistent, but who cared?). In most cases, being the victim of a purge meant death and permanent imprisonment of the afflicted family, including even distant relatives.

However, in 1956, Kim Il Sung faced a major and unexpected political challenge. His unabashedly Stalinist ways provoked dissatisfaction among top officials, much influenced by the ongoing thaw in Moscow. Some of these high-ranking party dissenters obviously wanted to use Khrushchev's de-Stalinization as an opportunity to advance their own careers, while others might have felt genuine compassion for the plight of the masses bearing the major burden of the Stalinesque policies. The pro-Soviet and pro-Chinese factions within the North Korean leadership conspired to move the country toward a more moderate political line, akin to the policy of the post-Stalin Soviet leadership (then briefly supported by China as well). To make this possible, they wanted to oust Kim Il Sung from power. The Soviet and Chinese governments were aware and mildly supportive of the scheme. In August 1956, during a Central Committee meeting, the opposition openly challenged Kim Il Sung and his policies.

WITH FRIENDS LIKE THESE ...

One of the sad facts of Communist history is that most founding fathers of Communist states perished at the hands of their own comrades, becoming victims of the machine they had themselves created. North Korea was no exception. If anything, the founders of the North Korean state fared worse than their Chinese or, for that matter, Hungarian counterparts.

The subsequent fate of the members of the North Korean Politburo in 1949 is most illustrative in this regard. In Communist countries, the Politburo is the supreme executive committee of the party and state, superior to any other institution, including the Cabinet. The 1949 North Korean Politburo was technically the first executive board of the unified party. Before that, there had been two independent parties, one operating in the North and the other in the South.

The 1949 Politburo had ten full members. It was headed by Kim Il Sung, the Party chairman, who remained North Korean dictator until his death in 1994. He had two vice chairmen, Pak Hŏn-yŏng and Hŏ Ka-i.

Pak Hŏn-yŏng, the leader of the Korean Communist underground in the colonial era, was chairman of the South Korean Workers Party for many years. After the merger of the two parties, he became second in command of the unified Party and was also given the post of foreign minister in the DPRK government. However, in 1953 he was ousted from his positions and soon after arrested. In 1955, he faced a kangaroo court and was executed as an "American spy."

The other vice chairman, Hŏ Ka-i, was a seasoned Soviet bureaucrat of Korean extraction who was dispatched to North Korea to develop the local government and party machinery. In 1949 he was also the Party's first secretary. His close connections to Moscow made him the obvious first target when Kim Il Sung decided to distance the North from its Soviet sponsors. Hŏ Ka-i was accused of "political mistakes" in 1951, and in 1953 he was shot and killed in his home. Official reports claim that Hŏ Ka-i committed suicide, but it is possible that he was assassinated on Kim Il Sung's orders. We may never know.

Another member of the 1949 Politburo, Yi Sŭng-yŏp, a prominent leader of the South Korean left, was, at that time, responsible for the guerrilla movement in the South. In 1953, he became a major defendant at the largest show trial in North Korean history. Yi Sŭng-yŏp was said to be an American spy who was planning to stage a coup in the North that would pave the way for a large-scale American landing in Wonsan. Broken, Yi Sŭng-yŏp delivered the expected penitence and was sentenced to death.

Only two of the ten members of that initial Politburo were killed by their enemies rather than by their comrades. Kim Sam-yong, a leader

(continued)

of the Communist underground in the South, was arrested by the South Korean police and hastily executed in the first days of the Korean War. Kim Ch'aek, once a guerrilla fighter in Manchuria, was killed in an American air raid in January 1951.

Of the four other members, Kim Tu-bong was probably the most prominent. In 1949, he was the North Korean head of state. This was a largely ceremonial position well suited to the character of this outstanding scholar, a founder of modern Korean linguistics. He attempted to distance himself from daily politics. But this did not help: in 1957 Kim Tu-bong was purged, subjected to public humiliation, and disappeared from public view. We do not know whether he died in prison or was killed.

Another 1949 member, Pak Il-u, the then minister of the interior, suffered a similar fate. He was purged in 1955 and then disappeared. His fate remains unknown to this day.

Pak Chŏng-ae, the only female in the 1949 Politburo, survived longer than most of her compatriots. She was purged in the late 1960s and exiled in the countryside. She resurfaced in the late 1980s, after two decades, but never regained her influence.

Apart from Kim Il Sung himself, only one 1949 Politburo member, Hŏ Hŏn, died of natural causes. In 1949 he was sixty-three years old, in bad health, and had only two years to live.

Thus, out of the ten people who ran the country in 1949, only two avoided persecution and died natural deaths. Of the others, two were killed by the enemies of Korean Communists. The remaining six were all purged by their own comrades.

Should we see them as sincere idealists and tragic victims or should we remember that many of these supposed victims, while in power, had sent a striking number of people to the execution grounds? Maybe it would be best to leave these questions unanswered....

This challenge was crushed, largely because the younger generation of officials, deeply nationalist, hardened by war, and eager to see their country less dependent on Moscow, saw no need for the proposed liberalization and therefore rallied around Kim. Having defeated the challengers, between 1957 and 1959 Kim launched a new, more thorough purge of those party functionaries who had worked or had "excessively close" associations with the Soviets and Chinese.[10]

The purges of the 1950s led to a nearly complete reshuffle of the North Korean leadership. From the late 1950s onward, almost all top positions in the North Korean party-state came to be controlled by former Manchurian guerrillas and other Kim Il Sung appointees (including a small but growing number of his family members). They stayed in control, more or less unchallenged, until their own demise in the 1980s and 1990s.

Only a few of them had graduated from high school, and an absolute majority had no formal schooling whatsoever as, being children of poor subsistence farmers, they could not attend even primary school.[11] Their earlier experiences were also of little help in running a modern state. Nonetheless, they were unconditionally loyal to Kim Il Sung, sharing his vision of the country's future. And that was what really mattered.

BETWEEN MOSCOW AND BEIJING: THE FOREIGN POLICY OF KIM IL SUNG'S NORTH KOREA

As mentioned previously, until the late 1950s North Korea was essentially just another "People's Democracy"—a self-description used from the late 1940s by most Soviet client states and allies of the Soviet Union. In the late 1950s things began to change.

The transformations that began in the late 1950s had their origins in the Korean War and before. Personnel changes in the leadership were very significant. Communist leaders of the first generation were largely university graduates who combined a measure of nationalism with a modern and relatively cosmopolitan worldview. However, in the late 1950s they were replaced by former guerrillas whose worldview largely reflected the values and aspirations of East Asian peasantry living in small villages. Akin to radical leaders like Mao or Pol Pot, to a very large extent they wanted to actualize the utopian dreams of peasants (which of course didn't stop East Asian Communists from killing and starving peasants in droves). Another contributing factor was the impact of the Korean War.

This led to the militarization of North Korean society and helped to transform the entire country into a nearly perfect garrison state (or as the North Korean official propaganda prefers, "made the entire country an impregnable fortress").

Nevertheless, all these trends could develop only due to a massive geopolitical shift in the late 1950s—that is, the Sino-Soviet split. For nearly three decades, the two major Communist states had very contentious relations that sometimes skirted quite close to war. Each peddled its own version of Communism. The Soviet brand probably appeared more dull and no longer attracted the starry-eyed radicals on Western university campuses; however, it was much more permissive and liberal, much less indifferent to the daily needs of the average citizen, and more efficient (or should we say "less inefficient"?) economically. The Chinese brand of Communism was all about endless ideological mobilization, selfless dedication, and sacrifice to the cause and the omniscient leader.

Changes in post-Stalin USSR were crucial. In the decade following Stalin's death in 1953, the number of political prisoners in the Soviet Union decreased nearly five-hundred-fold, from some 0.6 million to merely one to two thousand.[12] Restrictions on the movements of collective farmworkers within the country were lifted (contrary to the assumptions of many Westerners, short-time trips within the country were never seriously restricted for the urban Soviet population). At the same time, large-scale housing construction programs were launched, and consumption goods became more affordable to the average Soviet citizen.

In China the same decade was marked by the collectivization of agriculture (or the abolition of individual land ownership) and the madness of the Great Leap Forward. These experiments looked attractive to the denizens of Paris's cafés, who (like Sartre) instantly switched their loyalty and enthusiasm from the USSR to Mao's China. To the Chinese themselves, this "bold social experimentation" produced the worst famine in modern history, leaving between twenty and thirty million people dead.

Initially, in the early 1960s, North Korea was much attracted to the austere and autocratic notions of Communism emanating from China. Mao's ideals resonated well with Kim Il Sung's own notion of the perfect Korea he hoped to build. In the vision of North Korean leaders, their realm should become a country where all of the people would work hard on huge state-owned farms and factories, breaking production records while possessing an unswerving ideological zeal and love for country. Everybody would be issued roughly the same ration of heavily subsidized food and basic consumption goods, and no selfish profiteering would be tolerated, so money would gradually become all but useless. Such a society would be led by a small army of devout and selfless officials and presided over by the omniscient Great Leader, whose word would be law. Obviously, at the time many common North Koreans would have found this ideal quite attractive (it is not incidental that peasant rebels across the globe frequently dreamed of similar things).

When he spoke of future prosperity, Kim Il Sung's promises were neither too wild nor too excessive. In 1962 he famously outlined his vision of the coming affluence by saying that in the near future all North Koreans would "eat boiled rice and meat soup, dress in silk and live in houses with tile roofs." This promise—repeated by the Great Leader on a number of occasions—does not sound too ambitious to us, but we should remember that for centuries Korean farmers could not afford to eat rice on a daily basis (barley or corn was their staple) and meat soup was reserved for special occasions. Moreover, only landlords could afford a tile roof, whereas the vast majority had to be content with a thatched roof. Thus, Kim Il Sung promised his subjects that his regime would eventually deliver a standard of living perceived as reasonably luxurious by pre-modern villagers—but not much more.

Kim Il Sung's initial decision to align with China was only partially driven by ideological considerations. Pragmatic political calculations played a role, too: after the failed 1956 conspiracy, Kim Il Sung and his supporters began to see the Soviet Union as a source of dangerously liberal ideas. They were also afraid that the then Soviet line of opposing personality cults might easily be used against Kim Il Sung, whose own personality cult so obviously followed Stalinist patterns.

After the 1956 crisis, relations between North Korea and the Soviet Union began to deteriorate, reaching the point of almost open hostility between 1962 and 1963. References to the Soviet Union almost disappeared from the official media, and Soviet advisers were sent packing. The same fate met the few hundred Soviet and Eastern European wives of North Koreans who had studied overseas and married women from other Communist countries. Their North Korean husbands being ordered to divorce them, the women were summarily expelled from the country. By 1960 all North Korean students were recalled from the ideologically suspicious Soviet Union and Eastern Europe, and only two decades later were these student exchanges restarted—albeit on a significantly smaller scale.

Pravda and *Rodong Shinmun*, the major official newspapers of the USSR and North Korea, respectively, were engaged in open polemics: *Rodong Shinmun* accused the Soviets of being exploitative and ready to take advantage of Korea's weakness. *Pravda* lamented the ingratitude of the North Korean leaders who suddenly fell silent on matters of aid from the USSR (indeed, since approximately 1960 and until after the collapse of the Soviet Union in 1991, North Korean media seldom admitted the very existence of continuing economic aid from the Soviet Union). In late 1956 Yi Sang-jo, the then North Korean ambassador to Moscow, wrote a highly critical letter to Kim Il Sung and then asked Moscow for asylum. His request was granted by the Soviet government—nearly unprecedented in the history of the Communist bloc.[13]

Pyongyang's relations with Moscow partially recovered after 1965. Changes in the Soviet leadership—specifically the replacement of impulsive and reform-minded Khrushchev with the more conservative Brezhnev—did play a part, but there were more important reasons. First, when relations turned sour in the early 1960s, Soviet economic assistance declined, and China proved to be neither willing nor able to compensate for this loss. Second, in 1966 China itself plunged into the bloody turmoil of the Cultural Revolution. For the North Korean elite, the Cultural Revolution was the embodiment of utter chaos; it might have been seen in Pyongyang as even more dangerous than Soviet liberalization. Indeed, privately, when talking to Brezhnev in 1966, Kim Il Sung described the Great Proletarian Cultural Revolution as "massive idiocy."[14]

Actually, the late 1960s was a period of grave crisis in relations between North Korea and China. Ambassadors were recalled, and tensions along the border mounted—much later, in May 1984, Kim Il Sung recalled in his confidential talk with East German leaders how much patience was necessary to deal with Chinese soldiers intruding into North Korean territory.[15] In a telling sign, during the late 1960s Kim Il Sung even asked Moscow for permission to use Soviet airspace for air travel by North Korean government delegations, thereby revealing the fear that North Korean planes might be intercepted and forced to land by the Chinese.[16] Chinese Red Guard groups openly criticized Kim Il Sung, describing him as a "Neo-Feudal ruler" living the life of luxury and self-indulgence.[17]

From the early 1970s North Korea finally switched to an "equidistance" policy, which continued until the early 1990s. It was essentially a policy of balancing the two mutually hostile sponsors: China and the Soviet Union. North Korean politicians and diplomats discovered that the Sino-Soviet rivalry, in spite of inherent instability, gave them remarkable political opportunities as well. With appropriate guile they could extract aid from both sponsors without giving much in return.

Aid was increasingly important: in spite of ferocious ideological campaigns, from the late 1960s the North Korean economy, once the most advanced in continental East Asia, was sliding toward stagnation. Without a constant influx of foreign aid, North Korea was on the path toward economic nonviability.

Neither Moscow nor Beijing had any illusions about North Korea. They knew perfectly well that they were being manipulated but saw no viable alternative to providing Pyongyang with aid. Partially, their policy was driven by the need to keep North Korea as a stable buffer zone protecting both China's North East and Russia's Far East against the US military presence in Japan and South Korea. However, to a larger extent, the rival Communist giants were paying North Korea to remain neutral in their mutual quarrel. Of course, both Moscow and Beijing would have liked to see Pyongyang join their respective side unconditionally, but, since this was not going to happen, they were at least determined not to let North Korea join the opposite camp. With remarkable skill, North Korean diplomats

extracted aid from their two quarreling benefactors without having to re-
ciprocate to either of them.

In the early 1970s North Korea quixotically tried to rid its economy of
its dependence on Moscow and Beijing through borrowing heavily on international markets. At that time, immediately after the oil crisis of 1973,
Communist regimes were considered to be exemplary debtors while the
international market was awash with newly generated petrodollars. Therefore, securing loans was not that hard. Probably, North Korean leaders
hoped to use this additional income to overcome the slowdown that was
taking hold of their economy. The scheme did not work: the loans were
wasted on a number of prestige-boosting and/or ill-conceived projects.
Very soon, Pyongyang began halting its interest payments and, between
1979 and 1980, became the first Communist state to default. This left them
with significant debt—$600 million in principal plus $1.2 billion in ac-
crued interest as of 2007.[18] This foray into the world of high international
finance ended in debacle and seriously damaged North Korea's credit
rating.

Around the same time, from the mid-1970s, more unseemly incidents
began to occur. With increasing frequency, North Korean diplomats and
officials were discovered traveling with large amounts of contraband: illicit drugs, counterfeit currency, and other smuggled goods that they tried
to sell. In late October 1976 the Norwegian police caught North Korean
diplomats selling four thousand bottles of smuggled liquor and a large
quantity of smuggled cigarettes. In those days, the Scandinavian governments imposed hefty taxes on alcohol, which made the smuggling of
tax-free liquor an extremely profitable business. It was estimated that the
DPRK Embassy in Norway sold liquor and cigarettes with a black market
value of some one million dollars (in 2011 prices, this would be at least
three times that amount). Similar activities were uncovered in three other
Nordic countries—Denmark, Finland, and Sweden. The scale of operations in Sweden was probably the largest and the scandal was extensively
covered in the local press. One night, mischievous Swedish students af-
fixed a sign reading "Wine and Spirits Cooperative" to the entrance of the
DPRK Embassy—to the great annoyance of its occupants.[19]

Around the same time, the North Korean authorities began to deal in far more dangerous substances. In May 1976 Egyptian customs officials discovered the presence of hashish in the luggage belonging to a group of North Korean diplomats—the first in a long chain of incidents of this type. The North Korean operatives even drew knives, but were overpowered. Happily for them, their diplomatic passports saved them from prosecution. Soon afterward, a similar incident again occurred in Norway where in October 1976 North Korean diplomats were caught handing over a large amount of hashish to local drug dealers. In the subsequent decades, North Korean officials and diplomats have occasionally been caught smuggling drugs in various parts of the world.

Apart from drugs, North Korea also appears to have produced and disseminated high-quality counterfeit US currency (the so-called "super notes"), though it should be added that evidence in this case remains largely circumstantial.[20]

It is often speculated that these smuggling operations were related to a new policy that affected North Korean missions overseas: once the economic slowdown made its mark in the mid-1970s, missions had to follow the self-reliance principle. That is, North Korean embassy officials had to pay for their own operational expenses from funds its staff somehow generated by themselves.

It seems, however, that, contrary to popular misperception, these illegal activities never developed into major hard currency earners. Even from the regime's point of view, smuggling and counterfeiting did more harm than good: these incidents made the North Korean government look odious without bringing in much income. In the early 2000s there were signs that those activities were finally discontinued or scaled down, but one wonders why this did not happen earlier.[21]

Another bizarre feature of North Korean foreign policy of the 1970s was their spy agencies' strange obsession with abductions. These operations began earlier: in the late 1950s North Korean intelligence attempted the abduction of a number of dissenters from the USSR. Not all operations were successful: Ho Chin (Lim Un), a young poet and dissenter, managed to escape from his kidnappers and was granted asylum in the USSR, where he eventually became a prominent journalist and historian. A young North Korean musician was far less lucky, however: he was kidnapped by North Korean agents from downtown Moscow and was never seen again. This led to a major crisis in relations between Moscow and Pyongyang, with the Soviet Union expelling the North Korean ambassador—another event with few parallels, if any, in the entire diplomatic history of the Communist bloc.

In the late 1970s the major targets of these operations were Japan and South Korea. Unlike earlier incidents, these kidnappings did not target dissenters or defectors. Abductees were average men and women. In many cases, it seems that the abductions were opportunistic, with North Korean commandos taking any person who was unlucky enough to stroll along some Japanese beach where the commandos were lying in wait. Indeed, these abductions were so bizarre that many reputed journalists and scholars (overwhelmingly—but not exclusively—of leftist inclinations) in the 1980s and 1990s wasted tons of ink insisting that North Korea had nothing to do with the strange disappearance of Japanese citizens in the 1970s.

These people were made to look foolish by Kim Jong Il himself. In 2002 Kim Jong Il admitted responsibility for the abductions and ordered the return of a number of survivors back to Japan. The admission was extended to improve relations with Japan but had the opposite effect. Accusations that had been often perceived as the fantasies of the right were suddenly proven to be completely correct, and the Japanese public exploded. The Japanese government demanded the immediate return of all abductees. In response, the North Korean authorities stated that all survivors had been returned home and that all other abductees had already died (this was in 2002). Few believed this statement, and as a result trade and exchanges with Japan, once quite important for the regime, were completely frozen.[22]

Thus, North Korean leaders were paradoxically punished for their rare attempt to be honest and admit past wrongdoings. No doubt they have learned their lesson and from now on will probably think twice before admitting to more of their past misdeeds.

Obviously the Japanese were abducted to take advantage of their native language skills and their knowledge of Japanese daily life in order to train

North Korean agents. For example, Yaeko Taguchi, a former hostess kidnapped in 1978 (she was then age twenty-two), trained Kim Hyŏn-hŭi, a North Korean intelligence agent whose cover was to be a Japanese national. However, the entire operation was strange indeed, and one cannot help but agree with Charles Armstrong's witty remark: "Perhaps Kim Jong Il had watched too many spy movies and was attempting to make them into reality."[23]

This decision to rely on abductees was rather strange, considering the North Korean authorities could count on the enthusiastic support of a number of people who spoke Japanese as their first language and had firsthand knowledge of modern Japan. Those people were members of Chongryon (Chosen Soren) a powerful pro-Pyongyang group of Koreans in Japan.

Some 700,000 ethnic Koreans lived in Japan in the early 1950s. Most of them emigrated in the 1930s or early 1940s, either voluntarily moving in search of a better life, or forcibly sent there by the colonial authorities as providers of cheap labor. In 1952 ethnic Koreans were formally deprived of Japanese citizenship. In Japan, ethnic Koreans were subjected to considerable discrimination and were relegated to unskilled or semi-legal occupations. This ensured their affinity with the Japanese left, but eventually it was pro-Pyongyang leftist nationalists who succeeded in organizing them.

In the late 1950s, a majority of ethnic Koreans in Japan opted for North Korean citizenship, even though only a tiny minority of them had come from what became North Korea after 1945. Those "overseas citizens of the DPRK" were the eventual creators of Chongryon.

In the late 1950s and early 1960s, pro-Pyongyang activists successfully persuaded many ethnic Koreans to "return" to the North from Japan. These returnees numbered an impressive 93,000, an overwhelming majority of whom had never previously been to the country to which they now repatriated themselves. They desired to escape discrimination and envisioned contributing toward the building of a perfect new society in their native land. They were seduced by North Korean propaganda, but, as recent research shows, Japanese right-wing politicians secretly also promoted the migration with the intent of eviscerating a potential "fifth column" within Japan.[24]

Most of the returnees were gravely disappointed, to put it mildly, by the destitution they saw upon arrival. However, they soon realized that they had gone beyond the point of no return. They were stuck in a destitute police state where they (and their children) found themselves in a strange position: they were simultaneously both a privileged and discriminated-against group. On the one hand, the returnees were seen as ideologically unreliable. On the other hand, most of them received money transfers from family members who remained in Japan (and who had been wise enough not to go to the "Socialist paradise"). This allowed them to enjoy a life that was quite agreeable by North Korean standards. It was permissible for the returnees to ask relatives back in Japan for money as long as their letters included an obligatory eulogy to the Leader and his system.

Remittances began to dry up in the early 1990s, with predictably grave results for second- and third-generation returnees. The main reason was a generational shift. The immediate relatives of returnees began to die off, and the next generation was ever more disinclined to send money to people whom they had never met. Around the same time, Chongryon membership began to dwindle as the younger generation of ethnic Koreans increasingly accepted Japanese citizenship or applied for a South Korean passport. Nonetheless, until the early 1990s, money transfers from Japan were a major source of income for Pyongyang.

DEALING WITH THE SOUTH

The Korean War did not end in a peace treaty. Only an armistice—a ceasefire—was signed in 1953. Tellingly enough, the ROK government refused to become a signatory. The actual reasons were complicated, but officially the logic was that a ceasefire was tantamount to recognizing the North Korean state.

Until the late 1960s, foreign governments had to choose the Korean state they would have diplomatic relations with. If a foreign nation granted diplomatic recognition to Pyongyang, this meant severing diplomatic ties with Seoul (and vice versa). This principle quietly ended in 1969, and since then it has become possible for a government to maintain diplomatic relations with the two Korean states simultaneously.[25] However, conflict between the two Koreas has remained unresolved.

For the first few years after the armistice in 1953, North Korea's government did not show much interest in South Korean issues, as Kim Il Sung was preoccupied with rebuilding the economy and eliminating real and potential rivals within the top leadership. Many in Pyongyang also assumed that no revolution was likely to break out in South Korea. After all, leftist forces were all but wiped out by police terror, and many fled to self-imposed exile in Pyongyang.

WOMEN'S WORK?

Soviet Communism, as well as its local variants, had a strictly male face. Top Communist leaders of the 1960s and 1970s were aging males in badly tailored suits. Women were remarkably underrepresented at the apex of Communist power.

This was not always the case. In the early 1900s revolutionary Marxism was arguably the most feminist of all major ideologies of the era. It did not limit itself to calls for legal gender equality, but went one step further by demanding full economic and social equality for men and women.

In the Soviet Union of the 1920s and 1930s, there was, essentially, an affirmative action program. The exploits of female pilots, engineers, and military officers were much extolled by the media.

However, this was to change in the late 1930s, when the government of Stalin's Russia discovered the political usefulness of the traditional family and the values associated with it. From then on, while the importance of female labor in the workplace was not disputed (and, indeed, continued to be encouraged), the primary social function of women was to be wives and mothers.

When Soviet troops brought Communism to Korea in 1945, it was in its most nationalist and anti-feminist stage. Legal measures aimed

(continued)

at bringing about gender equality came into effect. The 1946 Gender Equality Law abolished concubinage, eased restrictions (mainly social in nature) on divorce, and enshrined female property rights in law.

That said, North Korean female participation in higher-level politics remained low. Out of some 260 cabinet ministers between 1945 and 2000, a mere six were women. It was a common assumption in the Kim Il Sung era that North Korean women should not aspire to have careers in politics or administration. The conventional wisdom was that a girl should look for a proper husband and, if possible, for a job that would leave her enough time to fulfill her primary duties as a mother, wife, and daughter-in-law.

Actually, work was not seen as a necessity. Unlike other Communist nations, the North Korean state was quite positive in its attitude toward women who wanted to become housewives. In the Soviet Union and Eastern Europe of the 1970s, a full-time housewife was a very rare creature, while in the North Korea of the same time, maybe up to one-third of all married urban women stayed at home (no exact statistics are available).

Unsurprisingly, there were few female faces among the top leadership. In the 1940s and 1950s, North Korea had a small number of female politicians, left over from the earlier period of heroic (and feminist) revolutionary Marxism. The most remarkable of them was Pak Chŏng-ae (born Vera Ch'oe), once a Soviet intelligence operative and later a Politburo member and ardent supporter of Kim Il Sung. The latter did not save her from being purged in the 1960s, however.

Another example was Ho Chŏng-suk, daughter of prominent leftist lawyer Hŏ Hŏn. She herself fought in the Chinese Civil War, even becoming a political military commissar of a regiment. In North Korea she rose to the position of justice minister and in this capacity oversaw the initial stages of North Korea's Great Purge. In the 1960s, however, Ho Chŏng-suk was pushed out of top-tier politics and relegated to ceremonial positions.

From around 1960 virtually all women in top political positions in the North derived their power as a result of being members of the ruling Kim family. For instance, there is Kim Sŏng-ae, the second wife of Kim Il Sung. She obviously had some political aspirations in the 1970s, but her ambitions were cut short by the rise of her stepson Kim Jong Il, who had her sidelined. Another important woman of the Kim family is Kim Kyŏng-hŭi, Kim Jong Il's younger sister—one of the regents who assisted Kim Jong Un in the early stages of his rule and the wife of unfortunate Chang Song-t'aek.

In North Korean society the relative power of women increased dramatically after the collapse of the state Socialist economy. In the 1990s males were expected to continue attending to their nonfunctioning factories, while women, who were—or could easily become—housewives, were free to engage in the nonofficial economy. As a result, women became the breadwinners in the majority of North Korean families.

This increase in income predictably produced a remarkable change in the gendered division of labor as well as in gender relations in general (hence, for example, a rise in the number of divorces initiated by women). In the countries of Eastern Europe, the collapse of state Socialism generally led to a massive decline in gender equality. Conversely, in North Korea, the years of crisis led to the empowerment of women—at least the ones who did not perish in the famine.

Apart from that, Kim Il Sung also understood pretty well that the Soviet Union was not going to approve of any major attack on South Korea—and with a large US presence in the South, such an attack would have been (and still would be) suicidal at any rate.

However, events of the early 1960s made Pyongyang reconsider its passive approach to the unification issue. For one thing, the sudden outbreak of the April Revolution in 1960 led to the collapse of the Syngman Rhee regime in Seoul. The April Revolution produced an unstable democratic government that was soon overthrown by the military. Kim Il Sung saw these events as proof that a revolution in South Korea was possible. Indeed, in the 1960s and 1970s, mass opposition movements were a common sight in South Korea, and huge rallies on the streets of Seoul encouraged optimism in Pyongyang.

The decline of Soviet influence in Pyongyang also stoked hopes for unification, as Kim Il Sung envisioned that he could take advantage of a favorable turn of events in the South without worrying excessively about Moscow's position.

Another event that had significant impact on North Korean thinking was the steady escalation of the war in Vietnam. Indeed, Vietnam and Korea had a lot in common. Their histories and cultures have remarkable similarities, and after the Second World War both countries were divided into a Communist North and capitalist South. Like their North Korean comrades, Vietnamese Communists once reluctantly accepted a ceasefire under pressure from Moscow and Beijing. However, unlike the North Koreans, the Vietnamese Communists did not keep the promises they had made under duress and began to increase their support for Communist guerrillas in the South Vietnamese countryside. Eventually, this led to full-scale US intervention, but by the late 1960s, it had become obvious that this intervention was failing. For Pyongyang, Vietnam increasingly looked like an encouraging example.[26]

With the benefit of hindsight, it is clear that these expectations were unfounded, for, alas, South Korea was no South Vietnam. In the 1960s the South Korean government, surpassing all expectations, managed to engineer an economic miracle. Conversely, the South Vietnamese government was the embodiment of corruption, inefficiency, and factional strife. It should also not be forgotten that the brutal experiences of the North Korean occupation of 1950–51 made the vast majority of South Koreans staunchly anti-Communist. Whatever they secretly thought about the then government in Seoul, they saw Kim Il Sung as the greater evil. Last but not least, South Korean terrain made guerrilla operations difficult. At the time, before the successful reforestation program of the 1970s, most of South Korea's land was treeless and hilly, so guerrillas would be sitting ducks for helicopters and light planes.

Nonetheless, all of this became clear only later. In the late 1960s the North Korean government made another bid for unification—so violent and intense, actually, that some have gone so far as to describe it as the "Second Korean War."[27]

The North Korean plan for unification generally followed a well-established Communist pattern known as the "United Front" strategy. The strategy initially called for the creation (by North Korea) of a broad left-leaning opposition movement that would be led and manipulated by clandestine groups of South Koreans (or rather, Jucheists). The assumption was that a broad coalition would first overthrow the pro-American military regime. Afterward, the hidden pro-Pyongyang core would cast off and, if necessary, destroy their former allies, eventually emerging as the driving force of a truly Communist revolution.

Kim Il Sung and his people, being former guerrillas themselves, also pinned great hopes on the emergence of an armed guerrilla resistance within South Korea. Obviously, in emulation of the Vietnamese experience, they expected that a small number of North Korean commandos, often of South Korean extraction, would serve as a nucleus for a future South Korean guerrilla army.

In the 1960s, encouraged by signs of leftward drift among some South Korean intellectuals, Pyongyang undertook several attempts to establish an underground party in the South. The most successful of these attempts led to the creation of the "Revolutionary Party of Unification" in 1964. The party, however, never managed to reach prominence and was eventually destroyed by the South Korean authorities. Some of its leaders were executed, while others were sent to jail.

There have been other attempts to reestablish the pro-Pyongyang underground and recruit some promising young leftists to its ranks. As recently as 2013, Lee Seok Ki, a relatively prominent politician and a member of parliament from the far-left United Progressive Party, was discovered to have also been the head of a small, clandestine pro-Pyongyang organization. There is little doubt that such organizations continue to exist in South Korea—though we should not forget that they are politically very marginal and have little actual influence.

The allure of the Pyongyang model was strong among many anti-dictatorship activists in the South Korea of the 1970s and 1980s. The present author personally knows people who once commuted to Pyongyang via submarine (the usual way of getting agents or full-time activists out of and into South Korea). In three cases that he is personally aware of, these trips and a short exposure to Pyongyang life led to immediate disillusionment with North Korea.

Indeed, it is hard to deny that Korean leftists, self-proclaimed "defenders of human rights and enemies of authoritarianism," have demonstrated a surprisingly high level of sympathy—or, at least, toleration—for the hereditary Stalinist dictatorship in Pyongyang. As mentioned earlier, some prominent leftist activists have been occasionally sponsored by Pyongyang. However, one should not believe in the conspiracy theories popular within the South Korean right. Both the revival of the South Korean far-left and the remarkable popularity of Generalissimo Kim among its followers have little to do with Pyongyang's spies. Rather, they reflect the peculiarities of South Korean capitalism and the South Korean political structure. On balance, North Korea's United Front strategy has been unsuccessful.[28]

Aside from attempts to create a Communist underground, in the late 1960s the North Korean government undertook military operations aimed at destabilizing the government in Seoul. However, these efforts also ended in failure.

On January 21, 1968, thirty-one North Korean commandos infiltrated Seoul. Their goal was to storm the presidential palace and slaughter everyone inside. Obviously, Kim Il Sung believed that this bold attack, to be attributed to the local guerrillas, would be good for the "forthcoming" revolution in Seoul and might singlehandedly spark a mass armed resistance. The raiding party was intercepted at the last minute, however, and an intense firefight ensued in downtown Seoul. One commando escaped back to the North, where he received a hero's welcome and eventually became a general; another was captured alive, eventually becoming a Protestant pastor in South Korea. All the others were killed. The raid is often known as "The Blue House Raid," after the name of the presidential residence in Seoul.

Another attempt to foment revolution followed in late 1968. Some 120 North Korean commandos landed on the East Coast, where they hoped to establish a Vietnamese-style guerrilla base. They took over a few villages and herded villagers into ideological indoctrination sessions where the farmers were harangued about the greatness of the Great Leader, the happiness of their northern brethren, and the assorted wonders of the soon-to-come Communist paradise. But the inflexible, doctrinaire North Korean propagandists were less persuasive than their North Vietnamese counterparts and failed to impress the villagers. Thus, the expected uprising did not happen, and the commandos were hunted into extinction by the South Korean military.

At around the same time, the North Koreans began to escalate tensions in the DMZ, often attacking South Korean and American border patrols. In January 1968, almost immediately after the Blue House Raid, the North Korean Navy captured the US naval intelligence ship *Pueblo,* and kept the ship and its crew in captivity for more than a year. Although the episode was seen as being part of a grand Communist strategy, the oral tradition of the Soviet diplomatic service holds that, on the night after the seizure, Soviet experts spent sleepless hours looking for an excuse that would allow the Soviet Union to avoid entering into a potential war between the United States and North Korea. Finally, they found one: the 1961 treaty between the USSR and the DPRK stated that the Soviet Union had a duty to defend its ally against acts of military aggression, but because the *Pueblo* seizure was an act of aggression by North Korea, the Soviet Union had no duty to intervene.

However, between 1971 and 1972 it became clear that all these adventurous and sometimes bloody efforts had come to naught. South Korea's "toiling masses" were not going to take up arms and go to the mountains. The average South Korean remained anti-Communist or, at least, deeply suspicious of North Korea.

In this situation, North Korea's leaders made a U-turn and began secret negotiations with the South on the assumption that some kind of provisional coexistence (until the forthcoming revolution) was necessary. In July 1972 the North and South issued a Joint Communiqué that theoretically committed both to the goal of eventual peaceful unification. It was rhetoric pure and simple, but it created a framework within which the two Korean states began to talk and interact when they considered it necessary. The policy of mutual nonrecognition continues to this day (and is likely to endure for the foreseeable future), but since 1972, Pyongyang and Seoul have usually maintained direct contact of various kinds.

There were, however, some occasional relapses into revolutionary adventurism. In 1983 North Korean intelligence operatives planted a powerful bomb in Rangoon, Burma, where the South Korean president was on a state visit. Due to an operative's mistake, the device was detonated too early, and the president survived the explosion; however, a number of dignitaries were killed. The three North Korean operatives, none of whom spoke Burmese, could not escape. Two were taken alive after unsuccessful suicide attempts, and another was killed after a firefight with Burmese soldiers. Not only the Burmese (never staunch opponents of Pyongyang), but even the Chinese were annoyed by this adventurism.

Another act of blatant violence was the bombing of a South Korean passenger jet in November 1987 by two North Korean intelligence officers. Obviously, this was done in order to create the impression that Seoul would be an unsafe venue for the coming Olympic Games of 1988. The bombing killed 115 crew members and passengers (many of whom were construction workers on their way back from the Middle East). One of the two agents was captured and another committed suicide, but the overall political impact of the operation was close to zero: the 1988 Olympic Games were a great success.

There might have been other undisclosed or aborted operations of a similar kind, but on balance, from the mid-1970s the North Korean leadership came to the conclusion that a South Korean revolution was unlikely to happen any time soon. Support for South Korean "revolutionary forces" was never completely dropped from Pyongyang's agenda, but as time passed, its significance steadily diminished. From the early 1990s, when the economy began to fall apart, Pyongyang's agenda became dominated by the necessity of defense, not offense.

THE COMMAND SOCIETY

In the decades during Kim Il Sung's rule, North Korea became a society where the level of state control over the average citizen's public and private life reached heights that would be almost unthinkable in any other country, including Stalin's Russia.

Icons

The personality cult of the Kim family has long been a peculiar and often bizarre feature of North Korean society—and like any cult, it has iconography. Normally, four members of the Kim family are considered worthy of depiction—Generalissimo Kim Il Sung, Marshal (from 2012, posthumously, also Generalissimo) Kim Jong Il, Marshal Kim Jong Un, and General Kim Jong Suk (the latter being Kim Il Sung's first official wife and Kim Jong Il's mother). Some other members of the family are occasionally depicted as well, but the images of those four are virtually omnipresent and come in many forms.

North Korea is a country of portraits. From the 1940s, depictions of Kim Il Sung were common, but from the 1970s, it was decreed that every house should have a portrait of the Great Leader. The state bestowed upon the people such portraits and directed them to put these icons in their living rooms. They were to be placed on a wall devoid of any other adornments and cleaned regularly.

From 1972, Kim Il Sung's portrait was also placed at the entrances of all factories, railway stations, and airports. From the mid-1980s, the portrait was also to be present in all railway and subway carriages, but, for some unknown reason, not in buses or trams. In the late 1970s, North Koreans were directed to place standardized portraits of Kim Jong Il alongside those of his father.

A further layer of complexity was added in the 1990s. From then on, every single Korean house was to have three portraits: one of Kim Il Sung, one of Kim Jong Il, and yet another of the two great men talking about some highly important matters of statecraft. Privileged officials, however, were lucky enough to be issued with a different third picture, the visage of Kim Jong Suk. Due to reasons unknown, offices still have portraits of the Dear Leader and Great Leader only.

Another important icon of the personality cult is the badge that all adult North Koreans have been required to wear on all occasions since the early 1970s. This badge usually depicts Kim Il Sung. (In some rare cases, badges feature a portrait of Kim Jong Un, alone or alongside the visage of Kim Il Sung.) There are a great number of badges, and an

(continued)

experienced observer can learn a lot from the type of badge a North Korean wears. For instance, officials of some important government agencies are issued their own particular type of badge.

Of course, we should not forget statues. The first statues of Kim Il Sung appeared in the late 1940s, but the vast majority were erected in the 1970s and 1980s. Most counties and cities have their own statue of Kim Il Sung, centrally located. If such a statue is absent, the symbolic center will house a large mural depicting one of the Kims. Similar murals can be found at major crossroads in cities and, occasionally, in the countryside.

During every major official holiday, all North Koreans are expected to pay a visit to a local statue and, after a respectful bow, leave flowers honoring the Generalissimo (usually Kim Il Sung, but in some cities other members of the Kim family can be commemorated as well). The largest and most important statues are located on Mansu Hill in downtown Pyongyang. In April 2012 the first statue (Kim Il Sung) received company when the likeness of Marshal (now Generalissimo) Kim Jong Il was erected next to his father. The original statue of his father had a facelift: a broad smile and pair of glasses were added to his face, which had been up until then very austere and stern looking. Interestingly, in Kim Jong Il's lifetime, very few statues of the man were erected.

In an emergency, statues and portraits are to be protected whatever the cost, as any sacred object should be—and North Koreans are reminded that they must safeguard the images. For example, in 2007 the official media widely reported an incident that allegedly occurred in August of that year.

During severe flooding, Kang Hyong-kwon, a factory worker from the city of Ich'on, was trying to make his way to safety through a dangerous stream. Before leaving his flooded house, he took the two most precious things in his life—his five-year-old daughter and portraits of Leaders Generalissimo Kim Il Sung and Marshal Kim Jong Il. Suddenly overwhelmed by the current, he lost his grip of his daughter, who fell into the swollen water, but still managed to keep hold of the sacred images. The media implored North Koreans to emulate Kang Hyong-kwon, a real-life hero.

Private initiative was almost completely eliminated from North Korean economic life. Even the role of money diminished greatly, as few items could be freely bought and sold in Kim Il Sung's North Korea. In 1957 private trade of rice and other grains was banned, so that grains (by far the most important source of calories in the diet of the average North Korean) could be distributed by the state alone. From that time until around 1990, grains could be acquired almost exclusively through the public distribution system (PDS). Every North Korean was declared eligible for a fixed daily grain ration, which was provided for a token price.

The exact size of the ration depended on one's job; the average working adult received a grain ration of 700 grams a day, a housewife would be given merely 300 grams, while a person doing heavy physical work (a miner or, say, a jet fighter pilot) was eligible for the highest daily ration of 900 grams. The ratio of rice to other (less nutritious) grains in a ration depended largely on where you lived. During the "affluent" 1970s, the privileged inhabitants of Pyongyang received more than half of their rations in rice, while in the countryside nearly the entire ration came as corn and wheat flour, with rice being a luxury food reserved for special occasions.

In 1973, when the economic situation began to deteriorate, rations were cut for the first time. A typical adult's ration of 700g was reduced to 607g. The next cut came in 1987, when the same standard daily ration went down to 547g. Officially, these cuts were considered to be "voluntary donations," but nobody asked North Koreans whether they were willing to "donate" their food to the state.

Rationing was not restricted to grain. Additional foodstuffs such as soy sauce, eggs, cabbage, and other basic ingredients in the traditional Korean diet were rationed as well. Meat was distributed irregularly, a few times a year—usually before major official holidays. Fortunately, fish and other types of seafood were more readily available. In autumn, there might be the occasional distribution of apples, melons, and other fruits.[29]

Basic consumer goods were also rationed, even though the mechanism of their distribution varied. Items such as wristwatches and black-and-white TV sets—the major symbols of consumerism during the 1960s and 1970s—were usually distributed through one's work units. In some cases, valuable items were given to distinguished individuals as "presents of the Great Leader." This particular form of distribution was clearly also good for the ideological health of the nation: it reminded North Koreans of the wisdom and benevolence bestowed upon them by the Great Leader, who kept them fed and well-provided with daily necessities.

Contrary to what has often been claimed, private markets were never banned in North Korea. They operated under many restrictions and were small in scale, but they existed nonetheless. However, the average North Korean of Kim Il Sung's era seldom shopped at them. Items on sale at the marketplace were overpriced and usually seen as unnecessary luxuries. Average North Koreans were seldom prepared to spend more than half of their monthly wage on a chicken (this was the market price in the early 1980s). In most cases, North Korean consumers were quite content with what they got through the rationing system. Moreover, every able-bodied North Korean male was required to work for the state, and this require-ment was enforced very strictly. In the late 1950s small private workshops were nationalized, and all farmers were forced to join agricultural coop-eratives. These "cooperatives" were essentially state-run and state-owned farms in all but name. Farmers worked for the same standard 700g daily ration, the only difference being that in their case, rations were distributed not twice a month, as in the cities, but rather once a year, soon after the harvest.

The forced switch to "collective" state farms was a common feature of nearly all Communist states, but even so, North Korean state farms re-tained some peculiarities. Most significantly, farmers were allowed only tiny private kitchen gardens. In Stalin's Soviet Union, a farmer usually had a private plot, the size of which might exceed 1,000 m², while in Kim Il Sung's North Korea, private plots could not exceed 100 m², and not all farmers were allowed to have plots even that small. The assumption was that farmers, being deprived of any additional source of income and calo-ries, would have no choice but to devote all their time and energy to toil-ing in the fields of the state.[30]

This is very different from the Soviet prototype. Soon after the forced collectivization of agriculture in the 1930s, Soviet farmers' individual plots still provided more than half the country's total production of potatoes (a major source of calories in Russia in those days) and a significant share of other vegetables. Nor did this situation change much in subsequent decades. In the early 1970s Soviet consumers obtained more than 60 percent of their potatoes and eggs from the private agricultural sector; the private sector also produced 40 percent of their fruit, vegetables, meat, and dairy products.[31] A similar situation was to be found in Communist Vietnam, where farmers were allocated 5 percent of the total land to be used as their private plots. Throughout the 1960s and 1970s, farmers in North Vietnam earned between 60 and 75 percent of their income from the private cultivation of these "5-percent plots," even though the plots were not officially allocated fertilizer or other state-supplied resources.[32]

When it came to finding a job, North Korea was similarly strict, even by Communist standards. After graduation from high school, all North Koreans were assigned to jobs. Those who were judged to be both academically gifted and politically reliable would be allowed to sit for college entrance exams. Changing one's job was possible, but had to be approved beforehand by the authorities and required much paperwork (the only exception being women, who often became full-time housewives after marriage).

One of the most striking peculiarities of Kim Il Sung's North Korea was the extent to which the daily lives of its citizens were monitored by the authorities. The place of residence could be changed only with the approval of authorities, normally in cases when real or alleged needs of the national economy would require somebody to be allocated to a new job in a different place. Women were the exception since they were allowed and indeed were expected to move into the husband's household after marriage and could, if they wished, be allocated a new job in the husband's area.

Additionally, not merely longtime residence but also short-term travel had to be approved by the authorities beforehand. A North Korean was not allowed to travel outside his or her native county or city without a special travel permit issued by the local police. The only exception was visits to counties/cities that had a common border with the county/city where he or she had official household registration. If caught traveling without permit, a North Korean would be arrested and then "extradited" back to the jurisdiction of residence for investigation and "appropriate punishment." Moreover, the issuance of a travel permit required justification unless the person was going on official business. A travel permit clearly specified the intended destination and period of travel and had to be produced when purchasing a ticket or when one stayed overnight either in a hotel or with friends. A trip to certain special areas, such as the city of Pyongyang or districts near the DMZ, required a distinct type of travel permit that had to be confirmed by the Ministry for the Interior—and such "confirmed number permits" were exceedingly difficult to get.

Incidentally, the "travel permit" system set North Korea apart from other Communist countries. Being a native of the Soviet Union, the present author was surprised to discover the average Westerner's belief that Soviet citizens needed official permits to travel domestically. This was not the case in the post-Stalinist Soviet Union (and for the vast majority of the urban people, it was not the case even under Stalin). There were *areas* within the Soviet Union that were closed to the average traveler, but these areas were few and far between. The right to reside in a city of one's choice was indeed limited, but short-term domestic travel was essentially unrestricted in the former USSR.

In the enforcement of domestic travel control, as well as in general surveillance, a special role was played by a peculiar North Korean institution known as the *inminban*, or "people's group." These groups still exist, even though their efficiency as surveillance institutions has declined since the early 1990s.

A typical *inminban* is comprised of twenty to forty families. In neighborhoods consisting of detached houses, that is, in the majority of North Korean neighborhoods, one *inminban* includes all inhabitants of a block, while in apartment buildings an *inminban* includes all families sharing a common staircase (or two to three adjacent staircases if the building is not so large). *Inminban* membership is, essentially, inescapable: every North Korean regardless of age or sex belongs to an *inminban*.

Each *inminban* is headed by an official, always a woman and usually middle-aged. Her duties are numerous. Some of these duties involve neighborhood-related issues (garbage removal, for example) while many others are related to surveillance. The head of an *inminban* is required to learn about the income, assets, and spending habits of all of her charges. The present author once interviewed a number of former *inminban* heads for a research project and was surprised to hear most of them cite a statement they probably heard often during their training sessions: "An *inminban* head should know how many chopsticks and how many spoons are in every household!"

The police supervise the *inminban's* activities. Every *inminban* is assigned a "resident police officer" who regularly meets its head (in fact, even her appointment must be confirmed by this officer). During such meetings an *inminban* head must report suspicious activities that have come to her attention.

The *inminban* also plays a major role in enforcing control over the movement of people. Every evening the head of an *inminban* is required to fill in a special register where she records all outside visitors who intend to spend the night on her turf. If a relative or friend stays overnight, the household must report this to the head of the *inminban*, who then checks the person's ID (if the overnight visitor comes from outside the city or county, his/her travel permit is checked as well). A few times a year, specially assigned police patrols, accompanied by the head of the *inminban*, conduct midnight random checks of households just to make sure that all people spending the night there have registered themselves properly. Additionally, they check the seals on radio sets to ensure that the tuning function remains disabled so that the sets cannot be used to listen to foreign broadcasts (more on that later).

Alongside the *inminban* system, there is another ubiquitous system of surveillance and ideological indoctrination—so-called "organizational life." Every North Korean must belong to an "organization" that both controls and directs his/her social activities. To simplify things a bit, virtually all North Koreans are expected to join the Party Youth organization at the age of fourteen and, subsequently, a minority of them might then join the ruling Korean Workers' Party. Contrary to rather widespread belief, party membership in itself is not a privilege: actually, the KWP rank and file is subjected to even stricter demands than the general populace. However, during the Kim Il Sung era, party membership was much coveted by the upwardly mobile and ambitious, since it was a necessary prerequisite for *any* social advancement (only KWP members were eligible for promotion in nearly all cases).

Those who are not lucky enough to join the KWP would remain in the Party Youth organization until they turned thirty and then become members of the Trade Union organization at their workplace (farmers enter the Agricultural Union instead of the Trade Union). Even housewives are not left outside this ubiquitous web of surveillance and indoctrination: if a woman quits her job after marriage, she automatically becomes a member of the Women's Union, where the "joys" of "organizational life" await.

It is significant that every single North Korean is a member of one of the earlier-mentioned five "organizations" at his/her workplace and simultaneously a member of the *inminban* in his/her neighborhood. This is still the case even though the significance of the system began to decline in the 1990s, as party discipline and state control became lax during the famine.

"Organizational life" usually consists of frequent and soporifically long meetings. Typically, there are three meetings every week, each lasting one or two hours. Two meetings are dedicated to ideological indoctrination: their participants are lectured on the greatness of the Great Leader Kim Il Sung and his family, the glorious achievements of the Korean Workers' Party, and the incomparable triumphs of the North Korean economy. The diabolical nature of US imperialism and sufferings of the destitute and oppressed South Korean population are also discussed frequently (as we will see later, however, in the recent decade, the fate of South Koreans has started to be presented in a slightly different light).

One of the three weekly meetings is, however, quite different from the other two. It is known as a "Weekly Life Review Session" but better recognized under the descriptive translation as "Self-Criticism and Mutual-Criticism Session." Such a session usually involves all participants (that is, every North Korean above the age of fourteen) delivering a brief report about their personal misdeeds and unsound actions during the previous week. Following this, another member of the same cell is expected to criticize the person in question for the same or different misdeeds. Of course, in real life these sessions are akin to theatrical performances, since people are street-smart enough to not admit anything that might lead to serious consequences. Typically, individuals admit to being late to their shift or not sufficiently diligent in taking care of portraits of the Great Leader (surprisingly, the latter is seen as a minor deviation). Nonetheless, these self-criticism and mutual-criticism sessions help to keep the population in line and in some rare cases even lead to the exposure of significant ideological deviations.

One of the truly unique features of Kim Il Sung's North Korea was the re-emergence of hereditary groups, each having a clearly defined set of privileges and restrictions. In this regard, Kim Il Sung's North Korea was surprisingly reminiscent of a pre-modern society, with its order of fixed and hereditary castes (or "estates," as they were sometimes known in pre-modern Europe).

Starting from 1957, the authorities began to conduct painstaking checks of the family background of every North Korean. This massive project was largely completed by the mid-1960s and led to the emergence of what is essentially a caste system. This system is known in North Korea as *sŏngbun*. According to the *sŏngbun* system, every North Korean belongs to one of three strata: "loyal," "wavering," or "hostile." In most cases, people are classified in accordance with what they or their direct male ancestors did in the 1940s and early 1950s.

Children and grandchildren of former landlords, Christian and Buddhist priests, private entrepreneurs, and clerks in the Japanese colonial administration, as well as the descendants of other "suspicious elements" (like, say, courtesans or female shamans), are classified as part of the "hostile" stratum. This involves a great deal of discrimination. For example, people born into this caste cannot be accepted to prestigious colleges or reside in major cities—even if they are the culprits' great-grandchildren.

Conversely, people whose direct male ancestors greatly contributed to the establishment or defense of the Kim family regime are usually members of the "loyal" stratum. This privileged caste includes prominent officials, descendants of fallen heroes of the Korean War, and others whose deeds are lauded by the regime. As a rule, only members of this group are eligible for the most prestigious jobs.

One cannot change one's own place in this hierarchical system, and the children will automatically get the same status. Only in exceptional cases can a humble "bad sŏngbuner" be reclassified and promoted—for example, by saving a portrait of Kim Il Sung from a flooded house or doing some equally heroic feat.

As stated earlier, *sŏngbun* is inherited through the male line; the present author knows one family in which the wife is a descendant of revolutionary guerrillas and hence has an exceptionally good *sŏngbun*. Nonetheless, her husband is the progeny of a minor landlord, and hence, the children of the couple (incidentally, one of the most perfect long-married couples I've seen in my life) were not eligible for admission to good colleges. Such unequal marriages were unusual: like any other stratified society, in Kim Il Sung's North Korea, the young and, especially, their parents were not enthusiastic about "marrying down." Marriages, therefore, were usually concluded between families of roughly equal social standing—and, indeed, countless times my North Korean interlocutors cited *sŏngbun* as an important, even decisive, factor in their selection of a marriage partner.

The *sŏngbun* system might appear blatantly unjust to someone with modern sensibilities, but it is clearly a highly efficient and effective way to keep people in line. In Kim Il Sung's North Korea, every aspiring dissenter knew that it was not only he or she who would pay dearly for an attempt at resistance. Potential challengers were aware that their immediate family would remain the target of discrimination for generations. Needless to say, this made people even less willing to change the system.

All Communist regimes believed (and with good reason, one must admit) that their people must be kept isolated from potentially dangerous knowledge from the outside world. Few, if any, of these regimes, however, could rival both the intensity and extensiveness of North Korea's self-imposed information blockade. This exceptional reclusiveness was a result of North Korea's peculiar and vulnerable position as part of a divided country.

This set of extreme isolationist policies was first introduced around 1960. The regime probably initially instituted them to ensure that the North Korean people would not be influenced by the dangerously liberal ideas emanating from the "revisionist" Soviet Union. From around 1970, it was the fabled "economic miracle on the Han River" in the South, however, that became the major source of political anxiety for North Korea's leaders. The ruling elite understood that average North Koreans must be kept ignorant of the comparative affluence enjoyed by their southern brethren. With the passage of time, the gap between the two Koreas grew exponentially, and the political importance of maintaining complete control over external information grew accordingly.

North Korea is the only country in the world to have banned the use of tunable radios in peacetime. From around 1960, all radios officially sold in North Korea have fixed tuning, so that one can only listen to a small number of official North Korean stations. If one buys a radio in a hard currency shop or brings one in from overseas (which is legal), the owner has to immediately submit the radio to the police, whereupon a technician will permanently disable its tuning mechanism. Since a technically savvy person can easily repair a radio that has been so tampered with, all privately owned radio sets have to be sealed. During the earlier-mentioned random household checks, *inminban* heads and the police are required to make sure that these seals remain intact.

This presents a remarkable contrast with the Soviet Union, where, after Stalin's death, listening to foreign broadcasts—even those deemed to be "subversive" in nature—became a perfectly legal activity. In the Soviet Union, foreign stations were frequently jammed, but this jamming was ineffectual outside major cities. Moreover, high-quality shortwave radios could be freely purchased in Soviet shops. A 1984 research project stated that in an average week, some 14 to 18 percent of Soviet adults listened to the Voice of America, 7 to 10 percent to the BBC, and 8 to 12 percent to Radio Liberty.[33] By the prevailing standards of the Communist bloc, the Soviet Union was not particularly permissive: in East Germany, for example, more or less everybody watched West German TV. Such decadent permissiveness surprised North Koreans. This author remembers the shock of a minor North Korean official who learned from him (in the mid-1980s) that it was perfectly legal to listen to foreign broadcasts in the USSR. Stunned by such outrageous liberalism, he asked: "And what if the programming is not ideologically healthy?"

In the late 1960s the authorities undertook a massive campaign aimed at the physical destruction of foreign books (for the most part Soviet and

Japanese) that were then privately owned by North Koreans. In libraries, all foreign publications of a nontechnical nature were (and still are) to be kept in a special section, with only people possessing a proper security clearance authorized to read them. Remarkably, even in the 1970s, no exception was made for publications of "fraternal" Communist countries: Moscow's *Pravda* and Beijing's *People's Daily* were deemed to be potentially as subversive as *The Washington Post* or Seoul's *Chosun Ilbo*.

The North Korean authorities were aware that dangerous information could penetrate the country not only via radio or print but also through unsupervised personal interactions between North Koreans and foreigners. They therefore took care to reduce such interactions to a bare minimum. North Koreans have always been aware that close contacts with foreigners outside one's clearly defined official duties are potentially dangerous.

When the present author lived in Pyongyang in the mid-1980s as a Soviet exchange student, he and other such students had to deal with an impressive array of restrictions placed on their daily lives. For instance, they were not allowed to attend classes together with North Korean students. They could not visit private homes, nor could they go to certain museums. In an interesting twist, they were not allowed to enter the catalog rooms of major libraries. And, needless to say, most adult North Koreans would avoid personal contacts with them. These restrictions (like, say, a ban on visiting movie theaters) were sometimes hard to understand, but the overall underlying tendency was clear: the authorities strove to eliminate the possibility of uncontrolled interactions between ideologically contaminated Soviet students and North Koreans. Furthermore, they sought to limit access to information that they did not want to leave the country.

Finally, in a truly Orwellian twist, the North Korean authorities took care to isolate the populace not only from the foreign media but also from the official publications of earlier years. All North Korean periodicals and a significant number of publications on social and political topics were regularly removed from common-access libraries and could only be read by people with special permission. Periodicals like *Rodong Shinmun*—the country's main newspaper—were removed regularly; as a result, all newspapers published more than ten to fifteen years ago become inaccessible for the laity. This rule was obviously introduced to ensure that changes in the policy line of the regime would remain unnoticeable to the populace. During the 1970s and 1980s, the government did not want the average North Korean exposed to the paeans Kim Il Sung delivered to the great Soviet Army and Comrade Stalin during the 1940s and 1950s. Nor did they want them to be aware of the harangues against "Soviet revisionism" that were common in the Korean press of the early 1960s.

A COUNTRY OF CAMPS

Kim Il Sung's regime was brutal, but one of its most peculiar features was the emphasis placed on the prevention of ideological deviation rather than open state terror. People who expressed ideologically unwholesome ideas were first dealt with through the institutions of "organizational life" and/or the *inminban* system. A majority of the people were fully aware that they could be the object of surveillance at any moment, so they knew better than to break the rules or express the slightest doubts about official ideology. Nonetheless, political persecution was still very much a part of life in Kim Il Sung's North Korea. After all, even with all the advantages of unceasing surveillance and control, arbitrary arrest and the institutionalized use of violence were also important for maintaining internal stability and ideological conformity.

As a result, North Korea has an extensive system of prison camps whose number of inmates was estimated to be some 150,000 in the early 1980s and perhaps as many as 200,000 in the early 1990s. These figures are estimates based on analysis of aerial photos and testimony from prison camp survivors and former guards, since the government of North Korea has— predictably—never admitted the existence of the prison camp system, let alone published official statistics about its scale.[34]

Only in the early 2000s did the prison population begin to contract, reflecting the relative liberalization of the regime. Still, in 2012 the political prison camp population was estimated to be at the level of 80,000 to 120,000.[35] This is roughly half of what it used to be in the heyday of Kim Il

Sung's rule, but it still constitutes by far the highest ratio of political prisoners to the general population worldwide.

The earlier-mentioned figures indicate that during the Kim Il Sung era, some 0.6 to 0.7 percent of the country's population were political prisoners. In North Korea it is easy to distinguish between normal and political prisoners because there are two distinct prison systems. The numbers involved are slightly higher than the ratio of political prisoners to general population of the Soviet Union in the last years of Stalin's rule. Indeed, the North Korean system of persecution owed much to Stalin's model, but it also had some peculiarities that likely developed under the influence of Mao's China.

To start with, the system is unusually secretive. The macabre tradition of show trials, so typical of Stalin's Soviet Union, was discarded by North Korea's policymakers long ago. Until December 2013's public purge of Chang Sŏng-t'aek, the last show trial took place in December 1955, when Pak Hon-yŏng, the most prominent first-generation Korean Communist, was sentenced to death as a US and Japanese spy. From then on, Kim Il Sung's victims began to disappear without a trace. The government simply did not bother informing the public that some prominent dignitary was found to be a lifelong South Korean saboteur or an American spy (if such reports were issued at all, they were classified and given only to the elite, not the population at large). In some cases, the disappearance did not mean death—years later, the person would make a sudden comeback, with no explanation given for his/her long absence. Much of the time these unfortunate people were sent into internal exile with their immediate family, and more occasionally they may have spent a spell in a political prison camp.

There are some indications that as a rule, political criminals in North Korea were (and still are) not even present at their own trial and do not know the term they are sentenced to serve. The hapless person in question is normally intercepted by security agents at work or on the street and hauled to an interrogation facility. The person does not get to make a phone call (and until recently it was unlikely that their home would have a phone from which they could make a call in any case).

After interrogation, the unfortunate victim was shipped to a camp. This was in stark contrast to the USSR, where even at the height of Stalin-era purges, a mock trial—lasting ten minutes or less—was deemed necessary to keep up the appearance of "Socialist legality." When the condemned met an overworked execution team, victims at least became aware of what political crime they had allegedly committed. David Hawk notes that "forced disappearance" might be a more suitable way to describe what is normally referred to as "arrest" in North Korea, and he is right.[36] Indeed, in North Korea only common criminals have the luxury of a formal trial, however biased and unfair it may be.

As mentioned previously, unlike the former USSR and most other countries, in North Korea there is a clear separation between camps that handle common criminals and camps reserved exclusively for political prisoners. The latter are known as *kwanliso*, and as of 2013 there are four such camps in operation. In the past, there were about a dozen of them, but in the course of time some were closed while those remaining were expanded.

The "family responsibility" system is also a remarkable feature of the North Korean society, created in Kim Il Sung's era but relaxed substantially in the mid-1990s when Kim Jong Il ascended to power. According to the system, if someone was arrested for a political crime, his entire family—technically speaking, all people who shared his household registration address and were his relatives—would be placed in a political prison camp, although they were separated from the criminal and usually faced more relaxed conditions of imprisonment (that were nonetheless exceedingly harsh). This is another difference with "justice" under Stalin in the USSR, where only family members of the most significant victims of the purge were sent to the camps.

Actually, the family responsibility principle might be counted among the factors that contributed to the regime's stability. While the repressive system in North Korea remains very secretive, it has always been public knowledge that if somebody says or does something politically improper, not only the culprit but also the entire family disappears. People who might otherwise be prepared to risk their own lives are understandably deterred by the prospect of their entire family paying a terrible price as well—including, perhaps, descendants yet unborn.

A typical example of the family responsibility principle is the fate of Kang Ch'ŏl-hwan, arguably the best known of all former inmates of the North Korean prison system. In 1977 Kang was sent to Camp 15 together with his family. He was only seven years old at the time and remained in the camp for ten years. The reason for his imprisonment was an old conflict between his grandmother, a former activist of Chongryon, and Han Tŏk-su, the notorious leader of ethnic Koreans in Japan, who also enjoyed significant political clout in Pyongyang. The Kang family had been among those Koreans who chose to return to the "Socialist Motherland," and his grandfather, a successful businessman, contributed significant amounts of money to the construction of the Kim Il Sung statue on Mansudae Hill— recently "refurbished" (see front cover photo). However, after the family had lived in North Korea for a while, Han decided to settle old scores, and they were all sent to a camp—only Kang Ch'ŏl-hwan's mother, the daughter of a successful North Korean spy, was spared. Children are common in these camps, and therefore there are schools for them. Political police personnel act as teachers (Kang Ch'ŏl-hwan "graduated" from such a school).[37]

This story is interesting in another regard, too: while it was Kang's grandmother whose nationalist-cum-revolutionary zeal got the entire family in trouble, the major punishment was inflicted on Kang's grandfather, a rather apolitical businessman. This is a remarkable, albeit paradoxical, reflection of the deeply patriarchal nature of North Korean society, where men are often held responsible for the serious misdeeds of "their" women—on the assumption that the man, being the "natural" head of the household, ought to keep an eye on everything that happens there and put a stop to any improper activity.

Inside the camps, there are zones with differing regimes: softer "zones of revolutionization" and stricter "zones of absolute control." In the latter, prisoners are deprived of the right to live with their families and are subjected to exceptionally harsh conditions. It is assumed they will never be released.

On the other hand, "zones of revolutionization" are relatively mild by the standards of Gulag-style prison camps. Such zones are believed to have existed only in two camps—Camp 18 and Camp 15 (the former was recently closed). Inside these zones inmates are usually allowed to stay with their families and live in individual houses or family quarters. They work and are free to move within their camp zone (or revolutionization zone) and somewhat spared the regimented existence usually associated with a prison. Model prisoners might even be allowed to have children— of course, those children remain with their parents inside prison fences. In most cases, the inmates are completely cut off from the outside world, so their friends and relations do not know exactly what has happened to them—and, being conditioned by the experience of life in North Korea, they know better than to ask too many questions. The most important difference between the two zones of the North Korean prison camps is that people can occasionally be released from the "zones of revolutionization"—and this is the reason why we know so much more about these zones than about the "zones of absolute control."

It seems that as a rule, family members of a political criminal who live in the "zones of revolutionization" are released when the main culprit dies—but nobody knows for sure. Normally, the main culprit is sent to a different place, usually the "zone of absolute control," from which he has almost no chance of emerging alive.

The camp routine consists of ten to twelve hours of backbreaking labor, followed by boring indoctrination sessions. There is one day of rest per month, and if inmates do not meet their production quotas, they are punished both with beatings and a reduction in rations. Even full rations are barely enough for physical survival, however, and consist almost exclusively of poor-quality corn.

To make sure that no deviation, let alone dissent, will remain undetected, the North Korean political police, known as the Ministry for Protection of State Security (MPSS), have an extensive network of informers. Defecting officers of the MPSS, some of whom the author knows personally, claim that under normal circumstances there is supposed to be one informer for every fifty adults in the entire population. If this directive is followed, it means

that some 250,000 to 300,000 North Koreans are now paid police informers—and many more have had such experience at some point in their lives.

THE WORLD ACCORDING TO KIM IL SUNG

What did Kim Il Sung expect his beloved subjects to think? What were the
precious ideas that the North Korean state spent so much time trying to
protect from foreign pollution? A look at the North Korean ideology of
Kim Il Sung's era reveals a peculiar mix of Stalinized Leninism and
Maoism, heavily spiced with rather extreme forms of nationalism and a
touch of Confucian traditionalism.

Perhaps the most striking part of the North Korean "ideological land-
scape" from the late 1960s was a personality cult of Marshal (eventually
Generalissimo) Great Leader Kim Il Sung, the Sun of the Nation, the Ever-
Victorious General. Initially, his cult was patterned on the cults of Mao
and Stalin, but by the early 1970s it reached an intensity that was incomparable to any leadership cult in the modern world.

Mao and Stalin were presented officially as the successors of Marx,
Engels, and Lenin—the legitimate disciples of the deceased Communist
sages. In other words, they were just the most recent among the incarna-
tions of Marxist wisdom and omniscience. The visual representation of,
say, Stalin's "historical significance" was oft-reproduced group portraits in
which Stalin's profile was superimposed next to those of Marx, Engels, and
Lenin—obviously, in order to demonstrate their equality and succession
in ideological terms. In China, another version of the same group portrait
was also popular, with Chairman Mao superimposed next to Stalin so that
the image simultaneously depicted the five alleged founding fathers of
Chinese-style Communism.

Kim Il Sung was never presented in such a way. North Korean propaganda of the early 1950s sometimes referred to Kim Il Sung as "Stalin's
loyal disciple," but this was done at a time when the alleged primacy of the
Soviet Union still remained a core element of the regime's ideological discourse. Such references disappeared by the late 1950s.

In later times, some ideological indebtedness to Marx and Lenin was begrudgingly admitted, and their portraits could sometimes be seen in North Korea as well (it seems that the last publicly displayed portrait of Marx was removed in April 2012, when the country celebrated the dynastic succession of Kim Jong Un). Nevertheless, these references were to a large extent intended for overseas consumption—devices used to placate visiting dignitaries from other Communist countries or to forge better ties with politically useful Western progressives. For the domestic audience, Kim Il Sung was not presented as an heir to, a disciple of, or the recipient of the guidance of any foreign leader, philosopher, or thinker. He was the founding father of North Korea in his own right, the Creator of the Immortal Juche Idea and the Greatest Man in the Five Thousand Years of Korean History. "National solipsism" (to borrow Bruce Cumings's apt term), the tendency to see Korea as the decisive element in the world—past and present—has always been an important feature of the North Korean worldview and meant essentially that Kim Il Sung was the greatest human being to have ever graced planet Earth.

Since the early 1970s, all North Koreans over age sixteen have been required to sport a badge with Kim Il Sung's visage when they left their homes. Kim Il Sung portraits have to be hung in every office and home; from around 1980, portraits of his son and successor Kim Jong Il were displayed alongside the father (in the 1990s the portrait of Kim Chŏng-suk, Kim Il Sung's wife and Kim Jong Il's mother, was added, too). There are complex regulations that prescribe how the pristine condition of the sacred images should be maintained. If the portraits are damaged, such an incident is carefully investigated, and the people responsible for the maintenance of the portraits are punished if found guilty of neglect. For decades, the North Korean media has been replete with stories extolling the heroic deeds of North Korean citizens who willingly sacrificed their lives to save the portraits of the Great Leader and his son.

Statues of Kim Il Sung have been erected across the country, with the largest statue, twenty-two meters high, built on Mansu Hill in Pyongyang in 1972. The statues have become centers of elaborate rituals. For example, on the Great Leader's birthday and some other major official holidays, every North Korean is supposed to go to the nearest statue and, after a deep bow, lay flowers at the feet of the great man's visage.

The names of Kim Il Sung and (later) Kim Jong Il are to be typed in bold script in North Korean publications (Kim Jong Un's name began to be typed in bold script in late December 2011, a few days after his father's death). Every major article needs to start with a proper quote from either Kim Il Sung or Kim Jong Il. No exception is made even for purely academic publications, including, say, works of liquid state physics or molecular biology. Fortunately for scientists, throughout his long life Kim Il Sung delivered many speeches and signed many articles, so a proper quote can always be found.

The list of titles of Kim Il Sung and his immediate family members began to be formalized in the 1970s. Thus, every North Korean knows how to distinguish between the "Great Leader" (Kim Il Sung) and "Dear Leader" (Kim Jong Il) and is also aware that "three Great Generals of Paekdu Mountain" are Kim Il Sung; his wife, Kim Jong Suk; and their son, Kim Jong Il. After Kim Jong Il's death and the ascendency of his son, Kim Jong Un, the latter was given the title of "Supreme Leader."

Official propaganda established that the Kim family had played a major role in the last 150 years of Korean history. For example, in the 1970s, schools began to teach North Korean students that the March 1st Uprising of 1919, the largest outbreak of anti-Japanese, pro-independence sentiment, started in Pyongyang (not in Seoul, as actually was the case) and that its major leader was, of course, Kim Il Sung's father, Kim Hyŏng-jik. They also claim that Kim Il Sung, then merely seven years old, took part in the March 1st rally. In real life Kim Hyŏng-jik, like the majority of educated Koreans at the time, was sympathetic toward the independence movement and was even briefly detained for participation in anti-Japanese activities. Nonetheless, he was by no means a prominent activist, let alone a leader of the nationalist movement.

Official North Korean historiography did not admit the role played by the Korean Communist Party in spreading Marxism in Korea in the 1920s. This is not surprising given that nearly all of the founders of this party were eventually purged by Kim Il Sung. According to North Korea's official narrative, the history of Korean Communism began in 1926, when Kim Il Sung allegedly founded the Anti-Imperialist Union. As befitting the greatest human being who ever lived, Kim Il Sung is alleged to have single-handedly begun the Korean Communist movement at the tender age of fourteen. It goes without saying that precious few in North Korea are sufficiently audacious as to question the superhuman qualities of Kim as well as the other members of his illustrious family. After all, the recent edition of Kim Jong Il's works includes in its first volume the documents that were allegedly produced by the Dear Leader in 1952 (at the time, Kim Il Sung's eldest son was ten years old).

One recurring feature of this official narrative is an attempt to play down or conceal the foreign influences and connections of Kim Il Sung and his family. As part of this systemic manipulation, the official narrative does not admit that Kim Jong Il was born in the Soviet Union on a military base in the vicinity of Khabarovsk. After all, the successor to the Juche Revolutionary Cause and future head of the ultra-nationalist state could not possibly have been born on foreign soil! North Korean propagandists therefore invented a secret guerrilla camp that allegedly existed on the slopes of Mount Paekdu in the early 1940s, enabling Kim Jong Il to be born on the holiest of Korean soil.

In an interesting twist, in the 1990s, when the Soviet Union was safely dead and Soviet influence was no longer seen as a danger, North Korean official media finally admitted that Kim Il Sung did spend the early 1940s in the Soviet Union. However, this admission did not lead to disavowal of the Paekdu Camp story, which by that time had become a cornerstone of the official propaganda. Nowadays, a North Korean is supposed to believe that in the early 1940s, Kim Il Sung lived in Soviet exile but still personally led daring guerrilla raids into North Korea (Soviet documents indicate that this was not the case). Allegedly, he did so in the company of his pregnant wife, and she gave birth to their first child on the sacral—and purely Korean—slopes of Mount Paekdu. To support these improbable claims, North Korean authorities built a "replica" of the Paekdu Secret Camp, complete with a log cabin where Kim Jong Il was allegedly born, and made it a site of obligatory pilgrimage.

The complete control over information flows within society, combined with isolation from the outside world, gave North Korea's propagandists opportunities their peers elsewhere could not even have dreamed of. They could successfully hide from their people even knowledge that would be considered common in many other societies. At the same time, they could exaggerate or create nonevents with impunity.

As a result, in the media of Kim Il Sung's era, North Korea was presented as a People's Paradise, a place where the entire population lived in a state of unimaginable happiness. North Korean cultural products of the time—unlike the works of Soviet art in the Stalin period—seldom if ever mentioned the existence of internal enemies. Rather, North Koreans were presented as happy children living under the fatherly care of the omniscient Great Leader. In a remarkable gesture, North Korean banknotes bore the motto "We have nothing to envy," thus reminding North Koreans that they were the happiest nation under heaven.

Much in line with this old approach, in 2011 the North Korean media published a worldwide rating of happiness. It stated that the happiest people live in China, with North Koreans coming in second (obviously, they were so moderate in their claims because by that time, North Koreans had become aware that China had a much higher standard of living). The two lowest rankings were held by the United States and South Korea.

THEIR MAJESTIES AND THEIR WOMEN

As is the case in any dynastic state, the personal and sexual lives of the rulers are by definition political. All candidates for the top job are chosen by their predecessors, and this means that family affairs are difficult to distinguish from the affairs of state.

The personal lives of Kim Il Sung and Kim Jong Il are quite convoluted and full of unexpected drama. TV producers should be happy about this, since stories of passion and jealousy in Kim-era Pyongyang will likely achieve high ratings for future TV programs.

Kim Il Sung was married three times. Not much is known about his very first wife—even her existence is sometimes questioned. She is believed to have been another guerrilla, and most think that the first marriage was childless.

By the late 1930s, Kim Il Sung had entered his second union, with Kim Jong Suk. She was also a guerrilla, crossing the Soviet frontier in late 1940 together with Kim Il Sung. Barely literate but kind to and popular with her comrades, she gave birth to three children. Their first son was Kim Jong Il, who would eventually become the North Korean leader.

Kim Jong Suk died in childbirth in 1949. Soon afterward, Kim Il Sung married Kim Song-ae, who had worked in his office at the time. Kim Song-ae remained invisible in North Korean politics until the late 1960s, when she briefly made an attempt to position herself as an important member of the top leadership. She was soon eclipsed by the rise of her stepson, Kim Jong Il. Kim Song-ae bore three children. When Kim Jong Il was finally chosen as successor, they were sent to prestigious diplomatic jobs far away from Pyongyang—a move that provided them with an agreeable lifestyle while rendering them politically harmless (Kim Song-ae's eldest son continues to serve as North Korea's ambassador to Poland).

In his youth, Kim Jong Il had the reputation of a playboy. Indeed, he was popular with girls—not only because he was the crown prince but also because he seems to have been charming (at least if available sources are to be believed). He had a good sense of humor, knew much about cinema and popular culture, and, in spite of being slightly overweight, loved riding motorbikes.

It seems that Kim Jong Il never formally registered a marriage, so the line between a proper wife and a live-in girlfriend was blurry. However, of all of Kim Jong Il's women, only two have significance as far as dynastic policy is concerned.

Kim Jong Il's first known partner was Song Hye-rim, a stunning movie star who had to divorce in order to move in with Kim Jong Il. In 1971 she gave birth to Kim Jong Nam, the Dear Leader's first son. However, Song Hye-rim never managed to win the approval of Kim Il Sung, Kim Jong Il's mighty father—obviously because she was a

(continued)

daughter of South Korean Communists, whom Kim Il Sung never trusted. At any rate, Song Hye-rim's relationship with Kim Jong Il collapsed in the early 1970s. Song Hye-rim was sent into comfortable exile in Moscow, where she died in 2002.

Her son, Kim Jong Nam, also developed uneasy relations with the rest of the family. Since the early 2000s, he has lived in Macao and occasionally did not act to his father's liking (including granting remarkably frank interviews to foreign journalists).

In due course, Kim Jong Il fell in love with another beauty, Ko Yŏng–hǔi, a dancer from a family of ethnic Koreans in Japan. She had two sons, Kim Jong Chol and Kim Jong Un (the current leader). For a while in the late 1990s, Ko acquired minor political clout, but like her predecessor, she died at a relatively young age in 2004.

After Ko Yŏng–hǔi's death, Kim Jong Il reputedly developed relations with the strong-minded and ambitious Kim Ok, his former secretary. Her somewhat special standing was confirmed when Kim Ok appeared at some funeral ceremonies after Kim Jong Il's death in December 2011.

It was against such a backdrop that in late 2008, Kim Jong Il finally chose his third son, Kim Jong Un, as his successor. The third ruler of the Kim dynasty, Kim Jong Un subsequently broke with all these conventions when in July 2012 he began to appear in public with his young and stunningly beautiful wife, Ri Sol Ju, of whose background not much is known (it is, however, known that she loves expensive Dior handbags).

Indeed, there was a striking contrast between North Korea and the outside world. Predictably, the Communist states were presented as relatively prosperous. Even so, the propaganda of the Kim Il Sung era did not spend much time eulogizing the achievements of Soviet cosmonauts or Hungarian milkmaids. This was remarkably different from other states of the Communist bloc, as Kim Il Sung saw other Communist countries as both dangerously liberal and a source of ideological corruption and hence did not want to encourage excessive attention to their real or alleged achievements.

Propagandists also presented the countries of the Third World, especially those that styled themselves as "Socialist," in a favorable light. When it covered the developing world, the North Korean media loved to dwell on the great popularity of Juche ideology across Asia, Africa, and Latin

America. If *Rodong Shinmun* of the 1970s was to be believed, perusing the works of Kim Il Sung was a favorite pastime of many an African villager.

For a brief while, attempts to create a worldwide Jucheist movement were an important part of North Korea's internal and external propaganda. Nearly all of these propaganda operations took place in the Third World. In the developed West, such ideological offerings had few takers, while maintaining such a movement there would be costly. A notable exception was the North Korean support of the Black Panthers. Eldridge Cleaver, the leader of the BPP's international affairs sector, once described North Korea as an "earthly paradise" and expressed his admiration for Kim Il Sung's soldiers, who, in his mind, were "the first to bring the U.S. imperialists trembling to their knees" (the relevant documents were recently discovered and published by Benjamin R. Young).[38] However, such zealots were exceptional in the West, where even the most radical groups felt uneasy about Kim Il Sung's adulation.

In the Communist bloc, Juche propaganda had an even lower chance of success than in New York, London, or Geneva. After all, the surveillance apparatus in these Communist countries was powerful enough to ensure obedience to the most correct brand of Communist ideology—that is, the brand endorsed by the local leadership. Ordinary people in Communist countries also tended to be unsympathetic toward Juche, which they typically saw as an amusing caricature of their own official ideologies.

Thus, North Korean diplomats and spies concentrated their propaganda efforts in the developing world. In the 1970s they created a network of study groups and research centers dedicated to the propagation of Kim Il Sung's ideology and heavily subsidized by Pyongyang. It soon became clear, however, that the scheme did not work as intended: many entrepreneurial activists were happy to receive cash, but their commitment to the Great Leader was doubtful, as was their ability to influence the politics of their home countries. Nonetheless, the subsidies for the worldwide Juche movement, while reduced around 1980, were never completely stopped, since the movement was all too useful for domestic purposes. The North Korean leadership understood that it would be good to present North Koreans with the sight of exotic foreigners who ostensibly had come to

North Korea to lay flowers at the statues of the Great Leader and confess their unwavering admiration for the Greatest Man on Earth. The government of North Korea had to pay for return air tickets and accommodation, but given the domestic political impact, it seems to have been a good investment.

During the Kim Il Sung era, the media would report that inhabitants of the Communist bloc and Third World were doing relatively well, but the implication was that they were still inferior to the North Koreans. Things were different in the countries of the West—above all in the United States, the embodiment of all things evil. The United States was a country run by aggressors who made a living by robbing the world of its resources. According to a short sketch of American history found in the super-official Korean Central Yearbook, the United States was a nation founded by pirates and inhabited by blood-thirsty warmongers and sadists. From kindergarten, North Koreans were exposed to endless tales about acts of sadistic brutality perpetrated by the "disgusting Yankees" during the Korean War. They were also reminded that the same acts were still committed in South Korea by these evil monsters (one of the most common names used for Americans in the North Korean media was "the American imperialists, the two-legged wolves").

Indeed, the worst place on Earth to live was South Korea, "a land without light, a land without air." Until the late 1990s, South Korea was presented as a destitute American colony, whose population lived in abject poverty. In movies and paintings of the time, the South Korean cityscape looked positively hellish. People dressed in rags, lived in shacks, and looked for edible garbage at the dumping grounds near US military bases. Disgusting "Yankees" were often present in the picture as well—fat American soldiers with hugely protruding noses and ugly, caricatured Caucasian features, riding in jeeps (if such a jeep hit a Korean girl, they would laugh approvingly) or standing on major crossroads with automatic rifles, always ready to kill innocent Koreans.

The First Year textbook—intended for eight- or nine-year-olds—presents North Korea's children with an enlightening picture: "A school principal in South Korea beats and drives from school a child who cannot pay his tuition on time."[39] In high school, teenagers learn that "Nowadays, South Korea is swamped with seven million unemployed. Countless people stand in queues in front of employment centers, but not even a small number of jobs is forthcoming. The factories are closing one after another, and in such a situation even people who have work do not know when they will lose their jobs."[40] Needless to say, these horror stories are pure fabrications—primary education is free in South Korea, and even in the worst times of economic crisis there have never been "seven million unemployed."

Of course, the narrative is not free from heroic tales of resistance. Many brave and fearless South Koreans secretly publish works of Kim Il Sung and Kim Jong Il, hold revolutionary meetings in basement rooms adorned with portraits of the Great and Dear Leaders, and, while imprisoned, never err in their loyalty to the Juche idea while heroically enduring the torture inflicted upon them by the "puppet South Korean" police.

The explicit assumption was that an overwhelming majority of South Koreans envied their prosperous and happy brethren in the North and dreamed about a day when they, too, would enjoy life at the bosom of the Kim family. Only the large US military presence and the treachery of a handful of shameless collaborators prevented this great dream from coming true.

To what extent did the average North Koreans of Kim Il Sung's day believe this propaganda? By the late 1980s, a majority of the North Korean population had no personal memory of times when things were seriously different. They also had no access to alternative sources of information. There must have been some skeptics, especially among better-educated people or among those who had some experience of interacting with foreigners or living overseas. But the skeptics were wise enough to keep quiet. In North Korea, the unusual intensity of propaganda was combined with a self-imposed information blockade. It also helped that official propaganda repeated the same basic stories and messages for many decades. This ensured that the official worldview seemingly remained unquestioned by the majority. After all, most North Koreans had their own lives to live and were not much concerned about how sincere in their statements Juche worshippers from Venezuela or Zimbabwe really were.

THE SILVER LINING IN A SOCIAL DISASTER

This description of Kim Il Sung's North Korea is probably quite unappealing to the average democratically minded person. Indeed, it is fair to say that in the 1960s, Kim Il Sung managed to create a society that was arguably the closest approximation of an Orwellian nightmare in world history—and then managed to maintain this society for nearly thirty years.

Most people reading this book—including the author himself—have a very different set of life experiences and values. One would probably imagine, therefore, that the average North Korean would constantly feel restive and dissatisfied living under such a regime. However, this was not the case. When living in North Korea, the author was very surprised at how normal people's lives seemed. North Koreans of the Kim Il Sung era were not brainwashed automatons whose favorite pastime was goose-stepping and memorizing the lengthy speeches of their Leaders (although both these activities were an obligatory part of their lives). Nor were they closet dissenters who were waiting for the first opportunity to launch a pro-democracy struggle. They were also not—in the main—students of subversive ideas who studied samizdat texts (and not only because samizdat simply could not possibly exist in such a thoroughly controlled system). And yet it was clear that they were also not just docile slaves who did nothing but sheepishly follow all orders from above.[41]

BE READY FOR BODY COUNT

Given the North Korean regime's habit of politicizing everything, one should not expect North Korean math textbooks to be free from politics.

Let's have a brief look through the second-grade math textbook for North Korean primary schools, published in 2003 (or officially Year 91 of the Juche Era). This textbook is a masterpiece of politicized math, and I would like to introduce some representative gems from this treasure trove.

Admittedly, the majority of the questions in the textbook are not political—indeed, they have no backstory at all. Kids are required to deal with abstract numbers and areas. However, some 20 percent of all questions are different—they include a story to make the math appear more interesting and relevant. Some of the stories are quite innocent—about a train timetable or kids' games, for example. But some are not.

For instance, take an engaging problem from page 17: "During the Fatherland Liberation War [North Korea's official name for the Korean War] the brave uncles of the Korean People's Army killed 265 American Imperialist bastards in the first battle. In the second battle they killed 70 more bastards than they had in the first battle. How many bastards did they kill in the second battle? How many bastards did they kill all together?"

On page 24, the "American imperialist bastards" fared better and were lucky to survive the pious slaughter: "During the Fatherland Liberation War the brave uncles of the Korean People's Army in one battle killed 374 American imperialist bastards, who were also brutal robbers. The number of prisoners taken was 133 more than the number of American imperial bastards killed. How many bastards were taken prisoner?"

The use of math for body counts is quite popular—there are four or five more questions like this in the textbook. As every North Korean child is supposed to believe, his South Korean peers also spend days and nights fighting the "American imperialist bastards." Thus, this, too, creates a good opportunity to apply simple math.

On page 138 one can find the following question: "South Korean boys, who are fighting against the American imperialist wolves and their henchmen, handed out 45 bundles of leaflets with 150 leaflets in each bundle. They also stuck 50 bundles with 50 leaflets in each bundle. How many leaflets were used?"

Page 131 also provides kids with a revision question about leaflet dissemination: "Chadori lives in South Korea, which is being oppressed by the American Imperialist Wolves. In one day he handed out 5 bundles of leaflets, each bundle containing 185 leaflets. How many leaflets were handed out by the boy Chadori?"

That said, North Korean children are not supposed to be too optimistic. Life in South Korea is not just composed of heroic struggle but also great suffering. On page 47 they will find the following question: "In one south Korean village, which is suffering under the heel of the American imperialist wolf bastards, a flood destroys 78 houses. The number of houses damaged was 15 more than the number destroyed. How many houses were damaged or destroyed in this South Korean village all together?"

(continued)

These sufferings are nicely contrasted with the prosperity enjoyed by happy North Koreans. On the same page, the question about destroyed South Korean houses is immediately followed by this question: "In the village where Yong-shik lives, they are building many new houses. 120 of these houses have 2 floors. The number of houses with 3 floors is 60 more than the number of houses with two floors. How many houses have been built in Yong-shik's village?"

Indeed, feats of productive labor often become topics of North Korean questions, with robots, tractors, TV sets, and houses being mentioned most frequently. Interestingly, in some cases questions might produce results that were clearly not intended by the compilers. For example, on page 116 one can find the following question: "In one factory, workers produced 27 washing machines in 3 days. Assuming that they produce the same number of washing machines every day, how many machines do they produce in one day?" One has to struggle hard to imagine a factory that manages to produce merely nine washing machines a day, but the irony clearly escapes the textbook's authors (after all, a washing machine is a very rare luxury item in North Korea).

Political activists love to say that everything is political. Whether this is true in general, I know not, but primary school math textbooks in North Korea clearly are.

Of course, there were both zealots and dissenters. We should not forget that there were also people broken by the system. However, on balance, the vast majority of North Koreans did not belong to any of these categories. Like most people of all ages and all cultures, they did not normally pay too much attention to politics, even though state-imposed rituals were performed and obligatory statements delivered. Those in Kim Il Sung's North Korea were mainly concerned about much the same things as those in other societies. They thought about their families. They hoped to get a promotion. They fell in love. They wanted to educate their children. They were afraid of getting sick. They enjoyed romance, good food, and good books and didn't mind a glass of liquor. The political and ideological was more prominent in their lives than in the lives of the average person elsewhere, but it still did not color most of their experiences.

On top of this, in the 1950s and 1960s the promises of Kim Il Sung's national Stalinism did look attractive to many North Koreans. Had they possessed the benefit of hindsight, they would have probably had second thoughts about their initial enthusiasm for—or, at least, acceptance of— the system. The grave consequences, however, did not become apparent until it was too late.

Indeed, for the average North Korean living in the 1950s, Kim Il Sung's system did not look uninviting. It assured modernity and economic growth (first in industrial output and then in living standards). It vowed to maintain material equality while opening avenues of social advancement to people of humble origins. It promised to deliver justice to pro-Japanese collaborators whom the average Korean of the colonial period hated. This system was not democratic to be sure, but its nondemocratic nature was probably seen only as a minor problem to a majority.

We should not forget that Kim Il Sung was imposing his system on a country whose population overwhelmingly consisted of the sons and daughters of pre-modern subsistence farmers. These people had never been exposed to democracy even in theoretical terms, and Kim Il Sung's system seemed to be better than what they had experienced before—as they were at the mercy first of a traditional absolute monarchy and then a remarkably brutal colonial regime.

Information from the outside world did not hint at the existence of at- tractive alternatives elsewhere. The developed West had unsavory associa- tions with colonialism and at any rate was too far removed and too little known to be a viable object of emulation. South Korea until the late 1960s did not constitute a particularly attractive alternative, either. Contrary to what many ideologically biased historians claim nowadays, even at its lowest ebb the South Korean regime of Syngman Rhee was remarkably more permissive than its North Korean counterpart. Nonetheless, it was brutal—from available statistics, between the years 1945 and 1955, the number of people massacred for political reasons was actually larger in the South than in the North (a result of ruthless anti-guerrilla campaigns). The South Korean regime also had a less equal distribution of wealth and to a large extent was dominated by former pro-Japanese collaborators. So, until the late 1960s, even a well-informed and unbiased observer would not have much reason to see the South Korean system as vastly preferable to Kim Il Sung's version of nationalist Stalinism. Some poorly informed and/ or less unbiased observers clung to this option even longer. As late as 1977, prominent economist Joan Robinson, radical Cambridge intellectual and vocal propagandist for China's "cultural revolution," prophesied: "Obviously, sooner or later the country must be reunited, by absorbing the South into socialism."[42] While judgments of a "radical" Western intellectual, especially an unabashed admirer of Mao's thugs, should not be taken too seriously when it comes to events in distant lands, it is telling that such a bold statement did not make Robinson a laughingstock during that time.

At the time—believe it or not—the material situation did not look so bad for the average North Korean. In the early 1960s tens of thousands of ethnic Koreans fled China for North Korea in order to escape the famine and chaos resulting from the Great Leap Forward and the other insane experiments of Chairman Mao. Those refugees were granted housing and assigned work by the North Korean authorities. A man who was part of this exodus recently recalled his surprise at walking into a North Korean shop for the first time and discovering plastic buckets of various shapes and sizes for sale. Everybody could buy these wonderful items without coupons, and there was not even a need to queue!

Compared to other countries with similar income levels, Kim Il Sung's North Korea demonstrated a measure of success in such areas as secondary education and health care. Propaganda exaggerated these successes, but they were real nonetheless.

Just before the famine of the 1990s, life expectancy in the North peaked at seventy-two, only marginally lower than the then life expectancy in the much more prosperous South. According to 2008 census results, which are largely seen as plausible by foreign experts, life expectancy at birth in the North is currently around sixty-nine years.[43] This is some ten years shorter than in the South, but still impressive for such a poor country.

In 2012 the infant mortality rate in North Korea was estimated by the World Health Organization to be twenty-three per thousand live births. This is significantly higher than China's twelve, but remarkably low compared to many developing countries with similar incomes. For example, in Chad infant mortality was eighty-nine per thousand births, and in Kenya it was forty-six. If the CIA estimates are to be believed, Chad and Kenya have roughly similar levels of per capita GDP as North Korea (actually, there are good reasons to suspect that the CIA estimates of the North Korean GDP are inflated, so the actual contrast might be even more dramatic).[44]

These achievements appear to be even more of a paradox given the serious and systematic underfunding of North Korean health-care facilities, even in the best of times. Most hospitals occupy derelict buildings with small crowded rooms, and their equipment is roughly the same as that used by Western doctors in the 1950s, if not the 1930s. Access to good drugs was also very limited. Doctors definitely did not constitute a privileged or well-paid group in North Korean society, as medical professionals in the North were no different from average white-collar clerical staff in their social standing and income.

Surprisingly, the primary reason for these remarkable achievements may have been the ability of the government to control everyone with little or no concern for privacy. These are the essentials for a police state, but they can be very conducive to maintaining public health through the use of preventative medicine.

The entire population of Kim Il Sung's North Korea was subject to regular health checks. The checks were simple and cheap—like, say, chest X-rays—but they helped to locate medical problems at early stages. The checks were obligatory, and no North Korean could avoid an inspection, since the entire state machine was mobilized to make sure of this. The same was the case with immunization. A Western doctor who frequently goes to North Korea with aid missions put it nicely in a private talk with the author: "For a health care professional, a police state is a paradise. The author came with his medical van to a North Korean village, the local official blew a whistle, and in 10 minutes everyone in the village was waiting in front of the van. Every single person! No excuse was tolerated and nobody dared to evade us. In other developing countries it was so different!"

Even the low salaries of doctors were not necessarily a bad thing. This allowed the rather poor state to support a large number of medical doctors—32.9 physicians per 10,000 persons, roughly the same rate as in France (35.0) and above the US level (26.7).[45] A relative shortage of nurses should be taken into account—North Korean doctors often have to perform tasks that in other countries are done by nurses. Nonetheless, the number of doctors is impressive.

This emphasis on cheap prophylactics and easy availability of basic—not to say primitive—health care is what made North Korea's medical achievements possible. After all, people of younger ages seldom die because of chronic conditions that require expensive treatment: untreated appendicitis is much more likely to kill somebody in his or her forties and fifties. Complicated diseases usually develop at an advanced age, while at earlier stages the majority of threats to life come from seemingly minor ailments that can be easily treated if identified early enough, when there is a doctor nearby.

Of course, even in the best of times there were serious problems with high-end medicine. The North Korean health-care system worked well when it dealt with fractured bones of tractor drivers or pneumonia among infantry soldiers, but it was poorly equipped to treat more complicated conditions. More sophisticated surgery was available only in exclusive hospitals for the regime's top brass (like Ponghwa clinic in Pyongyang). The lesser orders were (and still are) left to their own sorry fate if they were (or are) unlucky enough to catch something serious, with the status of the physically and mentally handicapped being especially low.

Education—above all, primary and secondary education—was another area where North Korea's police state scored remarkable success. Like basic medical care, primary education doesn't cost that much—especially if one has large class sizes and does not care about sophisticated equipment. After all, for running a village primary school, one needs a building, a blackboard, and a reasonably qualified teacher; however, one also needs to make sure that more or less all children of school age will attend school. The North Korean state managed to sort out these issues.

The emphasis on education is driven, in no small extent, by ideological concerns, since intense ideological indoctrination is an integral part of schooling. Significantly, the most important school subjects of the North Korean curriculum are "the revolutionary history of the Great Leader" and "the revolutionary history of the Dear Leader." However, one should not reduce the entire contents of North Korean education to the level of indoctrination and brainwashing: the average North Korean child acquires good skills in basic literacy and numeracy as well.

With regard to college-level education, the results are far more mixed. North Korean college students might be motivated, but the shortage of funds and excessive ideological controls adversely influence their performance (with a handful of military-related fields being an important exception). Some of the problems are structural, but many others are related to the persistent shortage of funds and resources. These shortages have become progressively more acute as time has passed.

Indeed, the major problem faced by the North Korean state and by North Korean society was a gradual economic slowdown. This became obvious around 1970. The official media kept insisting that the economy was growing by leaps and bounds, but the North Korean people could easily see from their own experiences that this was not the case. The system looked quite attractive in theory and briefly seemed to work well, but in the early 1970s it began its slow downhill slide.

THE BIRTH OF JUCHE, THE RISE OF THE SON, AND THE SLOW-MOTION DEMISE OF A HYPER-STALINIST ECONOMY

To solidify its newly acquired autonomy vis-à-vis both China and the Soviet Union, the North Korean regime felt compelled to invent an ideology of its own. This ideology came to be known as Juche. The usual explanatory translation of the term is "self-reliance," but this is misleading. A better translation would be "self-importance" or "self-significance"—that is, the need to give primacy to one's own national interests and peculiarities.

Juche was first mentioned by Kim Il Sung in a 1955 speech but remained marginal until the mid-1960s, when it was remodeled into the official ideology of the North Korean state. As a doctrine, it remained imprecise and vague, so one cannot help but agree with Brian Myers's remark: "a farrago of Marxist and humanist banalities that is claimed to have been conceived by Kim himself, Juche Thought exists only to be praised."[46]

North Korean ideologues failed. In the early 1970s they attempted to market the Juche Idea across the globe. Domestically, it worked fine. The Juche Idea was presented as the highest and most cutting-edge brand of radical progressive ideology worldwide. It justified the superiority of the North Korean leadership, who now could confront Soviet and Chinese ideological pressures by stating (or, at least, hinting) that the Juche Idea was inherently superior to both Maoist and post-Stalinist versions of Marxism-Leninism. Indeed, it would soon be deemed superior to Marxism itself. Kim Jong Il made this clear in an article first written in 1976:

> Both in content and in composition, Kimilsungism is an original idea that cannot be explained within the framework of Marxism-Leninism. The Juche idea which constitutes the quintessence of Kimilsungism, is an idea newly discovered in the history of human thought. However, at present there is a tendency to interpret the Juche idea on the basis of the materialistic dialectic of Marxism. [...] This shows that the originality of the Juche idea is not correctly understood.[47]

These statements might have massaged Kim Il Sung's ego—he was surely pleased to be able to style himself as a great theoretician of world significance in the same league as Marx, Confucius, and Aristotle. However, these boastful claims served a pragmatic function as well. When North Korean propagandists marketed Juche as a philosophy superior to good old Leninism, they created a doctrinaire justification for Pyongyang's political independence from Moscow and other self-proclaimed guardians of Marxism-Leninism.

In domestic politics, the most remarkable peculiarity of the period between 1965 and 1980 was the rise of Kim Jong Il. Kim Il Sung's unprecedented decision to designate his son as successor made North Korea the world's first and only "Communist monarchy." This was understandable: Kim Il Sung could see what happened in the Soviet Union, where immediately after Stalin's death the late strongman came to be bitterly criticized by the people who were once seen as his most trusted lieutenants. Kim Il Sung also obviously took note of the Chinese experience, where Chairman Mao's designated successor, Lin Biao, could not even wait until the chairman's natural death and tried to hasten the process by staging a coup. Kim Il Sung, who in the early 1970s was rumored to be seriously ill, therefore needed to find a successor whose legitimacy would be dependent on that of Kim Il Sung himself and who hence would be unlikely to use his newly acquired power to destroy Kim Il Sung's legacy. The choice came naturally: like countless powerful men in human history, Kim Il Sung decided that his son would be the perfect candidate for such an important job.

The rise of Kim Jong Il began in the late 1960s, when he was put in charge of the cultural sphere. Later, in 1974, he became a Politburo member, and finally, in 1980, at the 6th Congress of the Korean Workers' Party, he was officially proclaimed successor-designate to his father.

Young Kim Jong Il initially was not taken seriously by foreign analysts, who often predicted that he would not outlive his father for too long, at least politically. However, neither a string of stunning girlfriends (often dancers or movie stars) nor a well-known predisposition for vintage French wines and expensive Swiss cheese (not to mention first-rate sushi) prevented Kim Jong Il from becoming a charismatic politician and shrewd manipulator who eventually proved to be a match for his ruthless and street-smart father. He needed these skills, to be sure, since the power transfer (which began in the mid-1970s) occurred during a time when the North Korean economy began its slow-motion decline.[48]

At the time of the Korean peninsula's partition, the North effectively got a massive endowment. From approximately 1930, the Japanese Empire began to invest in Korea on a grand scale—and most of this investment went to the future North because of its strategic proximity to China and its large amount of natural resources. At the time, Korea was seen as a natural rear base for the future advance of the empire into China, and nobody in Tokyo dreamed that Korea could become an independent nation again. As a net result, by 1945, North Korea was the most industrially advanced region in East Asia outside of Japan. Meanwhile, the southern half of the Korean peninsula remained an underdeveloped agricultural backwater.

By 1940, what would soon become Kim Il Sung's "People's Paradise" produced 85 percent of metals, 88 percent of chemicals, and 85 percent of all electricity in Korea at that time.[49] The Hamhŭng chemical plant was the world's second largest, and the power generators of the Yalu River hydro-electric stations so impressed the Soviet experts in 1946 that they disassembled the machines for the purposes of reverse engineering. Needless to say, the massive US air raids during the Korean War destroyed a significant part of this sophisticated infrastructure. Nonetheless, many industrial facilities survived the war or were quickly repaired and put back into operation in the 1950s.

Making comparisons between a market economy and a centrally planned one is a notoriously tricky and imprecise business. In the case of the two Koreas, it is made even more difficult by the secretive nature of the Pyongyang regime: beginning around 1960, virtually all economic statistics were classified, and this remains the case at the time of writing. The only exception is population statistics and some data about food production that, since the 1990s, were occasionally provided to major international agencies. Everything else about the state of the North Korean economy is guesswork. Regardless, nobody doubts that until the mid-1960s (at the very least) in terms of basic macroeconomic indicators, the Socialist North was ahead of the capitalist South.

As stated earlier, by the late 1960s the North Korean economy had begun to slow down. This fact could not be hidden from the population; they could see it in the shops. The number of items sold freely without rationing coupons was steadily diminishing, and in the early 1970s retail trade essentially ceased to exist. The state-run public distribution system replaced it almost completely.

Nowadays a majority of elder North Koreans express their nostalgia for the late 1960s, which are still seen as a bygone era of great prosperity. This era was by no means a paradise of unlimited consumption, but in retrospect such nostalgia is easy to understand: from the early 1970s onward, living standards began to decline and never recovered again. This was especially unnerving for the North Korean leadership, who—unlike the common populace—knew perfectly well what was then happening in South Korea, which was experiencing one of the greatest economic success stories of the twentieth century. From 1960 to 1988, South Korea enjoyed one of the world's highest growth rates. Throughout this period, South Korea's per capita GDP, measured in constant 1990 dollars, increased almost fivefold, from $1,200 to $5,700.[50]

As a result of the "Miracle on the Han River" (as this remarkable economic transformation is popularly known), by 1980 South Korea became the most advanced nation of all continental Asia. The speed of this transformation was incredible. Nowadays, South Korea has the world's second largest number of high-rise residential buildings. It is rather difficult to believe that in 1963, when the first South Korean apartment block was constructed, it was impossible to sell the flats, since no one was willing to live above the second floor. South Korean television began to broadcast in color only in 1980, and the South Korean automobile industry, now the world's fifth largest, virtually did not exist until 1974 (ditto the ship-building industry).

The tremendous economic success of the capitalist South coincided with the deepening stagnation of the North. This was to have extremely important political consequences. In a sense, this yawning gap in economic efficiency might be the single most important factor in determining the political situation in and around the Korean peninsula nowadays.

The reasons for the failure of the Stalinist economic model have been studied thoroughly, and in North Korea's case they were essentially the same as elsewhere: distorted price information, lack of incentives for innovation and quality improvement, and an ingrained inability to handle data efficiently. Nonetheless, it is worth noting that many features of Stalinist state Socialism were especially pronounced in North Korea, and hence one should not be surprised that the failure of this model was also especially spectacular there. North Korea first accepted an inherently inefficient system of economic management and then modified it in ways that further amplified its already remarkable inefficiencies.

To start with, North Korea spent a remarkable proportion of national income on the military. In the 1990s this small country had a standing army of approximately 1.2 million people—the world's highest ratio of military personnel to the general population (to put things in perspective, it was roughly the same ratio as in the United States of 1943). Not surprisingly, military spending was also exceptionally high.[51]

Admittedly, there was some strategic logic behind this seemingly insane level of militarization. Until at least the early 1970s, if not longer, the North Korean government saw the forceful unification of Korea as a realistic political task and even as its major long-term strategic aim. In order to outgun the army of South Korea, a country with a population twice the size of the North, the state had to invest heavily in military hardware and also require an unusually long period of obligatory military service (North Korean males spend between seven and ten years of their lives under arms). Once South Korea began to pull ahead between 1965 and 1970, North Korea still strove to maintain its equality with the South by further increasing already high military spending. Burdened by this additional spending, the North Korean economy slowed even faster, and this slowdown in turn prompted North Korea's leaders to increase the military budget still further. This was a classic example of a vicious cycle, and the sorry results became only too predictable.

Another specific factor that exacerbated North Korea's economic woes was the policy of economic autarky. The slogan of "Self-Reliance" was borrowed verbatim from Mao's China in approximately 1960, even though few North Koreans were aware of its foreign origin. Indeed, the slogan was repeated ad nauseam in Kim Il Sung's time and—unlike many other slogans—seems to have been taken seriously. Kim Il Sung and his guerrilla comrades were devoted nationalists, but their understanding of economics was remarkably patchy. They believed that Korea should make the economy as self-sustaining as possible in order to minimize the political leverage that foreign states could use over it.

It was officially assumed that North Korea could and should produce everything of economic significance within its own borders. The leadership thought that only imports of raw materials were ideologically permissible, but even they should be kept to a bare minimum. It was also believed that provinces, cities, and even individual factories should take care of their own logistical requirements whenever possible and expect little from the central government.

At times this insistence on self-reliance may have appeared comical to an outside observer. For example, while reading through a North Korean newspaper, this author once came across an admiring report about workers at a Pyongyang granary who found a patriotic and politically correct solution for one of their logistical problems. They needed a diesel locomotive to move railway carriages filled with grain. Instead of ordering it from the state, however, they used the granary's small workshop to manufacture the locomotive. Their "revolutionary spirit of self-reliance" was lauded by the report, but it said nothing about the quality and reliability of this curious handmade contraption. This story reminds one of the notorious wooden trucks that Chinese villagers were ordered to make during the Great Leap Forward (and under virtually the same slogan of "self-reliance"). The North Korean media of Kim Il Sung's era unceasingly published eulogies to such dubious triumphs.

Given the small size of the North Korean economy, such deliberate rejection of economic specialization was a dangerous misjudgment. Among other things, this policy was aimed at reducing North Korea's dependence on foreign powers and—above all—on its major sponsors, the USSR and China. However, it probably yielded the opposite result: by making the cumbersome North Korean economy even less efficient, this policy actually might have *increased* North Korea's dependency on Soviet and Chinese assistance.

Indeed, Soviet and, to a lesser extent, Chinese aid was vital for the survival of the North Korean system. The scale of this support cannot be estimated with real precision, since much of this aid was provided indirectly through subsidized trade. For instance, Soviet foreign trade organizations were frequently ordered by the Kremlin to accept substandard North Korean goods in lieu of payment for Soviet merchandise, which would have been much more expensive had the market mechanism been in operation. Most of the trade between North Korea and its sponsors was nonreciprocal—essentially it was aid, thinly disguised as trade. The Soviet Union sent spare parts for MiG jet fighters, crude oil, and Lada cars to North Korea and was paid with canned pickles and bad tobacco that nobody wanted to smoke. Relations with other countries of the Communist bloc were not much different. It would be just a minor exaggeration to say that if we define "trade" as reciprocal exchange in goods, Kim Il Sung's North Korea conducted very little trade but rather swapped geopolitical concessions for economic subsidies.

As long as the Soviet Union and China, driven by their own geopolitical considerations, were willing to pump this aid in, the North Korean economy remained afloat, even though its growth rate was constantly declining. Nonetheless, from the early 1960s the very existence of Soviet and Chinese aid was seldom if ever openly admitted. Perhaps not only the average North Korean but even the decision-makers in Pyongyang did not fully appreciate how great their dependency on Soviet giveaways had become. The sudden termination of this aid in the early 1990s therefore delivered a sudden and fatal blow to Kim Il Sung's North Korea. A new society grew out of the ruins of this "national Stalinism," and—in spite of some superficial continuity from the former times—this new North Korea was in fact very different.

CHAPTER 2

Two Decades of Crisis

The system built by Kim Il Sung in North Korea was fatally flawed in that it was unsustainable economically. It could function only as long as Moscow and Beijing were willing to provide Pyongyang with systematic aid. As Moscow quickly ceased its support, Kim Il Sung's "Stalinism with national characteristics" consequently did not outlive the abrupt end of the Cold War.

Many observers initially expected that North Korea would share the fate of other Communist regimes and either collapse (like the Communist regimes in Eastern Europe) or initiate market-oriented reforms (like Vietnam and China). These expectations did not materialize: North Korea neither collapsed nor reformed itself. But a lack of government-initiated reform did not mean that North Korea remained unchanged. Post-1994 North Korea is very different from the country established and run by Kim Il Sung. It might be run by the same people (or their children and nephews) and the state's rhetoric might sound the same, but its society is fundamentally very different.

AND THEN THE WORLD CHANGED

In 1985 Mikhail Gorbachev became the general secretary of the Communist Party of the Soviet Union. He immediately embarked on a program of radical social, economic, and political reforms that ultimately triggered the collapse of the Soviet Union in 1991. Around that time, China's leaders learned how Communist sloganeering could be seamlessly combined with a rather Dickensian—but very efficient—form of capitalism. In turn, by the late 1980s, relations between the USSR and the PRC, which had been characterized by rivalry and discord since the late 1950s, became cooperative. The rivalry between Russia and the United States also lost its sharpness. In the early 1990s both the ex-Soviet elite and public saw the United States not as an enemy to contain and undermine but rather as a shining example to be admired and emulated (such a rosy view did not survive for long in Moscow, but this is irrelevant to our story).

Considerations that conditioned Soviet (and Chinese) policy toward North Korea for decades suddenly disappeared. Moscow and Beijing policymakers saw no more need to maintain North Korea as a buffer zone against the United States or to buy its neutrality in the Sino-Soviet schism. Concurrently, the economic transformation of the former USSR meant that newly independent Russian enterprises, formerly state operations, were no longer willing to ship their wares to North Korea without economic reciprocation. Russian businesses would be (and still are) quite happy to sell spare parts for MiG fighters or crude oil, but they expected to be paid for their shipments in hard currency and North Korea had very little hard currency. Sponsoring Pyongyang therefore became both politically unnecessary and economically unjustifiable.

Within the first perestroika years, bilateral trade between North Korea and the Soviet Union decreased roughly tenfold: from $2.56 billion in 1990 to a mere $0.14 billion in 1994. Incidentally, it has remained at roughly this level ever since ($0.1 billion in 2012)—further proof that without state subsidies and political pressure, Russian companies are not terribly interested in doing business with North Korea.[1] Since North Korea's trade with Communist countries was essentially aid in disguise, the dramatic drop in trade meant a comparable decline in the availability of free or subsidized products.

The start of the new era in the North is usually linked to Kim Il Sung's death in July 1994. However, the social transformation of the 1990s had almost nothing to do with this political change at the top. Some of the measures undertaken by Kim Il Sung in the last years of his long rule were strikingly similar to what would become the norm under his son.

Nonetheless, for the sake of convenience, we will describe this new era in North Korean history as the "era of Kim Jong Il."

The sudden disruption of foreign aid led to the collapse of the state economy. Being deprived of free spare parts and subsidized oil, many industries gradually stopped functioning. Since all vital economic statistics in North Korea are a state secret, the exact scale of this economic collapse is disputable. Even so, it seems that by the year 2000, industrial output in the state economy was approximately half of what it was in 1990. The Bank of Korea, whose North Korean economy-related assessments are widely believed to be the most reliable, estimates that North Korea's GDP from 1991 through 1999 decreased by 37.6 percent.[2] By the early 2000s, nonmilitary industrial output was believed to be barely 50 percent of 1990 levels.[3] Officially, most factories were not closed, and employees were still required to attend their place of work every day. Most workers had nothing to do except clean the rusting, idle equipment.

From the early 1990s, when official corruption started to grow exponentially, the most savvy and entrepreneurial among the managers of state enterprises began to make money by selling their non-operating equipment to China as scrap metal. In more extreme cases, old factories, often built during the Japanese occupation, became empty shells devoid of equipment.

In many regards, North Korean infrastructure has not changed much from the 1930s to the mid-1940s. With the exception of a few highways (off-limits to local traffic), paved roads are very rare outside major cities, and, as late as 2010, the railways continued to make occasional use of steam locomotives of 1930s vintage. However, in the mid-1990s, infrastructure suffered much more than it had up until then. Frequent electricity outages meant trains, which mainly relied on electric locomotives, could be days late—a remarkable state of affairs for a country the size of Pennsylvania.

But the worst blow was suffered by the agricultural sector. Like nearly all Soviet-style agricultural systems, that of North Korea was inherently and hopelessly inefficient. Modern farmers usually work well if they toil upon their own land and have some control over the harvest. This was not the case in North Korea, where the state owned the land and directly managed it in ways that even Joseph Stalin himself would have seen as excessive.

Structural inefficiencies were exacerbated by a multitude of technical and political errors. To start with, North Korean agriculture had become heavily reliant on the use of chemical fertilizer. Initially this policy decision made some sense because North Korea inherited highly developed fertilizer production facilities from the Japanese colonial period. But while this was the case, production itself was dependent on the supply of Soviet aid and was highly energy-intensive.

Another mistake was the heavy reliance on artificial irrigation that was made possible by the existence of large pumping stations. In some cases water had to be first pumped up a few hundred meters above the level of its natural source and only then directed toward the rice paddy fields. This worked well as long as electricity was plentiful and cheap. The decline in electricity output, however, made this system unsustainable.

Last but not least, the ill-conceived idea of terraced fields contributed to the succession of natural climatic disasters that hit from 1995 through 1996. This idea was once loudly lauded as a great, personal invention of Kim Il Sung's genius. Terraced fields might be perfectly suitable for the farming conditions of southern China, but not North Korea—as North Korean agricultural managers learned in due time and to their peril. Terracing increased soil erosion and made areas under cultivation more vulnerable to torrential rains. Such rains hit North Korea in the summer of 1995 and then again in 1996.

Official propaganda has always blamed subsequent events on these rains, which are described as "a once in a century natural calamity." The rainfall was indeed heavier than usual, but it is worth noting that the same rains produced almost no impact on the agriculture of South Korea, where the only notable result of the alleged "unprecedented natural calamity" was a marginal increase in the price of cabbage and onions. For the North, however, the floods of 1995–96 were the proverbial straw that broke the camel's back.

In order to feed its population, North Korea needs 5.0–5.5 million metric tons of grain (the exact figure is a subject of some debate between experts). Until the early 1990s, North Korean farmers managed to produce that much. Then the situation began to deteriorate precipitously. Deprived of fuel, electricity, and fertilizer, and with workers who had little incentive to care about the future harvest, the system collapsed. The 1996 harvest was a mere 2.5–2.8 million metric tons—half of what was required to keep the population fed.[4]

For the average North Korean, this agricultural collapse meant a sudden termination of the PDS (public distribution system), which had been the major source of food for the North Koreans since 1957. From around 1993, rations were increasingly delayed and/or only partially delivered. The delays began in more remote areas of the countryside but soon spread to major cities. After the floods, PDS rations ceased almost completely. Even the privileged population of Pyongyang was issued only partial rations, and there were periods (for example, in 1998) when distribution completely stopped even in the "capital of the revolution." Outside of Pyongyang (if that), only party cadres, police personnel, military officials, and workers at military factories continued to receive their rations, and even those privileged groups did not necessarily receive full allowances in the years between 1996 and 2000.

For the average North Korean, this was nothing short of a catastrophe. A twice-monthly trip to the grain distribution center was as vital as supermarkets are for American families. Famine ensued, and soon took on disastrous proportions.

The number of people who perished in the Great North Korean Famine of 1996–1999 will probably never be known with absolute certainty. Some NGOs put the number as high as three million whilst the North Korean government in confidential communications with certain foreign guests put the figure as low as 250,000. The first estimate is clearly a serious exaggeration, and the second is a face-saving underestimate.

At the time of writing, there have been three serious attempts to estimate the scale of this disaster impartially. In 2001 Daniel Goodkind and Loraine West concluded that excess deaths most likely numbered between 600,000 and one million in the period from 1995 to 2000.[5] In 2010, analyzing officially published results of the most recent (2008) North Korean population census, Pak Keong-Suk estimated that excessive deaths reached 880,000 in the 1993–2008 period, with the loss of about 490,000 being attributable to mortality increase, about 290,000 to fertility decline, and about 100,000 to outbound migration and its effect on fertility.[6] In 2011 Goodkind and West (together with Peter Johnson) revised their earlier estimates of excess deaths downward to 490,000.[7] Even if we accept the lowest estimate of 450,000–500,000, it still means that some 2.5 percent of the entire population perished in the disaster. This is roughly equal to the ratio of Chinese farmers who perished from starvation during the Great Leap Forward of the early 1960s. In other words, it was proportionately the largest humanitarian disaster East Asia had seen for decades. Nevertheless, the majority of North Koreans survived the famine. They did so by creating new ways to survive, both socially and economically. In essence, the North Korean people rediscovered capitalism, while the North Korean state had little choice but to relax its iron grip over the North Korean public.

THE SORRY FATE OF KATYA SINTSOVA

Have you ever heard of Katya Sintsova, the beautiful Russian girl whose naïve admiration for capitalism and its debased "democracy" brought ruin to her and her entire family? She was a girl whose sorry and lamentable fate is so reminiscent of the tragic fate of her country, which deviated from the true path of Socialism.

Katya Sintsova is a fictional (and highly implausible) character who appears in a North Korean short story entitled "The Fifth Photo." This short story was produced by a North Korean writer named Rim Hwawon and is quite representative of current North Korean writings about the collapse of Soviet and Eastern European Communism.

As Tatiana Gabroussenko remarked in her study of this peculiar kind of North Korean fiction, in the 1940s and 1950s the Russians were portrayed in North Korean literature as leaders and guides helping their Korean comrades. In the 2000s, however, it is the Koreans who are the shining example, the embodiment of Socialist virtue and looked upon as leaders. Russians nowadays are, conversely, presented as weak and naïve but still basically decent, noble human beings who flourish under the wise guidance of their North Korean friends.

For instance, in one of these stories the CIA plants a bomb on a US passenger airliner. The reason for this operation (and, as every North Korean knows, this is the type of operation the CIA does routinely) is to kill a Russian scientist who refused to cooperate with the US military-industrial complex. In the story, the Russian and his fellow passengers are lucky to have a North Korean on the same plane. The North Korean takes control of the situation and saves his fellow travelers from another vicious American plot.

Then we have Rim Hwawon's "The Fifth Photo." Katya Sintsova, its main character, is a beautiful Russian girl who comes from a family with impeccable Communist credentials. Her great-grandfather died a heroic death in 1919 during the Russian Civil War, her grandfather sacrificed his life fighting the Nazis, and her father was a selfless and hardworking party apparatchik of the Brezhnev era. Her brother became a top bureaucrat in the Moscow Party Youth Committee and was equally selfless and hardworking.

Katya was accepted to a top university because of her exceptional gifts in the arts. But at the university, she falls under the spell of "dangerous ideas." She begins to interact with people whose ideological bent is "less than healthy," including Westerners (the latters' behavior is seen by Rim Hwawon as especially outrageous). She becomes irritated that the contents of party meetings are so boring and is overcome by materialism and a lust for change.

An American seduces and impregnates her, after which she has an abortion. Meanwhile, her father dies, his last words being "Long live the Communist Party!" Katya loves him and feels sorry about his death but still considers him an old fool. This is when she meets the story's North Korean narrator, to whom she tries to sell photos from her precious family archive.

The narrator is an example of flawless revolutionary virtue, and his own daughter is free from all the frivolous, dangerous ideas that have ruined Katya's life—the exemplary North Korean girl dreams only of serving the Party and Leader even more ardently. The narrator's sons are brave officers of the Korean People's Army, always ready to fight

(continued)

the US imperialists. They are even treated to the highest honor imaginable, being granted an audience with the Dear Leader Marshal Kim Jong Il.

Katya, meanwhile, travels overseas in search of her American lover. An awful discovery awaits her: he was not really an American, but the descendant of an anti-Communist Russian landlord family. Almost a century before their lands were nationalized, and the vicious landlord's family has spent all their time dreaming of revenge. Katya's seduction was actually a part of a plot aimed at taking the lands back from the farmers and giving it to greedy and cruel landlords.

Katya Sintsova's sufferings don't end with this awful discovery, however. While alone and helpless in the brutal West, she suffers a car accident and loses a leg. In order to survive, she becomes a prostitute serving perverts in the city of Munich.

The message of this story is simple and easy to understand: Katya is Russia herself. She was lured into a trap by Western propaganda and the scheming descendants of landlords. Fooled into selling her great heritage, she ends up a pitiful prostitute at the bottom of the merciless capitalist heap. The story is written to serve as a clear warning to North Koreans not to listen to seductive voices from abroad but rather remain vigilant against their enemy.

CAPITALISM REBORN

In post-famine North Korea, the state-owned economy has been largely replaced by a diverse array of private economic activity. Such activities are usually associated with what is often labeled the "black market"—somewhat misleadingly, as we shall see later. It was recently estimated that, as of 2008, the share of income from informal economic activities reached 78 percent of the total income of the average North Korean household.[8]

However, as stated before, North Korea's social transformation is rather different from near-contemporaneous developments in China and the former Soviet Union in that it was neither initiated nor endorsed by the authorities. For political reasons to be discussed later, Kim Il Sung's socioeconomic system still remains the ideal for the North Korean elite. Nonetheless, this commitment does not go beyond words most of the time: the elite lack the resources and resolve that would make a revival of Kim Il Sung's "national Stalinism" possible.

When rations suddenly stopped coming, people began to either learn ways to cope with the new situation or die by starvation. For farmers the most natural reaction was to start growing their own food. This was not that easy because, unlike their Chinese counterparts, North Korean bureaucrats showed no inclination to disband the notoriously inefficient state farms. The state farms' fields were usually guarded, preventing farmers from using the best arable land for their production. A majority of farmers had to look for alternative places to farm for themselves.

North Korea is a mountainous country, and thus it is not too difficult to find steep slopes not used for regular agriculture. A quick look at satellite images demonstrates the presence of numerous small fields of irregular shapes and sizes located on many of North Korea's mountains. These are known as *sotoji* (literally, "small fields"). They are the private plots of North Korea's farmers and inhabitants of smaller towns. Generally, the farther away one lives from major administrative and political centers, the easier it is to develop such a field. In more remote parts of the country, *sotoji* now produce more than half of the harvest, but the nationwide average seems to be close to 20 percent.

While farmers developed illicit plots, the urban population reacted to the new situation by discovering private commerce. Most urban families began by bartering household items for food but soon switched to trade and household production. Beginning in 1995, huge markets began to grow in North Korea's cities and soon became the focal point of economic life in the country. Millions of North Koreans, women in particular, began to earn the family's income through trade and household handicraft production.

Women make up the majority of North Korea's market operators. Market vendors in North Korea are by no means the sort of street toughs one might encounter in the black markets of other countries. Instead, they are largely housewives and mothers who produce whatever they can and sell to whomever in order to keep their families alive.

This is partly due to the peculiarities of North Korean society itself. For decades, the North Korean state required every able-bodied male to be employed by a state enterprise. Married women of working age, however, were allowed to stay at home as full-time housewives.

When Kim Il Sung's system began to fall apart in the early 1990s, men continued to go to work. People expected that eventually things would return to what they thought of as "normal"—that is, to the old Stalinist system. They knew from their experience that people who show disloyalty to the state—for instance, those who collaborated with the South Korean authorities during the Korean War—are assigned a stigmatizing *sŏngbun* that is often permanent, as not only the offender but also their children and grandchildren face many official restrictions. Men believed that it would be wise to keep their "official" jobs for the sake of their families' future. On top of such status anxieties, men also faced massive pressure from the state's lower officialdom. An absentee worker ran the real chance of being sent to a prison for a few months of "labor re-education."

The situation for women was markedly different. They had spare time, and their involvement with private trade was seen as politically less dangerous—precisely because of the patriarchal nature of a society where only men really mattered.

As one would expect, soon thereafter, in the late 1990s, more successful businesswomen moved from retail to wholesale. In many cases, they were the members of once-discriminated-against groups who benefited most from the new situation. For example, until the 1990s, it was a major handicap for any social-climbing North Korean to have relatives overseas. In the 1990s the opposite suddenly became the case. Relatives overseas, especially in China, could often provide small amounts of capital (quite large by then North Korean standards), give sound business advice, and/or even create a formal or informal joint venture.

An acquaintance of the author is typical example. She was a young schoolteacher who, in the early 1990s, was asked by visiting Chinese relatives to buy them a large quantity of dried fish. She discovered that in merely a few days she earned well over her official *annual* salary and decided to become a professional trader. Being a woman, she could leave her job without repercussions.

By the early 2000s, some wholesalers had large sums at their disposal; they sometimes invested in new types of enterprise—eateries, storage facilities, and semi-legal transportation companies. Indeed, the growth of the market that initially centered on small-scale retail activities soon became far more diverse and complex.

The restaurant sector is illustrative in this regard. Between 1996 and 1997 state-run restaurants collapsed everywhere except for a few major cities. Private capital, however, almost immediately revived the industry, and private entrepreneurs now run most North Korean restaurants. Officially, they are not supposed to exist, and such eateries are technically state-owned. On paper, the state owns them and relevant municipal government agencies manage them. However, this is a legal fiction. Private investors make informal deals with municipal officials by promising them kickbacks, and then hire workers and buy equipment. The assumption is that a certain amount of the earnings from the business will be transferred to the state budget. In return, private owners run businesses with little or no state interference, investing and/or pocketing the profits. A 2009 study came to the conclusion that some 58.5 percent of all restaurants in North Korea are de facto privately owned.[9]

Similar trends exist in the retail industry. While the fiction of state ownership is maintained, many shops are essentially private. Manager-cum-owners buy merchandise from wholesalers as well as (technically) state-owned suppliers, and then market and sell the goods, pocketing the profits. Of course some of the earnings are paid to the state, but most is kept by owners. The earlier-mentioned study estimated that in 2009 some 51.3 percent of shops were actually private retail operations.[10]

Transportation has undergone similar changes. A large number of trucks and buses that traverse the dangerous dirty roads of North Korea are privately owned. Private investors discovered that grossly inadequate transportation facilities were a major bottleneck that the emerging North Korean merchant class had to contend with. Investors began buying used trucks and buses in China and bringing these vehicles into the North. Vehicles in the North are registered as the property of a government company or agency. The actual owner pays the manager of this agency an agreed price, usually on a monthly basis. Interestingly, the amount of money is contingent on the type of agency or company. The registration of one's truck with a military unit or a secret police department is most expensive, while some humble civilian agency (like, say, a tractor repair workshop) would charge the least. Owners sometimes prefer to pay more, however, because military registration plates might occasionally come in handy with the police.

Large transportation companies have now arisen: The author met an entrepreneur who owned seven trucks in North Korea. He used these trucks to move salt from salt farms on the coast to wholesale markets (incidentally, salt farms are increasingly private as well). This man also augmented his income by moving large sacks of cement that were stolen by workers from the few cement plants continuing to function in post-1994 North Korea. It was a nice income, but he expressed his surprise at the ingenuity of the workers who managed to somehow steal such a large amount of cement.

Indeed, one of the major problems for the state has been the growth of criminal and semi-criminal activities. Workers and managers steal from their factories virtually everything that can be sold on the private market. The large-scale looting of archaeological sites from the Koryo (10th–14th centuries AD) and Choson (14th–19th centuries AD) periods became a problem in spite of all efforts to stop it. Those caught smuggling antiques or selling equipment often faced severe penalties; there were even rumors about public executions of such miscreants. Nonetheless, the temptation was far too large.

Drug production started to boom around 2005. In earlier days, drugs were produced for clandestine export by government agencies, but private business also discovered the great money-making potential of addictive substances—and officials are not too eager to enforce the myriad bans and regulations (they usually get a slice of the profits, after all). Private production is usually concentrated on what is commonly called "ice," that is, methamphetamines. Drugs are marketed domestically and also exported to China, where authorities have had to step up border controls as a result. "Ice" has become surprisingly popular among younger North Koreans, so much so that in 2010, foreign visitors spotted antidrug posters in Pyongyang colleges. Incidentally, around the same time, the old state-sponsored drug production program was scaled down. Frankly, the entire project obviously did the regime more harm than good, damaging its international standing while bringing only a small return.[11]

Not merely in criminal activities but overall, China features prominently in the unofficial North Korean economy (and in the official economy as well, as we will see later). Nearly all trade links either begin or end in China. Part of this trade is unofficial, while other transactions are legal. North Korean merchants mainly import consumer goods from China—garments, shoes, TV sets, and so on. Food also constitutes a significant part of North Korean imports from China.

Paradoxically, thanks to this, the years of crisis became a time when the average North Korean began to dress well—or, at least, better than in earlier times. In Kim Il Sung's days, most people were clad in badly tailored Mao suits or military uniforms; now, even in the countryside, people on the street are dressed colorfully, usually in cheap Chinese imports.

To balance the trade account, North Korean merchants export to China whatever can be sold there. Apart from minerals, which are still usually handled by the state, they sell seafood, traditional delicacies, and Chinese medical herbs, as well as quite exotic items—such as "frog oil," a fatty substance extracted from live frogs of certain species that have to be harvested under special conditions.

China's ubiquity in the Northern economy has resulted in the "Yuanization" of the market: large-scale payments in post-famine North Korea are normally made in foreign currency. Dollars, yen, and Euros are not unknown, but it is the Chinese Yuan that reigns supreme. This situation has led to the emergence of money dealers who trade in foreign currencies and sometimes provide loans at the annual interest rate of 100 percent or more.

A particular form of entrepreneurial activity that is neither private nor state, the so-called foreign currency earning enterprise (FCEE), plays a special role in the new economy. Such enterprises have existed since Kim Il Sung's day, but have greatly increased in number, size, and reach from the late 1990s.

Unlike the Soviet Union, in North Korea, foreign trade was never under the exclusive control of a single state agency. In accordance with the "spirit of self-reliance," large North Korean companies and influential state agencies were allowed to sell anything they could on international markets. They would then use the earned foreign currency to import what could not be produced domestically. This practice was greatly expanded in the late 1990s when provinces, ministries, and even the military and police began to set up their own FCEEs. These enterprises did not usually limit themselves to what could be produced in-house, but looked for anything that could be sold for a profit.

Technically, the FCEEs are owned by the state, but they hire adventurous and entrepreneurial people whose job is to use the company's official clout and connections to earn as much money as possible. It is implicitly understood that these people pocket a large share of their earnings, but as long as they know their limit and provide their supervisors with sufficient kickbacks, profiteering is tolerated.

THE STATE WITHERS AWAY

The collapse of the state-run economy had far-reaching political and social consequences. In order to function properly, Kim Il Sung's system required a small army of enforcers and indoctrinators. A considerable workforce was necessary to ensure that every North Korean slept in a home where he or she was registered, did not travel to another city without a proper permit, and did not skip a self-criticism session. In the early 1990s the government discovered that it did not have the resources to reward the zeal of these overseers and indoctrinators. Of course, the regime did what it could to keep police officers and party officials on the payroll and issued them rations even in the middle of famines. Nonetheless, there were too many such people to be taken care of. Thus, in the mid-1990s, police sergeants, clerks in local government offices, and low-level indoctrinators faced the real threat of starvation. Like the average factory worker or schoolteacher, these small cogs in the bureaucratic machine depended on PDS rations for survival. When the PDS contracted dramatically, they were not considered important enough to remain on a new, much shorter, list of distribution targets.

A number of the author's North Korean interlocutors state that in the famine years between 1996 and 1999, the ones who statistically had the highest probability of dying were honest officials and clerks—those who did not take bribes, did not abuse their official position, and took the regime's promises seriously. However, most petty bureaucrats made a rational choice and adjusted their behavior to the brave new world, beginning to ignore illegal activities. In many cases, they had to be bribed to adopt such an attitude, but in other instances, they did so out of sympathy for the common people.

One of the best examples is the near complete loss of control over domestic travel. Theoretically, up to the time of writing, North Koreans are expected to apply for a travel permit if they plan to take an overnight trip outside the borders of their county or city. Starting from around 1996 to 1997, however, these controls became easy to circumvent. Nowadays, police officials can be bribed and permits obtained for a relatively small fee, the equivalent of $2 or $3. Alternatively, one can choose a cheaper but more troublesome option, and depart without any travel permit. For that, one must be ready to bribe police officers at checkpoints and in trains. Only the city of Pyongyang has not been touched by this relaxation, remaining off-limits to people from the countryside who do not have the proper papers—and such papers are still difficult to get.

Sometimes, North Koreans could and can get away with what used to be seen as political crimes. For example, possession of a tunable radio set has been a political crime for decades. This still technically remains the case, but nowadays a bribe of roughly $100 can buy a way out of punishment for someone unlucky enough to have been caught while listening to such a radio (police would probably even give the offending radio set back to the culprit). Of course, $100 is by no means a trivial amount of money for the average North Korean, since the average monthly salary between 1995 and 2010 fluctuated around the $2 to $3 mark. The actual monthly income of a household is much higher, at somewhere between $25 and $40 a month, since a majority of the North Korean families make most of their income in the unofficial economy.

Another result of the new situation was the near collapse of control over the Sino–North Korean border. Smugglers took advantage of the situation, paying bribes to ensure that border guards always looked the other way when necessary. For a large-scale smuggler, a bribe might be as high as a few hundred dollars, but for this amount he or she would be able to move sacks of valuable merchandise across the border (even being helped by the border guards themselves). Apart from smuggling, the government has relaxed its attitude toward official cross-border trips, which are usually justified by the need to visit relatives in China but often are of a commercial nature. From 2003, for the first time in North Korean history, authorities began to issue passports to North Koreans intending on traveling overseas as private citizens—provided they have the right connections, good family backgrounds, and the resources to pay the necessary bribe.

The very people who are supposed to enforce them ignore with impunity some regulations (often truly absurd). Theoretically, North Korean women in cities are not allowed to wear slacks because such attire is considered unbefitting a woman and "goes against the good habits and beautiful traditions of Korea." Women are also theoretically forbidden from riding bicycles in urban areas. There are even bans of some "subversive" types of haircuts. Police have occasionally enforced these nonsensical bans in the past but from around the mid-1990s, became increasingly uninterested. From time to time, ideological authorities will remind people of the moral harm that might be caused by a woman clad shamelessly in slacks, prompting police to levy fines on violators of the ban for a few weeks. These kinds of campaigns never last long, however, and seldom bear fruit.

Most of the earlier-mentioned changes are spontaneous in nature, being driven primarily by greed and need as well as by a loss of ideological fervor on the part of those who previously upheld the status quo. In some cases, however, the relaxation has been initiated by the authorities. For example, around 1996, illegal border crossing into China, hitherto a serious crime, was reclassified as a relatively minor offense. Around the same time, the Kim Il Sung–era family responsibility principle was relaxed. In the past, if a North Korean was arrested for political crimes, his or her entire family would be shipped to a prison camp. Now, such measures are used selectively, normally only in cases of crimes considered especially dangerous.

The general relaxation is quite palpable for anyone who has been dealing with North Korea for decades. Nowadays, North Koreans are less afraid of foreigners and more willing to discuss potentially dangerous matters. This does not usually mean that they will deviate from the official line too openly, but the limits of what is permissible have clearly widened in the last fifteen to twenty years. North Korean refugees also admit that in Kim Jong Il's North Korea, it is often possible to do or say with impunity something that would result in imprisonment or even execution in Kim Il Sung's era.

Take the story of Yi Yŏng-guk, the former bodyguard of the Dear Leader himself. Disillusioned with the North Korean system, he fled to China and attempted to defect to South Korea. He was kidnapped by North Korean agents in China and sent back home. In the not-so-distant times of Kim Il Sung, the fate of such a high-profile defector would have been sadly predictable: torture and death awaited any individual who betrayed the *personal* trust of the Great Leader. However, in the liberal 1990s, Yi was treated with surprising leniency: he was sent to a prison camp and then released (yes, released!) following the intercession of Kim Jong Il himself. He used the opportunity to repeat his escape attempt and reached Seoul.[12]

TAKING THE EXIT OPTION: NOT AN EXODUS YET, BUT . . .

From the mid-1990s, North Koreans began to move to China in large numbers. Such illicit emigration was not that physically difficult because most of the length of both the Yalu and the Tumen is shallow, narrow, and frozen in winter.

This being the case, between 1998 and 1999, when the famine was at its worst, it was estimated that anywhere from 150,000 to 195,000 North Koreans were hiding in China.[13] After 2005 the numbers shrank dramatically, but it is estimated that at any given moment, there are still about 10,000 to 15,000 North Korean refugees hiding in China.[14] Most of these people take refuge in villages and towns along the border, where ethnic Koreans constitute a majority of the population. Refugees do all kinds of odd jobs shunned by the locals: they wait tables at cheap eateries and labor at construction sites in the timber industry. Since women constitute a majority of refugees, many of them cohabit with Chinese men—sometimes being abducted but more frequently through personal choice.

Some of these unions end in disaster, while others work just fine. Indeed, such arrangements can be mutually beneficial: a Chinese-Korean man of advanced age and moderate income gets a wife, while a North Korean woman gets a sense of security and a standard of living unthinkable back home. The local Chinese authorities usually ignore such unions, especially if the couple has children. Nonetheless, a North Korean common-law wife (such unions cannot be registered officially) is still not free from the worst fear of any North Korean refugee in China: arrest and deportation.

THE NEW RICH

North Korea is a poor place, no doubt. Nonetheless, 2014 Pyongyang has a booming restaurant scene, and the traffic on its broad streets— once notoriously empty—is steadily increasing in volume. Well-fed North Koreans frequent newly opened sushi bars and beer houses as well as a local hamburger joint. On the streets of the North Korean capital, one can still see some visibly undernourished people but also a number of women clad in designer clothes.

Such is the case not only in Pyongyang but also in a number of other major North Korean cities. The growth of "grassroots capitalism" predictably has brought with it a remarkable level of income inequality.

But who are they—the North Korean new rich? How did they make their money—and how do they spend it? Mr. Kim, who is in his early forties, is a private owner of a gold mine. The gold mine is officially registered as a state enterprise. Technically, it is owned by a foreign trade company, which in turn is managed by the financial department of the Party Central Committee. However, this is a legal fiction, pure and simple: Mr. Kim, once a mid-level police official, acquired some initial capital through bribes and smuggling, while his cousin had made a minor fortune selling counterfeit Western tobacco.

They then used their money to grease the palms of bureaucrats and took over an old gold mine that had ceased operation in the 1980s. They hired workers, bought equipment, and restarted operations. The gold dust was sold (strictly speaking, illegally) to Chinese traders. The cousins negotiated with the bureaucrats from the foreign trade company on how much "commission" they should pay them—roughly between 30 and 40 percent. They now use the rest to run the business and enjoy life.

One step below this, we can see even humbler people, like Ms. Young, once an engineer at a state factory. In the mid-1990s, she began trading in Chinese second hand dresses. By 2005 she was running a number of workshops that employed a few dozen women who made copies of Chinese garments using Chinese cloth, zippers, and buttons. Some of the materials were smuggled across the border, while other materials were purchased quite legally, largely from a vast wholesale market in the city of Rason (a special economic zone that can be visited by Chinese merchants almost freely). Ms. Young technically remained an employee of a moribund state factory, from which she was absent for months on end. She had to pay for the privilege of missing work and indoctrination sessions through a monthly $40 deduction classified as a "donation." This is an impressive sum when compared with her official salary of merely $2.

The North Korean new rich must feel insecure. They are afraid of the state, because pretty much everything they do is in breach of some article of the North Korean criminal code. Indeed, technically any of the earlier-described persons could face an execution squad should the authorities wish to do so. They provide officials with generous kickbacks, and in recent years, massive crackdowns have been infrequent. Yet the fear lingers nonetheless.

It is, however, difficult to say that they try to keep a low profile. On the contrary, nowadays one can see a lot of conspicuous consumption in North Korea. It is no surprise that the new rich enjoy consumption.

(continued)

Some forms of consumption activities are impossible—for example, overseas trips are out of the question, and domestic tourism seems to be unfashionable: North Koreans, rich or poor, usually travel out of necessity, not for pleasure.

However, many outlets cater to the needs of the "masters of money" (*tonju*), as North Korean entrepreneurs are known. The new rich frequent restaurants where a good meal would cost roughly as much as the average North Korean family makes in a couple of weeks. They buy and renovate houses—technically the sale of real estate is illegal in North Korea, but in the last two decades North Koreans have developed many techniques that allow them to circumvent such restrictions. The new rich buy all kinds of household appliances: flat screen TVs, computers, large fridges, and motorbikes. Even private cars—the ultimate status symbol, the North Korean equivalent of a private jet—have begun to appear, and since around 2009, one can see traffic jams on the streets of Pyongyang, once famously empty.

In good old Confucian spirit, the new rich invest in the education of their children. A good teacher of a popular subject—like, say, English or Chinese—might earn a decent income nowadays. Less practical subjects are also in demand, although piano and dance lessons are deemed suitable for girls only.

Until the mid-1990s, every North Korean who had crossed over into China and had been unfortunate enough to be extradited back would face a few years of imprisonment at best and, upon release, lifelong discrimination. This is no longer the case because border crossing itself is now regarded as only a minor offense. When North Koreans are extradited or deported from China, they are usually investigated for a week or two (this investigation normally involves some beating). Investigators want to make certain that the offender has had no contact with South Koreans and non-Chinese foreigners in China, and that they have had no involvement with any Christian missionary group. If no such suspicious connections are discovered, the extradited refugee spends a few months in a milder type of labor camp and is then released. Upon release, many of them flee again. After all, they often have families and jobs back in China.

Some refugees decide to go all the way—to South Korea, though this is not as simple as it sounds. Long gone are the times when every North Korean who decided to defect and was lucky enough to get overseas could just walk into the nearest South Korean consulate or embassy and inform the cheerful staff that he had just "chosen freedom," as the Cold War cliché went. Nowadays, while a two-star general of the North Korean air force or a district party secretary can still count on an enthusiastic welcome, the same does not hold for a middle-aged housewife from a rural area—and such a housewife is the typical refugee seeking passage to South Korea over the past decade. As a rule (there are exceptions), South Korean missions in China prefer not to deal with the average refugee. This is explained not only by the fear of diplomatic complications with China but also by the reluctance of the South Korean government to increase the number of refugees in the South. At the same time, the fiction of "one Korea," still maintained by both Seoul and Pyongyang, means that every single North Korean is legally, and thus automatically, eligible for South Korean citizenship and consular protection. In reality, however, for a majority of the refugees, the only way to reach South Korea is to get to a third country (usually Thailand or Mongolia) where South Korean diplomatic missions, sometimes reluctantly, process refugees and issue them with travel documents and air tickets to Seoul.

For refugees, this means first traversing all of China, then illegally crossing the Chinese border into Mongolia or Laos. Such a trip is almost impossible for the average refugee, who speaks poor if any Chinese and has little money and no local knowledge. The only way, therefore, is to make a deal with a professional escape specialist known as a "broker." Such a broker assembles a group of five to fifteen aspiring refugees, arranges transportation and safe accommodation, and then escorts them to China's southern border (if the final destination is Bangkok) or to Mongolia. There, the broker orchestrates a border crossing and accompanies the refugees on their perilous trip across the Gobi Desert or the jungles of Laos.

Brokers usually do not work for the actualization of some lofty ideal. Some of them might have ideological convictions, but in the main, defection has long become a commercial operation, pure and simple. For a "no-thrills defection," one must pay between $2,000 and $3,000, while a VIP version of the service costs between $10,000 and $15,000. The expensive option usually involves a fake South Korean or Chinese passport, North Korean border guards escorting the defector across the border, and a comfortable air trip from a major Chinese airport straight to South Korea.[15] The cost of even the cheapest defection is exorbitant for the average North Korean refugee in China, whose wages are between $50 and $100 a month. Usually the sum is provided by relatives in South Korea or elsewhere overseas, most frequently by a family member who has managed to defect to the South first and probably now waits tables in Seoul restaurants (as we will see, most defectors are not exactly successful in South Korea).

As of early 2014, there were some 26,000 North Korean refugees living in South Korea. This does not sound like a large figure, especially if we consider that between 1961 and 1989—during the years of the Berlin Wall—an average of 23,000 East Germans crossed into West Germany *every single year*. However, it sounds far more impressive if we remember that as recently as 2000 there were merely 1,100 refugees residing in the South. This is by no means an exodus, but, for the first time since the end of the Korean War, there has emerged a significant group of North Koreans who managed to slip from the embrace of "the loving care of the fatherly leader."

These people are very different from the Communist bloc refugees who arrived in the West during the Cold War. The refugees from the Eastern bloc tended to be well educated and usually motivated by political convictions to at least some degree. Conversely, most North Korean refugees are women from impoverished areas along the border looking for both income somewhere above subsistence and security rather than the realization of lofty political ideals. Elite refugees exist but are well below 10 percent of the total. To generalize a bit, a typical refugee of the Soviet Union in the 1970s might be described as a young, brilliant, Jewish chess player. In contrast, the average refugee from North Korea is a rural housewife in her fifties.

It is important to remember, however, that refugees remain in touch with their families back home. It helps that most refugees come from the border areas whose population can cross the border more easily. People frequently call their families using Chinese cell phones, which work perfectly well on the North Korean side of the border. From around 2003, a number of relay stations were built just on the border, and this greatly increased mobile phone coverage (signals can be received miles away). This being the case, Chinese cell phones have become common among more affluent North Koreans in the borderlands (many of these people derive the bulk of their income through legal and not-so-legal trade with China). Monetary remittances from South to North Korea constitute a blatant violation of both South Korean and North Korean laws, but nonetheless seem to be frequent: a majority of refugees in the South use brokers to send money back to their impoverished native villages and towns. Brokers charge 25 to 30 percent per transaction, but the system is remarkably reliable and fast. The total annual amount of such transfers has been recently estimated at some $10 million—by no means an insignificant sum for the tiny North Korean economy.[16]

ARRIVAL IN PARADISE, AKA CAPITALIST HELL

The fate of refugees in South Korea does not bode too well for the post-unification population of North Korea (assuming that unification will happen one day). Most of them find themselves relegated to the low-income bracket and are often the object of discrimination by their newly found brethren.

North Korean refugees are eligible for aid that is quite generous by the standards of South Korea, a country where the social welfare system remains underdeveloped compared to Europe and the United States. For the first few years, refugees are paid a small stipend—not enough to live on but still helpful. They are also provided with subsidized rental housing and scholarships for vocational training. Those who are young enough can apply for university admission. They do not compete with South Korean high school pupils. Rather, they sit for their own, easier, exams.

The statistics, however, are discouraging. In December 2010, research confirmed that the average income of a North Korean refugee in the South is merely 1.27 million won ($1,170), that is, roughly 50 percent of the average

South Korean salary. Unemployment is high—depending on which of the few studies you believe and how you define "unemployment," it afflicts an estimated 10 to 40 percent of the new citizens. Even the most optimistic estimates are depressing at best if one takes into account that South Korea has one of the lowest unemployment rates among countries in the developed world. Only 439 defectors (merely 4 percent of all employed defectors) were working in skilled jobs, while 77 percent were employed in unskilled jobs.[17]

Furthermore, North Koreans discover that mainstream South Korean society looks upon them with a measure of suspicion. A sad story was recently told to the author by a North Korean acquaintance. In 2011 a South Korean television company wanted to make a TV show about North-South couples (i.e., North Korean refugee women married to South Korean men). Participants were promised significant monetary rewards, and thus many female refugees initially agreed to the proposal. Soon, however, most of the candidates called the program's producers to say that they would not participate in the program regardless of how much money was offered, as their husbands decisively opposed the idea. The reason was that they did not want their neighbors, co-workers, and social contacts to know they had married a North Korean woman. The North Korean female interlocutor said: "You know, here in the South it is sort of assumed that only down-and-out males who can't get a proper South Korean woman marry either mail-order brides from Southeast Asia or North Korean refugees."

Surprisingly, even refugees with elite educations can face big challenges in the South. Unless their job directly relates to dealing with the North (and the supply of such jobs is limited), they have great trouble finding any prestigious employment. This is partially a result of suspicions that most employers have about their skills and partially because of their inability to use the extended personal networks that are so central to success in South Korean society. These networks usually unite people from the same region, members of the same clan, or graduates of the same university. North Korean refugees usually do not belong to any of these groups.

Finally yet importantly, the graduation rate for refugee university students is low: a majority of those who enter university drop out. Even though the dropout rate in South Korean universities tends to be very low, North Korean students often discover that they lack what is considered basic knowledge and social skills—advantages their South Korean peers possess. Added to that, many of them have to work to make a living, unlike their South Korean classmates, who usually work merely for pocket money. To make up for the gaps in their background knowledge, they have to study harder than their South Korean peers do, but economic pressure makes this difficult.

A Normal Day in 2011 . . .

It is not that difficult to identify the most representative North Korean newspaper. Everyone knows it to be *Rodong Shinmun*, the ruling Korean Workers' Party mouthpiece. This is not a humble newspaper, but the voice of the Party and State itself.

Let's have a look at an issue published on July 11, 2011. The choice is completely random, and other issues do not look that different.

The entire front page was taken up by one large, unsigned article that informed the reader of the greatest event of late. The Dear Leader, Marshal Kim Jong Il, inspected the largest department store in the city of Pyongyang and provided its personnel with a wealth of managerial guidance on the best way to run this retail outlet. The article was accompanied by two pictures: one depicted the Marshal taking an escalator with some of his entourage, and another shows the Leader standing with the top management of the department store.

The upper part of the second page was occupied by a report of another great event: Marshal Kim had inspected the Pyongyang Zoo and taught its personnel a thing or two about animal rearing and zoo management.

The second page also included official telegrams sent to and received from China on a diplomatic event—the fiftieth anniversary of the treaty of friendship and alliance between China and North Korea. The page also had a small report about an event to commemorate the 117th anniversary of the birth of a humble rural school teacher, Christian missionary, and nationalist named Kim Hyŏng-jik. He happened to also be the grandfather of Marshal Kim Jong Il and the father of Kim Il Sung.

(continued)

The third page contained a half-dozen reports about labor enthusiasm and production achievements. Somewhat uncharacteristically, these reports almost exclusively focus on light industry—obviously resulting from the recent emphasis on the production of consumption goods.

An article in the bottom right corner is a bit of an eye-opener—it relates how housewives of a particular county created a model reconstruction brigade to work on irrigation projects in the area. A small picture depicts the construction site: women are neatly dressed but there is not a machine to be seen, so they use only shovels and their bare hands to line the walls of the irrigation canals with block-like rocks.

The fourth page was filled with reports of foreign visitors who had come to North Korea to express their admiration for the country's great achievements. Most delegations were Chinese, but it is reported that a group of Russian police officials also came to join the chorus and expressed their admiration for "the great successes of North Korea, achieved under the wise leadership of Comrade Kim Jong Il."

The fifth page dealt with South Korea and foreign policy. The largest article was titled "The Hatred of Treacherous Regime" and told North Koreans how much their South Korean compatriots hated the current South Korean administration of President Lee. There were reports of strikes, police abuse, and an unfolding scandal in the South involving US military use of defoliants at a military base.

A small photo depicted a student rally in Seoul, whose participants were demanding a 50-percent cut in tuition fees. The accompanying article did not even hint at the fact that such a cut was actually suggested by "the treacherous regime of Lee Myung Bak." Instead, it deliberately created the impression that South Korean students began this revolutionary fight spontaneously because they could not bear the prohibitively high burden of tuition fees.

The final page again dealt with foreign policy. It began with a large and boring (even by *Rodong Shinmun*'s notorious standards) article about the eternal friendship between China and North Korea. It also included reports from other parts of the world that talked about how much the people of the world admired Generalissimo Kim Il Sung, the founder of the North Korean dynasty. According to the newspaper, commemorative events to honor the memory of the late Generalissimo Kim were held in Romania, Nigeria, Congo, and Thailand.

> The sixth page also contained an article commemorating UN World Population Day. The article concentrated on gender inequality in the capitalist world and contained some statistics about the sorry fate of Western European women (clearly the world's greatest victims of gender discrimination).
>
> Another article on the sixth page dealt with the complex situation of the world food market. Obviously, it was published in order to tell readers that North Korea was not unique in having grave food shortages. Nonetheless, this article stood out because it was almost free from demagogy and indeed contained an interesting analysis of current international trends (perhaps the only piece in the entire newspaper that deserves to be called an article).
>
> Such is the daily fare of news and views provided to North Koreans by their media—day by day, for decades, without much change.

Despite these issues, it would be wrong to assume that North Koreans feel regret about their move to the South. There have indeed been a few cases of refugees fleeing the South in order to head back North. However, for every such case, there are hundreds of instances where individuals and entire families work hard to pay a broker in order to bring their relations to the South.

Nonetheless, the problems are real and are likely to increase in magnitude in case of unification. After all, refugees are a group of people who have consciously chosen a different life. It follows that they will face fewer problems adjusting to massive change than a group of people who will have a different life forced upon them. Therefore, when and if unification comes, these problems are merely a sample of the social and economic issues that will face the South Korean state and the North Korean people.

CHANGING WORLDVIEWS

Approximately a half-million North Koreans have "visited" China over the last fifteen-odd years, and most of them have eventually returned home, voluntarily or otherwise. They have to be cautious, but nonetheless manage to tell stories about China's prosperity—stories that are indeed shocking to any North Korean.

Once, while in Northeast China, the author had a conversation with a member of an NGO who occasionally brings junior North Korean officials to a sleepy, dirty Chinese town in Manchuria. I asked him about the typical reaction of these North Koreans, to which he responded, "They cannot sleep for the first couple of nights, and they are so shocked and overwhelmed by the prosperity of the place, by the bright lights and nightlife of the town." (To the present author, this particular Chinese town during the night looked more like an abandoned steel mill.)

Chinese prosperity might be overwhelming at first, but soon North Korean refugees discover that the Chinese—whom they regard as filthy rich—actually consider their own country poor in comparison to South Korea. Indeed, it is not difficult to learn a lot about South Korea when in Northeast China. South Korean satellite TV is widely watched by ethnic Korean families, and South Korean soap operas with Chinese subtitles are a staple of local TV networks. At any given moment, roughly one out of seven ethnic Koreans of the Yanbian area resides in South Korea, usually being employed there in some unskilled, badly paid job—the family of the author's research assistant's girlfriend employs a Korean from China to look after an ailing grandmother. It does not take long for a North Korean refugee to learn that more or less everything that he or she read in the official media about the South is a blatant and grotesque lie.

This discovery does not necessarily make him or her dream about going to Seoul—after all, such a step requires considerable resources, is inherently risky, and might simply not be to everyone's liking. Nonetheless, stories of the fairy-tale land south of the DMZ are shared with trusted friends and family members back home.

From around 2000, VCRs and, soon afterward, DVD players began to spread in North Korea in large numbers. These machines are both cheap and legal. It was assumed that North Koreans would use them to watch officially approved and ideologically wholesome fare, like, say, biopics of the Dear Leader and his extended family. However, North Koreans usually prefer to watch something different and rather more ideologically suspicious: smuggled foreign movies and TV dramas, often those produced in South Korea.

As always in the case of North Korea, statistics are highly unreliable. According to Chinese customs, 350,000 DVD players were exported to North Korea in 2006 alone—a large number for a country with a population of some twenty-four million.[18] It seems that in border areas and major cities, one out of every three or four families currently has a DVD player. A study by the InterMedia research group concluded that in 2009 the penetration rate was 21 percent and 5 percent for VCRs and DVD players, respectively.[19] From the author's own research, it seems that in the borderland areas of the country, some 70 to 80 percent of all households possessed DVD players by early 2012. We can be sure that more or less all of these families have watched South Korean programs. This content (unlike the DVD players themselves) is illegal, but small entrepreneurs in China make good money by recording them and then smuggling the copies across the border.

Even computers are becoming increasingly common among the more affluent segment of the population. Estimates vary, but one can surmise that the number of privately owned computers, or computers that can be accessed with relative ease, now definitely exceeds 100,000 and is likely to have reached a few hundred thousand. A Western diplomat recently related to the present author that USB memory sticks have become a popular fashion accessory among the privileged Pyongyang youth. The message is unmistakable: by sporting a USB, an individual demonstrates that he/she has access to a computer, one of the important status symbols in present-day Pyongyang. Nowadays, possession of a computer in North Korea is somewhat akin to ownership of a sports car in more affluent societies.[20] North Korean computers are not connected to the Internet, and only some of them have a dial-up connection with the national intranet, known as the Kwangmyŏng network. However, even without an Internet connection, a computer remains a powerful information dissemination device—largely thanks to USB and CD-R drives. The authorities are aware of these threats, and therefore all computers are registered and their hard drives subject to random checks (recently, the security bureaucracy created a special division—the so-called Bureau 27—to monitor and control privately owned computers). Frankly, however, one should be skeptical about the effectiveness of such checks: a teenage computer enthusiast will always outsmart an aging police officer, especially if the latter does not see a good reason to be excessively vigilant.

As to South Korean movies and TV dramas, North Koreans do not necessarily always believe everything they see. Their own movies have always presented a grossly embellished picture of life in North Korea, and they expect this to be the case everywhere in the world. For example, as the author's own talks with North Korean refugees confirm, few of them believed that the average South Korean family had a car when they saw their first South Korean TV dramas (in actual fact, more or less every South Korean family does own a car—as of 2010, the country with a population of 50 million had 13.6 million passenger cars). The interior of a normal South Korean apartment, frequently shown in movies, did not look plausible to them, either—they believed it to be a set, and that such a lifestyle (with that unbelievably large fridge in the kitchen!) would be available only to a select few. Nonetheless, they also know some things are difficult or impossible to fake—like, say, the Seoul cityscape with all its high-rise buildings and giant bridges—and they use these trustworthy images as visual clues, surmising that South Korea must be very rich indeed.

North Korean people are now increasingly aware of South Korea's prosperity. As one refugee, a woman in her late fifties, remarked to the present author, "Well, perhaps children in primary school still believe that South Koreans are poor. But everybody else knows that the South is rich." There are, however, two important caveats. First, it is not quite clear how far this new consciousness has spread beyond the borderlands and a few major cities. Second, while the average North Korean has begun to suspect that the South is ahead of the North economically, he or she seldom understands just how huge this gap really has become. After all, for the North Korean farmer or skilled worker, being wealthy means feasting on rice gruel every day (poorer people eat corn).

Since around 2000, even North Korean propaganda has begun to take into account this slow change of mind—after all, Pyongyang's agitprop shock brigades are not as inflexible as they appear to many foreign observers (those who are seriously interested in the changes in North Korea's propaganda should read the informative works of Brian Myers and Tatiana Gabroussenko).

In post-2000 propaganda, the alleged poverty of South Korea has ceased to be a topic worthy of mention. It is even grudgingly admitted that South Korea might be relatively affluent (of course, this affluence is described as part of a bubble economy, being propped up by the scheming US imperialists for their selfish interests, and hence inherently unstable). However, with all its wealth, South Korea is presented as a very unhappy place. The reason for this unhappiness is that South Koreans' national identity, their precious "Koreanness," has been spoiled and compromised by the domination of American imperialists who propagate their degrading and corrosive "culture." In the post-2000 propaganda narrative, South Koreans suffer not from hunger but rather from national humiliation as well as cultural and environmental degradation. South Koreans allegedly dream of liberation and envy happy Northerners. The latter may be experiencing some temporary economic difficulties but nonetheless have managed to keep their pure national essence intact and have not sold out to the big-nosed servants of Mammon (the North Korean stereotype of Americans is remarkably similar to anti-Semitic stereotypes).

Another recurrent topic of this new propaganda is the inequalities and assorted social ills that permeate South Korean society. As a matter of fact, by international standards, South Korea is a society of remarkable income equality (the "Scandinavia of East Asia," as sociologist Aidan Foster-Carter once remarked), but the South Korean left strongly believes otherwise. North Korean newspapers therefore happily reprint articles from the South Korean leftist media painting a grim picture of a country where the pampered few suck the blood of a destitute majority. Alleged environmental pollution has become another large topic. Interestingly, in the past, North Korea loved to present itself as a country of enormous steel mills and smoky factories, but now, after the industrial collapse of the 1990s, the propagandists have acquired a love of waxing rhapsodically about the alleged pristine environment of their country—and contrast it with the industrial pollution and environmental degradation of the South.

To what extent does this propaganda work? This, of course, remains to be seen. Most likely, a significant number of North Koreans buy this new propaganda line about "relatively-affluent-but-unhappy-and-debased" South Korea. However, the "yellow winds of capitalism" and an understanding of South Korean prosperity are spreading as well.

This growing awareness of the outside world is merely one of many changes that have occurred in the era of "capitalism from below." North Korean popular attitudes toward domestic issues are changing as well. People below the age of thirty simply have no experience of the comprehensive rationing under the old regime and are therefore not inclined to see the state as the natural provider of all life's necessities. Many above the age of thirty have learned that they can do without the state, and some of them have come to enjoy this new situation.

Once again, these trends should not be exaggerated. From regular interaction with North Koreans, the author has come to suspect that the average North Korean would prefer to return to the regimentation that characterized life under Kim Il Sung rather than confront the uncertainties of the subsequent era. After all, in Kim Il Sung's era, everybody who was not unlucky enough to wind up in a prison camp was certain that his or her subsistence-level rations would be forthcoming regularly. Sometimes people were malnourished, but they never starved. Around the time of Kim Il Sung's death in 1994, this old stability disappeared. It is likely that the less successful majority would prefer to go back to the comfort of regularly delivered rations, even if this means more boring indoctrination sessions and the greater risk of being sent to prison for a politically incorrect joke.

At any rate, North Koreans do not have much choice. They have had to adjust, thereby modifying their career aspirations as well. For example, in spite of a significant increase in the intensity of militaristic propaganda after 1994, many North Koreans try to skip obligatory military service. In the past, the seven to ten years spent in the military was seen as an investment because soldiers could easily join the Korean Workers' Party, thus acquiring the most essential prerequisite for social advancement. However, party membership is not as highly prized as it used to be: after all, for an upwardly mobile and adventurous individual, the marketplace provides a faster way to earthly success.

People have begun to ignore the institutions of state that were once created to keep them under constant surveillance. The notorious weekly mutual-criticism sessions as well as indoctrination meetings of various kinds continue, but they have become less frequent and have lost much of their earlier intensity. One can even skip boring official functions in order not to miss a profitable day at the market, even though this might require a bit of bribery.

Although completely unthinkable in Kim Il Sung's North Korea, even riots have begun to happen occasionally. In March 2005, for example, Pyongyang experienced what was probably the first riot in the city for sixty years. The riot itself began at Kim Il Sung Stadium during a World Cup qualifying match between North Korea and Iran. In the middle of the game, an argument erupted between a North Korean player and the Syrian referee. The North Korean player shoved the referee, was sent off, and violence erupted. Fans began to throw bottles, stones, chairs, and anything else close at hand toward the Iranian players and match officials. It took a few minutes before order was restored, while the stadium loudspeakers demanded that fans stay calm. The North Korean team eventually lost 2–0 and the violence promptly resumed, continuing for almost two hours after the match. There were clashes between police and fans, and for a while, Iranian players could not leave the stadium because of the unruly and outraged crowds outside. All of these events unfolded in front of foreign media, who did not miss an opportunity to take rare shots of North Koreans fighting with police. This was a patriotic riot, no doubt, driven by lofty and officially sanctioned emotions, but it nonetheless demonstrated that the foundations of social control were eroding.

Around the same time, market riots in the countryside—admittedly, less patriotic in their intentions—began to occur as well. The outbreak of public discontent usually happens at markets when vendors believe that their right to make money is being unfairly infringed by some capricious decision of the authorities. For example, between 2006 and 2007, when the government unsuccessfully tried to restart the PDS, some markets were closed, and a considerable part of the local population was deprived of the major source of its livelihood. This resulted in numerous protests, usually by middle-aged women. Reportedly, their cry was "give us rations or let us trade!"—not exactly a pro-democracy demonstration but still a challenge to established authority.

The North Korean authorities have been remarkably—and unusually— lenient when dealing with these market riots. Given the secretiveness of the North Korean legal system, one cannot rule out that some of the ring-leaders in such incidents might have been secretly punished. Nevertheless, many of those who participated in the disturbances received either light punishment or escaped punishment completely.

These signs of social relaxation should not be exaggerated. The North Korean state remains one of the most repressive regimes in the world. In spite of some cracks, its surveillance system is still second to none in efficiency and brutality. Nonetheless, the changes are palpable. North Korea is drifting away from Kim Il Sung's "national Stalinism." The implication is clear: the society Kim Il Sung built is slowly but inexorably crumbling and being replaced by something else quite different. As this happens, contradictions between the existing political order and the emerging social order could lead to more rapid change and—just as importantly— to the demand for more rapid change. Where these demands will end, we cannot yet be sure.

CHAPTER 3

The Logic of Survival
(Domestically)

To an outside observer, the behavior of the North Korean leadership often appears irrational. It seems that there is a tested and easy way out of their predicament—but for some reason they refuse to take it. This allegedly "sure and tested" way is the path of Chinese-style reforms that many people hope North Korean leaders will eventually follow, too. Upon closer inspection, however, the alleged advantages of the "Chinese solution" are far from certain. Indeed, while it would be very good for the North Korean people, Chinese-style reform may very well be dangerous, even fatal, for the elite of the country.

REFORM AS COLLECTIVE POLITICAL SUICIDE

The history of East Asia after the Second World War is, above all, the history of spectacular economic success. The world has not seen anything like this since probably the dramatic rise of Europe during the Industrial Revolution in the late eighteenth and early nineteenth century. Between 1960 and 2000, per capita GDP growth averaged 4.6 percent in East Asia, while the world average was a mere 2.8 percent.[1] It is difficult to believe now that in 1960 the per capita GDP of South Korea was slightly below Somalia, while Taiwan lagged behind Senegal.[2]

This remarkable economic expansion was presided over (or, rather, induced) by regimes that were decisively illiberal and undemocratic. These governments are often described as "developmental dictatorships"—largely because they combined authoritarian politics with an obsession for economic growth.

The "developmental dictatorship" strategy was pioneered by military regimes in South Korea and Taiwan (the latter between 1945 and 1988 was a one-party hereditary dictatorship, a bit like North Korea). These regimes combined anti-Communist rhetoric and some lip service to the principles of the "free world" with a market-driven but government-controlled developmental strategy. Lacking natural resources, they utilized cheap and comparatively well-educated labor and stressed economic efficiency. Later, the two economies diversified into high-tech industries. As a result, they were successful beyond anyone's wildest expectations.

From the mid-1980s, this "first generation" of developmental dictatorships was emulated by the state Socialist governments of China and Vietnam. In both countries, the Communist Party elite kept their red flags and quasi-Leninist decorum for the sake of domestic stability, but for all practical purposes switched to the economic, but not political, developmental model pioneered by Taiwan and South Korea. If anything, their version of capitalism was even more unabashed and brutal—the quasi-Communist regimes treated workers with greater harshness and demonstrated a remarkable indifference to the yawning gap between rich and poor. Nonetheless, the model worked again, and the "second generation" of developmental dictatorships also achieved spectacular results. Suffice to say that Vietnam, which experienced a famine as late as the mid-1980s, was by the mid-1990s the world's third-largest exporter of rice.[3]

Thus, in China and Vietnam, the (technically) Communist oligarchy presided over an unprecedented economic expansion while successfully maintaining domestic stability, enormously enriching its members in the process. They can see themselves—with good reason—as benefactors and even saviors of their countries. They also enjoy power and comforts that were beyond the dreams of their mentors, who began their careers in the brutal and austere times of Mao and Ho Chi Minh.

This option seems to be irresistibly attractive, but it has failed to inspire the North Korean elite. Over the last two decades, at every "sign of change" in the North, newspaper columnists and academic commentators alike have assured their readers that the unavoidable has finally happened, and that the long-overdue reform of North Korea has at last begun. The Joint Enterprise Law of 1984, the launch of the Rajin-Sonbong Special Economic Zone in the early 1990s, and the so-called 7.1 measures of 2002 were greeted with much fanfare of North Korea's alleged interest in reform. The present author recalls an article from 2003, written by a professor of marketing from Indiana, entitled "North Korea Moving from Isolation to an Open Market Economy: Is It Time to Invest or to Continue Observing?" Predictably, the suggestion was to invest before it was too late (to give that author his due, however, he did include cautionary warnings).[4]

Terence Roehrig, from the US Naval War College, expressing fairly typical sentiments of optimistic outsiders, said recently:

> To avoid the potential dangers of a sudden collapse in the DPRK, it may be a better route to promote a long-term, gradual transition that seeks to encourage the forces within North Korea and the ruling regime for change. Whether that regime is another member of the Kim family or a military/party collective of some sort, to further a process of economic opening and reform could lead to a subsequent path of political moderation and reform.[5]

Roehrig might be right when he is saying this—cynically speaking, it makes sense to persuade the Pyongyang leadership that its members would have a bright future in a reformed North Korea. However, the elite have not shown much inclination to be persuaded by this siren song. Some of them clearly suspect that reforms would become a shortcut to ruin and self-destruction. Such suspicions are most likely warranted.

Unfortunately for common North Koreans, Kim Jong Il and his entourage were decisively unwilling to emulate China. North Korean leaders have stubbornly resisted reform not because they are ideological zealots who blindly believe in the prescriptions of the Juche Idea (they do not, and the idea itself is too nebulous to be a practical policy anyway), nor because they are ignorant of the outside world. They are neither irrational nor

ideological; on the contrary, they are rational to the extreme, being perhaps the contemporary world's most ruthless Machiavellians. North Korea's
leaders are highly reluctant to carry out reforms because they appear to be
aware that the existence of South Korea makes such reforms potentially
destabilizing.

It is the existence of the rich and free South Korea that has made North
Korea's history so different from that of China or Vietnam. North Korea is
right next to a country whose people speak the same language and are officially described as "members of our nation," but who enjoy a per capita
income at least fifteen times (some claim even forty times) higher than
that of North Koreans.[6] Even if the lowest estimate is to be believed, it is
still by far the world's largest per capita income difference between two
countries that share a land border. To put things in perspective, the income
ratio between the two Germanies was merely 1:3, and even this was
enough to prompt East Germans to overthrow their regime as soon as
they had an opportunity to do so without fear of Soviet intervention. If
ordinary North Koreans become fully aware of the prosperity their brethren enjoy merely fifty miles or so from Pyongyang, the regime's legitimacy
would suffer greatly and may disappear completely.

One can only imagine the mind-blowing effect that might be produced by the sight of the average street in Seoul, a typical South Korean
department store, or, for that matter, the apartment of a humble, semi-
skilled manual worker. Perhaps fifteen years of flourishing market activities somehow have made North Koreans immune to the sights of
consumerist abundance at shops (after all, one can buy a lot in North
Korea now if one has the money to do so). But one can easily imagine
what will happen to a North Korean's mind when he or she discovers
that a South Korean worker—supposedly a slave of American neocoloni-
alism—enjoys the amenities and lifestyle that in North Korea are
available only for a tiny minority (like successful drug smugglers or
Central Committee officials).

Reforms worked in Vietnam and China because, simply put, there was
not a prosperous "South China" or "South Vietnam." The prosperity of, for
example, Japan or the United States is well known in China and Vietnam,

to be sure, but is not seen by the common Chinese person or Vietnamese person as politically relevant. After all, they are different nations with different histories, so their remarkable prosperity does not necessarily demonstrate the inefficiency of Communist Party rule.

Above all, of course, China is not going to become the fifty-first US state or the forty-eighth Japanese prefecture. Nor does China have a rich "other" with which to seek unification: Taiwan is too small to have a real impact on the average Chinese income in the event of unification. The leadership in Hanoi is in an even more enviable position, since South Vietnam ceased to exist in 1975. Thus, for the time being, the common Chinese person seemingly accepts the same bargain that the South Koreans and Taiwanese did in the 1960s: at least put up with authoritarian rule so long as stability and economic growth continue.

In North Korea, due to the allure of the rich and free South, such a bargain is less likely to succeed, and Pyongyang leaders of Kim Jong Il's generation have been well aware of this.

The reasons are relatively straightforward. Reform is impossible without a considerable relaxation of the information blockade and daily surveillance network. Foreign investment and technology, as well as individual initiative and innovation, are necessary preconditions for growth. Consequently, if Chinese-style reforms were to be instigated, a large number of North Koreans would soon be exposed to dangerous knowledge of the outside world, and above all of South Korea. A considerable relaxation of surveillance would be unavoidable as well: efficient market reforms cannot occur in a country where a business trip to the capital city requires a weeklong wait for travel permits, and where promotion is determined not by productivity but by political loyalty (including the ability to memorize the lengthy speeches of the Great Leader). Relaxation would entail information flowing into and around the country, and thus the dissemination of this information, as well as dangerous conclusions drawn from it, would become much easier. The situation is further aggravated by recent dramatic improvement in information technology. Such improvements make censorship far more difficult and therefore constitute a major political threat to the regime.

It is doubtful whether the North Korean population would acquiesce to enduring a further decade of destitution followed by a couple of decades of relative poverty and back-breaking work if they were to learn about the "other Korea"—affluent, free, glamorous, and attractive. Would they agree to tolerate a reforming but still authoritarian and repressive regime on the assumption that this regime will, on some distant day, deliver a level of prosperity comparable to that of present-day South Korea? The North Koreans, unfortunately for their leaders, are much more likely to react to the new knowledge and their newfound freedoms in a different way: by toppling the current regime and unifying with South Korea in order to partake in the fabulous prosperity of the wildly rich South.

One can easily imagine how discontent with the North Korean system, as well as information about the astonishing degree of South Korean prosperity, will spread: first, through the relatively well-heeled North Korean groups who are suddenly allowed to interact with South Koreans and foreigners, or who have better access to the foreign media and entertainment, and then down to the wider social strata. Once North Koreans come to the conclusion that they have no reason to be afraid of the usual crackdown, there is a good chance that they will do what East Germans did in 1989—first migrate en masse and then storm the walls.

There is another important distinction between North Korea and China—and, once again, this difference is created by the existence of the successful South. It is an open secret that Chinese party officials used the reforms to enrich themselves: the new Chinese entrepreneurial class to a significant extent consists of former officials as well as their relations and buddies. The situation in the post-Communist countries of the USSR and Eastern Europe is no different. With few exceptions, the political and economic life of those countries is dominated by former second-tier party apparatchiks who used their connections, experience, education, and, above all, their de facto control over state assets to appropriate government property and remake themselves into successful capitalists and/or politicians. It would be just a minor exaggeration to describe the collapse of Communism as a "management buyout," as Richard Vinen recently did.[7] On balance, in the 1990s, a younger generation of Eastern European and Soviet nomenklatura jettisoned the system they never really believed in and enormously increased their wealth, if not power, in the process.[8]

The predicament of the North Korean elite is very different. Its members stand little chance of becoming successful capitalists if the system is overthrown. In all probability, regime collapse will be followed by the unification of the peninsula—after all, this is what the average North Korean will likely want, on the (mistaken) assumption that unification will instantly deliver them the same level of consumption enjoyed by their southern brethren. The reality, however, is that in such a scenario, all the important positions in the new economy will undoubtedly be taken by people from South Korea—people with the requisite capital, education, experience, and political support. Capitalism in the post-unification North is likely to be built not by born-again apparatchiks (as was the case in the former USSR), but rather by the resident-managers of LG and Samsung, as well as assorted carpetbaggers from Seoul. The case of East Germany is illustrative in this regard: the top tier of East Germany's elite found themselves put on trial, and lower level bureaucrats were expelled from office (or saw their positions phased out). Furthermore, the author is not aware of a single case of one of these people becoming a successful businessman in unified Germany.

This fact is understood by at least some North Korean bureaucrats, but it seems that the majority has another, greater, fear. They know how brutal their rule has been. They also know how they would have treated the South Korean elite (and their descendants) had the North won the intra-Korean feud and do not see any reason why they would be treated differently by the South. This makes them very fearful of retribution. They are not merely afraid to lose power and access to material privileges (these privileges are quite modest, incidentally, by the standards of affluence in most other countries). They are afraid of being slaughtered or sent to prisons, suffering the same fate they have bestowed on their enemies for decades. This would be a fate much worse than that suffered by East Germany's former top-tier leadership.

A few years ago, a high-level North Korean bureaucrat with unusual frankness told a high-level Western diplomat: "Human rights and the like might be a great idea, but if we start explaining it to our people, we will be killed in no time." Such thoughts are seemingly pervasive throughout the elite. It is also not coincidental that many visitors to Pyongyang, including the present author, had to answer the same question quietly asked by their minders: "What has happened to the former East German party and police officials?"

This fear of the top elite in Pyongyang is probably the main reason why the country has remained so resilient in the face of such unenviable international and domestic conditions. This makes North Korea different from many other dictatorships. A clerk in Mubarak's Egypt, for instance, could assume that, Democrats or not, Islamists or not, under a new regime he would still sit at his desk and continue the old routine of, say, issuing permits for house construction. Ditto a military officer, who also would expect that under a new government in Cairo he would still command his battalion. Consequently, they did not see the revolution as a personal threat and might have even been supportive of the movement that shook Egypt in 2011 and 2012.

In North Korea things are different: the elite—pretty much everybody who is somebody—believe that there is nothing to be gained and much to be lost in unification with the South. These fears might be—and, indeed, are—exaggerated, but they are by no means groundless. It is important that their predicament stems from the existence of a successful South, not from particular policies pursued by a specific administration in Seoul. Even if the most pro–North Korean administration imaginable were to come to power in Seoul, it will not make South Korea less dangerous (perhaps, as we will see later, a friendly South is actually *more* dangerous—although this fact might not be currently appreciated in Pyongyang).

These ruminations on the part of the Pyongyang elite are necessarily hypothetical and speculative, but reasonable confirmation of this hypothesis has emerged recently, no less than from Kim Jong Nam, Kim Jong Il's oldest son who lives overseas in semi-exile (largely in Macao and continental China). Kim Jong Nam is the only member of the Kim family who talks to foreign journalists. They occasionally manage to intercept him in an airport or a lobby of an expensive hotel. With the passage of time, his short interviews have become more substantive in content and more politically frank. In 2010 he even went so far as to openly voice his disapproval of the hereditary power transfer that at that point was unfolding in Pyongyang.

His remarks have become even more candid in recent years, and in January 2011 he gave a lengthy interview to Yoji Gomi, a journalist for *Tokyo Shimbun*. Soon afterward it was revealed that since 2004, the maverick North Korean prince had maintained e-mail exchanges with Gomi, who in early 2012 published the content of these e-mails in a book.

The single most important topic in this book is whether Chinese-style reforms are feasible for North Korea. Kim Jong Nam clearly states his belief that market-oriented reforms would probably revive the North Korean economy. At one point, while addressing his half-brother Kim Jong Un (by that time already the successor to Kim Jong Il), he implored him to "have pity on the common people" and follow the Chinese example.

However, at other points in the book, Kim Jong Nam is far less certain about the potential positive impact of reforms. In his January 2011 interview, he said, "I personally believe that economic reforms and openness are the best ways to make life better for the North Korean people. However, given North Korea's position, there is reason to fear that economic reforms and openness will lead to the collapse of the present system." In the same interview, Kim Jong Nam reiterated this point: "The North Korean leadership is stuck in a bind. Without reforms the country's economy will go bankrupt, but reforms are fraught with the danger of systemic collapse."[9] This is a remarkably forthright—and completely reasonable—admission, and unfortunately it confirms that Kim Jong Il and his advisers understood perfectly well how dangerous the reforms would be for their survival.

If so, what is the best policy choice for the North Korean elite? The optimal course of action appears to be a continuation of the policies the current leaders and their predecessors have followed for the last two decades. Domestically, the regime's policy aim has been to keep the North Korean population under control, atomized, and, above all, isolated from the outside world. Internationally, the safest solution is pursuing an aid-maximizing strategy, which includes attempts to squeeze more aid from the outside world through diplomacy and blackmail.[10] This foreign aid helps to keep the inherently inefficient economy afloat, prevent another major famine, and allow the country's tiny elite to live a reasonably luxurious lifestyle while buying at least some support from "strategically important" social groups (the aid is usually distributed first to the military, the police, and the populations of major urban centers).[11]

As we will see later, this anti-reformist approach cannot completely stop the slow-motion changes that might, in the long run, make the system unsustainable. However, for Kim Jong Il this policy made perfect sense: he hoped that the system would last long enough for him to die a natural death. He was not to be disappointed.

Judged from Kim Jong Il's point of view, the policy was an overwhelming success, and most of his advisers and relatives (with the notable exception of Chang Sŏng-t'aek) remain in control of the country at the time of writing in early 2014. Given that a majority of more liberal and permissive Communist regimes have long been overthrown, this is no mean feat. Allegations of factional strife between noble reform-minded officials and belligerent hard-liners used to be a regular North Korea "news" staple (among the international, not domestic, media). There must, of course, be people in the North Korean government who favor reform, but under Kim Jong Il, their inclinations were heavily suppressed, either prudently by the individuals themselves or harshly by the regime.

What Kim Jong Il and his entourage wanted was a return to the year 1984—not that of the Orwellian dystopia (though strikingly similar), but the last year when Kim Il Sung's system was still functioning properly. The economic policies of the Kim Jong Il era were largely driven by the desire to revive the hyper-Stalinist model of the past. Conceivably, many people at the top sincerely hoped that this model might somehow work, but even if they did not succumb to such fantasies, they still felt like they had no choice: due to the existence of the rich South, the hypercentralized and highly controlled Stalinist economy seemed to them to have been the only system compatible with maintaining political stability. Such a perspective seems to be continuing.

PUTTING THE GENIE BACK IN THE BOTTLE: (NOT-SO-SUCCESSFUL) CRACKDOWNS ON MARKET ACTIVITY

When discussing North Korean "grassroots capitalism," it is important to remember that most new entrepreneurial activities are technically illegal, even if the government has little choice but to turn a blind eye to what is happening at the marketplace. In the midst of the famine, the North Korean authorities still sporadically cracked down both on markets and on so-called "capitalist profiteering." Usually, such crackdowns ended in naught, being quietly sabotaged by low-level officials who either depended on markets themselves or understood that excessive pressure was likely to further aggravate an already disastrous situation.

In 2002 Pyongyang's negative attitude toward the growing market economy appeared to change. On July 1, 2002, North Korean leaders introduced a set of measures that are frequently described in the foreign media as the "2002 reforms." With the word "reform" being regarded as too radical, even subversive, the state media never accepted this description, and the policy is officially known in North Korea as the "7.1 measures" (that is, "July 1st measures").[12]

As usually happens at the first sight of any change in North Korean government policy, the measures were heralded overseas as a sign of long-awaited reforms and received an enthusiastic reception in the international media. This started a wave of the usual speculation about North Korea finally doing the right thing and veering toward the Chinese way. Newspaper headlines were sanguine: "With Little Choice, Stalinist North Korea Lets Markets Emerge," "Signs That North Korea Is Coming to Market," and "North Korea Experiments, With China as Its Model."[13] This optimism was completely unfounded, as we shall see.

The 7.1 measures in fact included several policies. First, consumer prices were raised dramatically. For example, for decades rice was "sold" within the PDS at the purely token price of 0.08 North Korean won per kilogram. After the reforms, the price increased by a factor of 550 (!) to 44 won per kilogram, approximating the market price at the time. Official wages increased as well, albeit on a smaller scale. According to Yim Kyong-hun's calculations, retail prices on average increased by a factor of 25, whereas wages increased merely by a factor of 18.[14]

Second, the 7.1 measures introduced changes in the management of state companies, which increased the power and independence of state enterprise managers. Not only were they now allowed to use the market to acquire materials for production and sell the finished product, but they were also given more freedom to design incentives for workers—such as the right to pay performance bonuses.

Third, the 7.1 measures envisioned the establishment of "general markets" (chonghap sichang), a move that in the foreign media was often described (misleadingly) as "lifting the ban on private market trade." Of course, one could not possibly lift a ban that never really existed. By 2002 the vast majority of North Koreans were already earning a living through private market activities of some kind.

The formal establishment of general markets was a less significant change than might have appeared. Essentially, it was a belated and grudging acceptance of what the government knew it could not control. One might be surprised to learn that the majority of market vendors whom the present author interviews regularly (many dozens) simply have no idea about any of the reforms promulgated in 2002. They did not hear about the measures that supposedly legalized their businesses and "completely changed" their lives—and with good reason: the much-hyped measures had little impact on the actual working of the markets, apart from changing the official name and making them (eventually) a bit more regulated. Vendors continued to do what they had been doing for years.

Nonetheless, the 7.1 measures and associated policies indicated that Pyongyang acknowledged and, to an extent, accepted spontaneous "de-Stalinization from below." This relaxation did not last long, however. Soon thereafter, the North Korean authorities began to attempt to reverse the changes that had spontaneously occurred over the previous decade.

This approach—a backlash against the market—might have been bad for the economy, but it was certainly considered to be good for political orthodoxy (and hence stability). The leadership at the time thought that spontaneous liberalization was dangerous and therefore never felt at ease with the very concept of markets. Thus, in 2005 they chose to launch a decisive offensive against the informal economy.

By that time, the famine was over, even though malnourishment remained widespread (and still is). A large role in the economic recovery was played by generous foreign aid. However, it would be an oversimplification to think that it was foreign aid alone that put an end to the disaster of the late 1990s—the partial recovery was helped by the emergence of the private economy (private farming plots in particular) and the adjustment of what remained of the state sector. Improved harvests played a role, too. The North Korean government saw this mild but palpable improvement as a sign that it could do what it was always "programmed" to do—revive the pre-crisis system.

An interesting illustration of this attitude is a remark uttered by a North Korean official in October 2005. When asked by a visiting South Korean scholar whether the government indeed had restarted the rationing system, the official replied: "Now, when we have a good harvest and plentiful reserves of rice, are the private sales of rice at the market necessary?"[15] The underlying assumption is clear: ideally, the economy should be based on administrative distribution and rationing. Markets and retail trade are tolerated only in times of crisis, if that.

In October 2005, roughly when the earlier-quoted conversation took place, the government announced that the long-defunct PDS would be restored in full, albeit with some modifications. The North Korean populace was assured that from now on, everybody would be issued standard rations on a regular basis, as in the Kim Il Sung era, although the price of rations was fixed at the post-2002 official level—rice, for example, was to be 44 won per kilogram. By the time of the announcement, however, the actual market price for rice had already reached 800–900 won, and by 2009 was fluctuating around the 2,000-won mark, so the new PDS price of 44 won per kilogram still remained a token.[16] The decision to reinstate the PDS was accompanied by the revival of the government's monopoly on grain purchases. It was announced that private trade in grain would be banned—or, more accurately, authorities reconfirmed that the ban had always technically existed since 1957 and was never formally lifted; it had merely ceased to be enforced in the early 1990s.

The attempted revival of the PDS was presented as a sign of a "return to normality" and was officially referred to in North Korean parlance as the "normalization of food distribution" (*siklyang konkup chongsanghwa*). Most of the North Korean populace would agree with this description. After all, a majority of North Koreans have lived most of their lives under the PDS and therefore perceived the system as "normal."

The revival proved to be, at best, a partial success. By 2006 it was clear that less than half the population received the promised food rations. Ultimately, Kim Il Sung's system could not be, and therefore was not, re-vived. Anyone living outside of Pyongyang had to be a sufficiently impor-tant official or work at a military plant in order to get full or nearly full rations. The majority of the population received very partial rations at best, or often none at all.

In any case, the "reconfirmed ban" on the private sale of grain lasted for merely a few months. By late 2006 rice and corn were again bought and sold freely, as police and low-level officials were unwilling to enforce the new regulations. As we will see later, this has been the outcome of many attempts to revive the old system. Diktats from on high seldom meet open resistance but are nevertheless quietly sabotaged by low-ranking officials and the general populace.

Attempts to regulate or limit market activities intensified after 2005. In December 2006 the North Korean authorities prohibited able-bodied men from engaging in commercial trade. Men were allowed to transact in the markets only if the aspiring vendor was not the primary breadwinner of the household but a mere dependent.[17] Indeed, in Kim Il Sung's North Korea all men were expected to have a "proper" job—that is, be employed in the state sector.

Of course, in the new era, most state factories are nonfunctioning, and yet almost all adult males are forced to attend their workplaces anyway. There is a certain method to this seeming madness, however. The North Korean sur-veillance system operates on the assumption that every adult has a proper job with a state-run enterprise; thus, indoctrination and police surveillance are centered on the workplace, where all "organizational life" takes place.

The 2006 ban did not have much impact on actual market activities, however, since men in North Korea seldom trade to begin with. Conversely, the government's decision a year later, in December 2007, to extend the ban on market trade to women below fifty years of age was much more important.[18] The decision reportedly led to riots in March 2008, particularly in the city of Chongjin.[19]

For a brief while, police and officials tried to enforce the ban, so younger female vendors had to use a number of tricks. The most common way to evade regulations was to bring along an elderly mother-in-law or other aged female relative when going to market. If police asked questions, the vendor explained that it was actually her highly esteemed mother-in-law who was the trader, while she was there to briefly help the old lady. This ruse could work, admittedly only as long as the police were not too serious about enforcing the ban—and luckily for many North Koreans, they were not. Within a few months the ban was forgotten completely. Once again, quiet resistance had won.

Nonetheless, the North Korean government did not give up and struck against the markets again in late 2008. In November of that year, the local authorities were officially notified that beginning in 2009, private markets would be allowed to operate only three days a month. The sales of industrial goods (things like fans, rice cookers, and so on) would no longer be permitted, either. The leadership made explicitly clear that improvements in the North Korean economic and social situation would make markets obsolete.[20] At the last moment, for reasons unknown, the plan was canceled.

The anti-market policies of the North Korean authorities culminated in the currency reform of 2009. It was designed to destroy the unruly markets once and for all. However, it shared the fate of earlier anti-market measures: it failed, and its failure was truly spectacular.

SALARIES

What was the average income of a North Korean in the 1980s and how much does he or she earn now? These two questions sound natural and commonplace, but are rather difficult to answer—largely because wages in the North play a very different role from that of wages in a capitalist (or even a Soviet-style Socialist) economy.

(continued)

That said, in nominal terms the question is simple enough. In the 1980s the average monthly salary in North Korea was 70 to 80 North Korean won. It had risen to 100 won by 2000. After the 2002 reforms, salaries were increased dramatically, reaching an average of 3,000 won, and have remained at that level ever since. Nowadays, North Korean workers draw salaries in the range from 1,500 to 6,000 won.

As of 2013, the official exchange rate of the North Korean won is now fixed at 135 to the US dollar, but the market rate fluctuated significantly, between 5,000 and 7,000 won to the dollar. Thus, the official salary is equivalent to less than $1 a month. For the Kim Il Sung era, the application of the then market exchange rate would mean that an average salary of 70 won would be roughly equivalent to some $20. But these figures are essentially meaningless and even misleading.

Under Kim Il Sung, North Korea was the epitome of a rationed economy. Everything was allocated by the state, which, being the sole employer in the nation's economy, decided how much grain a worker should eat every day (usually 700g), how much soy sauce he or she should get, and how often pork or fresh apples should appear on the average North Korean's table. Markets existed, but the vast majority of North Koreans in Kim Il Sung's era got what they needed from the state-run distribution system.

North Koreans in this era, however, did not necessarily see the public distribution system (PDS) as one of control. For them, it was often seen as a social safety net, because rations were heavily subsidized almost to the point of being free.

A good example of this was the price of grain within the public distribution system, which was set between 0.04 and 0.08 won. The entire standard food ration (cereals, soy sauce, some vegetables, and a few eggs and fish) would in the 1980s cost between 5 and 10 won a month, or, in other words, some 10 percent of the then average monthly salary.

In North Korea of the Kim Il Sung era, wages differed little from pocket money. People could use it to buy stationery or movie tickets, or satisfy other supplementary needs, while essential goods and services were provided effectively free of charge through the rationing system. The best equivalent might be military service: a soldier in a conscript army is supposed to fight and work, while the state is expected to take care of his basic needs and also provide him with a certain amount of pocket money.

Among other things, this system created a remarkable degree of material equality, although even in the Kim Il Sung era, officials lived much better than the average person. For most, regardless of where they lived or what they did, life was very similar. Even for officials, privileges came not from higher salaries, but from access to special distribution channels. They were issued items unavailable to normal people, such as chocolate and cigarettes with filters.

Rations largely ceased in the early 1990s, with people discovering that in the new situation, they had to rely on the market to get food. This was not easy because, from the mid-1990s, the average monthly salary would suffice to buy merely two kilos of rice.

In 2002 the state attempted to change the situation by increasing the official price of rice to the existing market level while also dramatically increasing salaries to partially compensate for the hike. Obviously, North Korea's economic planners did not realize the consequences of a dramatic increase in the supply of money. After a few months of hyperinflation, the price of rice stabilized to compensate for the increase in the money supply, and North Korean workers, now paid some 3,000 won instead of 100 won a month, discovered that they could afford to buy the same two or three kilos of rice as before.

No wonder that North Koreans turned to a great variety of activities to earn the necessary cash to buy the necessities of life. Now, in 2014, refugees agree that the survival income for a family of three or four is 200,000 won (some $25 according to the current market exchange rate)—roughly ten times the official salary. It is thus no surprise that salary is not seen as a major indicator of either one's income or one's prosperity.

A DISASTER THAT ALMOST HAPPENED: THE CURRENCY REFORM OF 2009

In late 2009 North Korean leaders decided to inflict a major blow to the market system, wiping out capitalistic activities and punishing independent entrepreneurs (also known as "shameless anti-Socialist profiteers"), while also rewarding those steadfast few who remained loyal to the Party and Leader in the midst of turmoil. Actually, it seems that it was not so much the faceless "leadership" but rather Kim Jong Il himself who was the mastermind behind the botched "reforms" of 2009.

In 2009 the device employed was a tried and tested one: currency reform. Such reforms have been part of life in all Communist countries, but similar measures have been used in market economies to curb hyperinflation, too. The Soviet currency reform of 1947 initiated by Joseph Stalin himself can be seen as an archetypical operation of this type. This Soviet reform was later emulated by other Communist regimes, including North Korea, which underwent reforms of this type in 1959, 1979, and 1992.

The reform scenario is well known. One day, usually in the morning, the population suddenly learns that old banknotes are to become useless in a few days and should be swapped for new banknotes. For note exchange, strict limits are set on the amount of cash that can be exchanged (usually equal to a couple of months of salary), while bank deposits usually are treated with greater leniency and can be exchanged in somewhat greater quantities—but still within limits. The exchange period is made deliberately short, usually a few days only, and the number of places where exchanges can be made is also highly restricted.

The intended result of such a policy is a dramatic reduction in the money supply, which is very good for curbing inflation. In Communist countries, which tended to embrace this kind of currency reform, the policy has an important added benefit: it wipes out illegal savings of black market operators. People who have lived on their official salaries and/or tended to keep money in government-controlled banks suffered as well, but to a much lesser extent.

Accordingly, on the morning of November 30 (at 11:00 AM, to be exact), the North Korean populace learned that old banknotes would go out of circulation. As was often the case with such reforms, it was accompanied with devaluation: two zeros from North Korea's paper currency, the won, were to be lopped off, so 100 "new" won was supposed to buy as much merchandise as 10,000 "old" won. This would make prices roughly similar to what they used to be in the early 1990s, just before the collapse of the state-run economy. The change had to be completed in less than a week, and the exchange limit was initially set at 100,000 "old" won per person—equivalent to $30 at the then-going exchange rate. Panic ensued, since many North Koreans, especially those involved in private economic activities, had significant amounts of cash holdings in North Korean currency. Many a private businessperson faced ruin (as was intended by the reform's planners).

The reform had one striking peculiarity, however, which made it different from its prototypes and doomed it to failure. It was declared that all people who were employed by state-run factories and institutions—that is, virtually all those legally employed in the economy—would receive the same amount in the new currency in wages as they did in the old currency.

This measure effectively constituted a hundredfold (that is, 10,000 percent) overnight increase in salaries and wages. Take, for example, the case of a skilled worker who dutifully attended his or her nonfunctioning factory and was, before the currency reform, paid 3,500 won per month. After the reform, the worker was still to be paid 3,500 won per month. At the same time, the price of all goods and services was supposed to go down a hundredfold—for example, the price of rice was officially fixed at the level of 22 new won per kilo, instead of the pre-reform level of 1,800–2,000. This—theoretically!—implied that a salary of 3,500 "new" won would buy as much as 350,000 "old" won.

For a while, foreign observers were taken aback by such a seemingly irrational move and speculated about secret designs behind the plan—or even refused to believe the first reports about the promised 10,000 percent rise in wages. However, it soon became clear that no secret design existed and that reports were true indeed. Obviously, those who approved the plan did not quite understand that, by increasing salaries a hundredfold overnight, they would produce a tidal wave of inflation and no dramatic increase in living standards.[21]

North Korea has undergone currency reforms a number of times, and its financial experts are aware of similar reforms elsewhere—so one cannot help but wonder how such a bizarre feature made its way into the reform plan. One can speculate that planners initially intended to follow the well-established pattern and launch a standard confiscatory currency reform—that is, a reform in which most of the cash deposits would be appropriated by the state, and both salaries and retail prices would be decreased in equal proportions. However, it seems likely that at the last moment somebody intervened and ordered a dramatic revision of the plan by injecting a large increase in official salaries.

Whoever suggested this was unbelievably naïve, not to say ignorant, about the fundamental workings of an economy, where human beings have to divide limited resources and are not able to simply create resources with paper alone. One should not be so surprised, however, by such naiveté. Given the mechanics of the North Korean state, such a decision had to be initiated (or at least personally approved) by Kim Jong Il himself. The North Korean ruler was not known for having to worry about paying for groceries or saving for a new car (let alone for a rainy day). Kim Jong Il was indeed a brilliant powerbroker and a world-class diplomatic manipulator, but he had a reputation for being almost comically incompetent in matters of economic management—and the 2009 reform confirmed this widely held view.

One can easily imagine how the Dear Leader would look through a currency reform plan and say: "And what about poor workers? Shouldn't we reward them for remaining loyal to Socialist industry? Why not increase their salaries, so they will become more affluent than those anti-Socialist profiteers on the black market?" One would imagine that few, if any, officials would dare to explain the dire economic consequences of such generosity to the Dear Leader.

From the first hours, the currency reforms took a very messy turn indeed. People rushed to save their earnings and savings, and panic buying ensued. In a sense, this was expected to happen, but the scale of the panic was unusual. To ease the situation, the authorities adjusted the rules, increasing the maximum exchange limits, but this did not help. Unfortunately, further actions merely exacerbated the crisis.

The authorities obviously expected that the PDS would start functioning immediately, delivering rations to the masses, but this did not (and could not) happen. As one would expect, inflation began to accelerate. For a while the government kept issuing restrictions on the maximum market price for essential goods—for example, rice should not be sold for more than 23 won per kilogram. The market ignored these regulatory mandates. In rare cases when the regulations were enforced by the police, goods predictably disappeared rather than being sold at a price that was well below the market equilibrium. In an attempt to rein in the chaos (and, perhaps, to "punish" the stubborn merchants and vendors), the regime closed all markets in December. In early January 2010, hard currency shops, where the elite and new rich could buy quality goods, were closed as well. This latter decision delivered a blow to the highly privileged groups of the population. In January it did not necessarily help to be an army general, a spymaster, or a successful antiques dealer, as even those privileged people had trouble procuring the necessities of life.

For a brief while in January and February 2010, a major outbreak of public discontent seemed to be within the realms of possibility. Dissatisfaction was expressed with unprecedented frankness. It was the first time in decades when even highly privileged members of the Pyongyang elite openly criticized their government's actions when talking to foreigners. Russian students in Pyongyang were approached by classmates who did not bother to hide their anger about the currency reform, and North Korean diplomats sometimes made pointed comments to their foreign opposite numbers. A military attaché of one Western country (not exactly friendly from the North Korean point of view) told me of his opposite numbers having related that the North Korean government "doesn't quite understand what it's doing." One can imagine how angry a military intelligence officer in one of the world's most controlled societies has to be in order to share his frustration with an imperialist outsider.

It is not coincidental that around this time rumors about the impending collapse of North Korea began to spread. To an extent these rumors were probably circulated by South Korean conservatives then in control in Seoul, but the sense of insecurity was briefly shared by many people who had firsthand access to Pyongyang (not least by the Chinese, whose unease was palpable at the time).

Nothing serious happened, however. By April, normal life had resumed. Foreign currency shops and private markets were reopened in February, the rich and powerful stopped complaining, and humbler folks resumed their usual economic activities, which lay well outside the shrinking government-controlled sphere.

In the aftermath of the reform fiasco, the government withdrew all restrictions that had been introduced in the 2005–2009 anti-market campaigns. The local authorities were explicitly ordered in May 2010 not to intervene with the daily working of markets—as long as politically dangerous items, like South Korean DVDs, were not on sale. It was again unofficially permitted to sell grain at the market price, and traders regardless of age or gender were allowed to work unimpeded. Obviously, the government again implicitly admitted that North Korea in its present shape could not exist without active markets—its hyper-Stalinist rhetoric notwithstanding.

There were rumors at the time that the North Korean premier, soon to be ousted from his job, apologized for "mistakes" when talking behind closed doors to a gathering of officials in Pyongyang. There were also widespread rumors that Pak Nam-gi (a high-level KWP official, responsible for economic policy) was executed for his "counter-revolutionary activities and espionage." Allegedly, the old bureaucrat was accused of being a lifelong American spy who deliberately mishandled the reform in order to inflict damage to the North Korean economy.

At the same time, the entire issue of the currency reform was never mentioned in the open-access North Korean media. Even as the entire country was in an unprecedented state of chaos, not a single article in the official newspapers even mentioned what was going on. All information and instructions reached the North Korean populace through classified channels. Signs were put on notice boards at banks, markets, and shops, and announcements were occasionally made over cable radio whose programming could not be heard by outsiders (and often differed from one neighborhood to another). Yet references to the currency reform also could be found in the types of media that are inaccessible to the average North Korean and exclusively target a foreign audience—like, for instance, the pro-North newspaper in Japan (*Choson Shinbo*). Very strange indeed.

The government succeeded in getting the political situation under control but could not do much about the vexing law of supply and demand.

Thus, a tidal wave of inflation spread immediately after the reform—and what else would one expect after an effective 10,000 percent overnight increase in all wages and salaries? Within a few months, four-digit inflation wiped out whatever little gains state employees had received from the entire operation. By late 2010 the price of food and consumption goods stabilized at roughly the same level as before the currency reform (which could have been predicted by anyone who ever took Economics 101).

In essence, a bold attempt to deny the law of supply and demand ended pretty much like any challenge to the law of gravity inevitably does—with a resounding thud. It remains to be seen, however, whether North Korea's leaders have learned their lesson. The level of economic ignorance they demonstrated in 2009 makes one suspect that the Kim family (and, perhaps, many of their top advisers) cannot grasp even the basic mechanisms that govern a functioning economic system. Admittedly, this ignorance about modern economics does not prevent them from being shrewd politicians who recognize what they need to do in order to stay in power. They know how to maintain a world where they and their families will have no need to worry about such mundane matters as paying their bills.

Nevertheless, it is possible that North Korean leaders have learned a thing or two from their dangerous encounter with the world of market economies. Beginning in May 2010, attempts to reverse marketization were abruptly stopped. In essence, the government, burned by its 2009 failure, returned to the policy of the late 1990s: while markets were not officially endorsed, they were (and still are as of 2014), for all practical purposes, tolerated. These measures helped. Contrary to what many people assume, the last few years have been a time when North Korea's economic situation has been slowly improving.

STILL POOR AND MALNOURISHED, BUT STARVING NO MORE

If one reads newspaper reports about North Korea, one cannot help but get a very dire picture of an insane dictatorship whose leaders enjoy seemingly meaningless saber-rattling while their subjects live under the constant threat of another murderous famine. While such an image is not completely lacking in truth, things are far more complex (and better for many North Koreans) than one would think from indulging in much of this fare.

In the last few years, from time to time the major international newspapers have showered readers with predictions of looming mass starvation in North Korea (often with an implicit—and unfounded—assumption that this might provoke internal unrest and regime collapse). Such ominous headlines can be found more or less every year, usually in spring. In March 2011, *The New York Times* wrote: "North Korea: 6 Million Are Hungry." One year earlier, in March 2010, the *Times of London* warned: "Catastrophe in North Korea; China must pressure Pyongyang to allow food aid to millions threatened by famine." In March 2009, the *Washington Post* headline blared: "At the Heart of North Korea's Troubles, an Intractable Hunger Crisis." In March 2008, the *International Herald Tribune* ran a predictable headline: "Food Shortage Looms in North Korea."[22] Such prophecies of doom come every year, but famine does not.

Indeed, over the last few years there have been times when the food situation has deteriorated, perhaps nearly to the point of another outbreak of famine. Nonetheless, on balance, the last seven to ten years can be described as a time of modest but steady and undeniable improvement in North Korea's economic situation.

Economic statistics are murky, but they seemingly indicate that by 2005 North Korean GDP had roughly returned to the pre-crisis levels of the late 1980s and then continued to grow from this (admittedly, low) point. According to the estimates of the Bank of Korea, widely believed to be the most reliable (or, more accurately, the least unreliable) assessments of the North Korean economy, the GDP growth over the 2000–13 period averaged 1.4 percent per annum.[23] A moderate increase, to be sure, but an increase nonetheless. Of course, one can and should be skeptical about the exactness of the figure—Marcus Noland, one of the world's best experts on the North Korean economy, loves to repeat: "Never trust a datum about the North Korean economy that comes with a decimal point attached."

However, anecdotal evidence and observations generally support such mildly optimistic estimates.

Malnourishment remains common (this has been the case for decades), especially in the countryside, but after 2000–02, few if any North Koreans have starved to death. "Capitalism from below" has brought social stratification, but the new middle class can now afford items that were unheard of in Kim Il Sung's time. DVD players are common. Refrigerators remain rare but are no longer exceptional, bicycles are ubiquitous, and even a computer is not seen any more as a sign of extreme luxury.

The improvement is especially noticeable in Pyongyang, but by no means limited to the North Korean capital. The huge avenues of the North Korean capital, once infamous for their complete lack of traffic, are now reminiscent of the streets of 1970s Moscow—traffic is not too heavy, but clearly present. In older parts of the city, where the streets are not so wide, one can occasionally even encounter small traffic jams, once completely unthinkable. The electricity supply is still unreliable, but much better than it had been since the 1980s.

Visitors and richer Pyongyangites—some 10 to 15 percent of the new middle class—can feast on numerous delicacies in a multitude of posh private and semi-private restaurants that have sprung up around the city in recent years. One can enjoy Japanese sushi, pizza, and assorted Chinese delicacies. Most new restaurants have private rooms, which are used for the closed banquets of the bureaucrats and the new rich (intimately connected, but somewhat different groups). In some cases, they do not limit themselves to gastronomical pleasures but double as elite brothels. This was confirmed by recent official North Korean pronouncements: when Chang Sŏng-t'aek was purged in December 2013, the indictment mentioned both his fondness for private rooms in expensive restaurants and his dalliances with women.

For the average North Korean denizen, the upmarket restaurants are prohibitively expensive, dinner costing some $5 to 10 (excluding alcohol), but the most exclusive places charge up to $30 per patron. To put this into context, the average monthly salary of a university professor now equals some 80 cents. Nonetheless, there are cheaper places for the less successful—and those places are never empty.

Expensive shops stocking luxury goods are becoming more numerous as well. Gone are the days when a bottle of cheap Chinese shampoo was seen as a great luxury; nowadays, the privileged few can easily buy Chanel in a Pyongyang boutique.

Of late, the North Korean capital has seen a dramatic growth in the real estate market, and rapid growth in real estate prices, too. While technically trade in real estate remains illegal, entrepreneurial North Koreans have discovered loopholes in the regulations. Although North Koreans are not legally allowed to sell their houses, they are allowed to swap their houses as long as both houses are located within the same jurisdiction (same city or county). The rationale is that people occasionally have to move within their city or town in order to get closer to their workplace or school.

Using this loophole, people swap accommodations, with the difference in the value of the two paid to the person moving into the inferior unit. In the event that one side has money but no house, the side with the house sells it and takes up residence with relatives (thus exploiting another loophole in the regulations). Sometimes, swaps include numerous parties and can be quite complex, with multiple sides exchanging money for property, but due to the near absence of real estate brokers, the number of people involved in such chains usually does not exceed a few households.

As a result of these innovations and the steady (albeit uneven) economic revival of the country, over the last fifteen years or so, housing prices have increased dramatically. In one known example, a good apartment in downtown Pyongyang was purchased around 2000 for the then considerable sum of $5,000 but sold recently for $160,000—a thirtyfold increase! This alone speaks volumes about both the improvement of the economic situation in the country and the affluence of the emerging Pyongyang merchant class.

A good flat in Pyongyang can cost between $60,000 and $70,000, and the best houses can sell for prices in excess of $150,000. On the other hand, smaller old flats, often without bathing facilities, cost between $25,000 and $30,000, and huts on the city outskirts might be even cheaper.

A renovation boom is also noticeable: older urban buildings seldom featured a shower room, so now such rooms are installed by the more affluent townsfolk (complete with Chinese water heaters, of course).

It is often assumed that starvation and destitution bring revolution, while economic growth and social development improve the probability of survival of governments. Much of the time, this is indeed the case, but there are many exceptions to the rule. Counterintuitively, the slow but palpable improvement in the economic situation in North Korea might actually prove to be the regime's undoing. North Korea may have grown, but without a dramatic structural transformation it is not going to achieve a growth rate that would be comparable to that of China or South Korea. Therefore, the huge income gap between North Korea and its neighbors, the major potential source of political trouble, will persist or even widen further. At the same time, as North Koreans worry less about their daily rice (or corn), they have more time to think, talk, and socialize—and this is not good for the regime. Contrary to what one might think, people seldom start revolutions when they are really desperate: in such times they are too busy fighting for physical survival. A minor but seemingly insufficient improvement in people's lives is what authoritarian regimes should fear most.

A visible and rather dramatic increase in relative inequality is likely to make the situation worse. In the bygone days of North Korean Stalinism, there was a great deal of inequality, but it was well hidden, and most were relatively equal in their poverty. The Kim family and immediate relatives enjoyed a luxurious lifestyle indeed, but the average mid-ranking official in the 1970s had access only to rather limited luxuries—leather shoes, a few meals of pork a week, and sometimes an apartment with a flush toilet (and an unreliable supply of hot water). Even such moderate luxuries were never advertised and indeed were carefully concealed from commoners.

Conversely, the new rich flaunt their wealth. Most North Koreans view such conspicuous consumption as evidence of ill-gotten gains. Expensive cars are to be seen everywhere, and posh restaurants of today are also far more visible than the clandestine distribution points where the privileged few once got their canned salmon and leather shoes. This is not to say that the poor of North Korea are worse off now than they were a decade ago;

the oft-repeated cliché that the "rich get richer and the poor get poorer" clearly does not apply to post-famine North Korea. Nevertheless, the highly visible and socially unjustifiable growth in the income gap between the top 5 percent and the majority of the population is bound to be unnerving and potentially destabilizing. The decades-old tradition that emphasized social equality makes such developments yet more repulsive in the eyes of the average North Korean.

Of course, all these developments leave us with a puzzle: where does this growth come from? While the exact answer to this question is impossible (given the fact that we lack accurate economic and social statistics on North Korea), the growth seems to be the result of three related developments. First, the North Korean market economy has taken off. In spite of a multitude of restrictions (and resulting inefficiencies), North Koreans produce many goods and services for themselves (and the outside world), and this is one of the major reasons for the economic recovery we can see. Second, foreign aid should not be discounted—this aid, squeezed from rather reluctant sponsors by North Korean diplomats, has surely had a real impact on the economic situation. Third, the attitude of North Korean officials matters much as well. Factory managers are no longer cogs in an ossified and inflexible state economic planning system, but, rather, increasingly see the factories they run as their own private property; they use their initiative to make money and pocket the proceeds (as well as pay their employees). None of this is sufficient explanation, and more work needs to be done in the future. We will probably not understand entirely North Korea's partial recovery until we get access to the country, its people, and the government's archives. Nonetheless, this rough sketch provides some clues for what we will probably find if and when the regime collapses.

CHAPTER 4

The Supreme Leader and His Era

THE BELATED EMERGENCE OF A "YOUNG GENERAL"

Since the early 1970s North Korea has been a family dictatorship, an absolute monarchy in all but name. Consequently, it was expected that Kim Jong Il would eventually anoint one of his sons as successor. Rumors about a coming succession have widely circulated in the media since the mid-1990s. International media outlets have from time to time run stories where, whilst citing "well-informed sources" inside North Korea, they claimed that Kim Jong Il had "just made a decision" about the succession. Until 2008, however, all these reports came to nothing. For some unknown reason, Kim Jong Il was not in a hurry to anoint a designated heir until almost the end of his reign.

In discussing Kim Jong Il's alleged choice, the media named a number of "approved candidates"—including all three of his known sons, as well as his brother-in-law, his sister, his daughter, and even his then-current mistress.

For a while during the 1990s, most people expected that Kim Jong Il would choose his eldest son, Kim Jong Nam, as his successor. This did not happen, however. In May 2001 Kim Jong Nam was apprehended by the Japanese immigration service while attempting to enter Japan on a fake Dominican Republic passport. He was accompanied by two women (one of whom was obviously his wife while another was seemingly a servant), and also had a child with him. When questioned by immigration authorities, Kim Jong Nam admitted his identity and claimed that he had just come to visit Disneyland.

It was widely reported that this incident led to a falling-out between Kim Jong Nam and his father, but these oft-repeated claims are based on hearsay. After all, this was not his first trip to Japan under an assumed name with a fake passport. Members of the Kim family at the time frequently used fake identities when traveling overseas, so the scheme would hardly have raised the ire of the ruling Kim. Nonetheless, since the late 1990s Kim Jong Nam has spent most of his time in Macao and China, seldom visiting Pyongyang.

Kim Jong Nam's relations with Pyongyang obviously took a further turn for the worse after his half-brother's ascension to power in 2011. There have been persistent rumors about attempts against Kim Jong Nam's life, allegedly arranged by his half-brothers. It is also remarkable that Kim Jong Nam now enjoys rather cozy relations with the Chinese government, which, as he has admitted in interviews, supervises him closely.

China is now the major player when it comes to North Korea's future, and the close Beijing connection of a runaway Korean prince might be of real significance in the future. Nonetheless, at present Kim Jong Nam seems to be completely cut off from daily affairs in Pyongyang. Interestingly, his son is now studying in Europe. This young man made some headlines when South Korean journalists discovered his Facebook account in which the young prince mentioned his preference for democracy over Communism—and also his YouTube posting where he expressed guilt about the sorry fate of common North Koreans.[1]

In any case, Kim Jong Nam lost whatever possibility there was of succeeding his father. Kim Jong Il, when he finally made his decision, chose his youngest son, Kim Jong Un, who was probably born in 1983 (though his exact age is not known). Of all Kim Jong Il's children, Kim Jong Un was the least known to the outside world, and even his name for a long time was misspelled in the media.

Admittedly, even after Kim Jong Un's sudden ascension to power, the biographical data remained sketchy and often unreliable. If North Korean official publications are to be believed, Kim Jong Un spent his youth serving incognito in the Korean People's Army. This seems to be a propaganda fantasy: in actuality, Kim Jong Un passed his teenage years in Switzerland, where he attended an expensive international high school. One should not be surprised about such an upbringing: since the early 1990s, Switzerland has become a place where many top members of North Korea's aristocracy send their progeny to study. Kim Jong Un attended the school under a pseudonym and is remembered by his former classmates as a somewhat shy boy who loved pizza and enjoyed watching sports on TV. At any rate, his Western education suggests that he probably speaks fluent English and perhaps some German, and has some idea of how the modern world operates. Obviously, after a few years in Switzerland, Kim Jong Un was brought back home and received some individual training at Kim Il Sung University.

Kim Jong Un emerged as heir apparent after his father confronted his own mortality. In late 2008 Kim Jong Il suffered a stroke, and it was seemingly this event that led him at last to make the long-delayed decision. In early 2009 word spread among North Korea's bureaucrats and the Party faithful that a new genius of leadership had emerged from within the ancient lands of Korea. By the summer of 2009, propaganda began to target virtually all segments of North Korean society, and the name of the "Young General Kim" or "New Star General" was frequently invoked at regular indoctrination sessions. North Koreans were also made to study a song extolling the virtues of the new leader. Propagandists did not explicitly state that the new shining star of political wisdom was somehow related to Kim Jong Il or Kim Il Sung, but few people had any doubt about the family to which the new mysterious genius must have belonged.

The succession became semi-official in September 2010, when the Korean Workers' Party (KWP) held a conference, the first official convention of the Party since the 1980 KWP Congress. On the eve of the conference, Kim Jong Un was promoted to the rank of four-star general, and for a brief while the "four-star general" (Taejang in Korean) was the most popular way to refer to him. At the conference, Kim Jong Un was appointed deputy chairman of the Central Military Committee of the Party, a previously unimportant institution that for a while was brought to the administrative forefront of the North Korean government.

From then on, the North Korean media began to report extensively on Kim Jong Un's activities. He often appeared in the company of his father while visiting military units and model factories, or chatting with steel workers and tractor drivers. Paeans to the wisdom and talent of the Young General began to appear in the media with increasing frequency, hence little if any doubt could be entertained about his intended future.

To promote the new leader, North Korean propaganda went to great lengths to emphasize the continuity with established patterns of family rule. When Kim Jong Un was first introduced to the North Korean public in September 2010, he appeared clad in a Mao suit, which was identical to the attire his grandfather used to sport in the 1950s—this suit remains his favorite attire at the time of writing. A Mao suit looks anachronistic even in North Korea, thus the Young General's choice of clothes has clear political connotations—it shows that he is the rightful successor to the dynasty once founded by his grandfather. It helps, of course, that Kim the Third bears a striking resemblance to Kim Il Sung (and not just because he is unusually stout for a North Korean). He also sports a haircut very similar to that of his grandfather. Indeed, for a while, the North Korean media described Kim Jong Un as "Kim Il Sung of today."

To emphasize continuity with his father, another similar visual message has been employed. In winter the youngest Kim has appeared in front of the cameras in a gray parka and fur hat, completely identical to those of his father. By using such methods the North Korean government has sought to remind the North Korean populace that their country was destined to be run by the reincarnation of Kim Il Sung and Kim Jong Il—but, given that Kim Il Sung enjoyed more popularity, the connection between the heir apparent and his grandfather was emphasized with special intensity.

At the time of his promotion in 2010, Kim Jong Un did not appear to be a well-prepared successor. He spent a large part of his childhood overseas, while as a youngster he led a secluded life in the palaces of the Kim family. He probably does not know much about the country he has to run. At the time, observers assumed that for a while after his father's death Kim Jong Un would remain a figurehead, assisted by a team of experienced senior advisers.

This seems to have been Kim Jong Il's initial plan, too. At the time of Kim Jong Un's promotion, Kim Jong Il's sister, Kim Kyŏng-hŭi, and her husband, Chang Sŏng-t'aek (also spelled Jang Song Taek), also rose to the summit of political power in North Korea. Kim Kyŏng-hŭi, who spent most of her life as the top manager of North Korea's light industry (not exactly a success story), was, in 2010, promoted to the rank of four-star general—together with Kim Jong Un himself. Kim Jong Il obviously reasoned that the relatively young and childless Kim-Chang couple (then in their mid-sixties, their sole child having committed suicide in 2006) would make the best regents for his inexperienced son if Kim Jong Il himself died prematurely or became incapacitated. Another person who obviously was meant to supervise the inexperienced leader was Vice Marshal Yi Yŏng-ho, the head of the North Korean General Staff and de facto commander of the armed forces. Kim Jong Il had thus made sure that his son would be guarded and guided by experienced dignitaries if ever the need should arise.

As briefly mentioned earlier, when the appointment of Kim Jong Un became certain, his semi-exiled half-brother Kim Jong Nam hinted that the hereditary succession itself might be problematic. In October 2010, during an unusually long and frank interview with the Japanese Asahi TV, he said: "Personally I oppose a hereditary succession for a third generation, but I presume there were internal reasons. We should abide by such reasons if there are any."[2] In January 2011, in a shorter interview with *Tokyo Shimbun*, he was more frank: "Even Chairman Mao Zedong of China did not enforce hereditary succession. [Hereditary succession] does not fit with Socialism, and my father was against it as well. [...] My understanding is that [the power succession] is intended to stabilize the internal system. North Korea's instability leads to instability in the region."[3]

THE SUDDEN DAWN OF A NEW ERA

When, at noon on December 19, 2011, the people of North Korea saw the anchorwoman on TV, they probably guessed instantly what had happened. Clad in mourning attire and tearful, the announcer delivered the big news. North Koreans were informed that Kim Jong Il had died two days earlier, during the morning of December 17th. It was stated that he was on his famous palatial armored train en route to provide on-the-spot guidance somewhere in the countryside. The latter has since been questioned, but the exact circumstances of his death are not that important. Whenever and however Kim Jong Il died, the seventeen-odd years of his rule came to an abrupt end.

At the time of Kim Jong Il's sudden demise, nobody doubted that Kim Jong Un was meant to become his successor. Nonetheless, it is often overlooked that by December 2011 Kim Jong Un had not yet been explicitly proclaimed successor to his father. It might be surmised that Kim Jong Un's official promotion to heir designate was initially scheduled to take place amidst the expected gala celebrations of Kim Il Sung's hundredth birthday in April 2012. However, Kim Jong Il died prematurely before these plans could be brought to fruition. Of course, the way the official media treated Kim Jong Un left no doubt about his destiny. Nonetheless, at the moment of Kim Jong Il's death, Kim Jong Un was technically merely a four-star general, one of a dozen top military officers—four-star generals, vice marshals, and marshals.

This uncertainty, however, had little if any impact on subsequent events. When the announcer explained to the North Korean people how devastated they were by Kim Jong Il's sudden demise, she also assured them that things would be all right, since Kim Jong Un was firmly at the helm of the country as the new leader.

Within days of Kim Jong Il's death, the North Korean media extolled the masses to switch their loyalty to Kim Jong Un. In quick succession, Kim Jong Un was made Supreme Commander of the Korean People's Army, acquired the title of Supreme Leader, and, a few months later, was made Marshal. His name also began to appear in bold script in official publications. In a curiously Orwellian twist, North Korean propagandists edited older copies of the regime's major official newspaper, *Rodong Sinmun*, so in the online archive the name of the Supreme Leader now appears in bold, even in issues from early 2011 when it used not to be.

In most other dictatorships, such an embarrassingly young and politically inexperienced dictator with somewhat dubious credentials would almost certainly face a challenge from within the inner circle. This has not happened in North Korea (so far), and with good reason: Pyongyang's elite are aware that any instability might have grave consequences for all of them. In other words, it seems that North Korean leaders have internalized the dictum of Benjamin Franklin, who famously and sagely advised, "Gentlemen, we must now all hang together, or we shall most assuredly all hang separately."

For all his own shortcomings, a glaring lack of experience being chief among them, this young and slightly comical-looking, rotund man is still the embodiment of legitimacy in North Korea. He belongs to the Paekdu bloodline—a semi-official North Korean term for Kim Il Sung's family—and he is the son and grandson of the country's two former top leaders. In the modern world, this might appear to be a weak, even bizarre, foundation on which to build a state. But the North Korean leadership, surrounded by a hostile world and presiding over potentially restive subjects, has nothing better—and one should not forget that for millennia the vast majority of human beings lived in societies where supreme political power was, essentially, hereditary.

Immediately after Kim Jong Un's ascension, on December 30th, the National Defense Commission issued a statement in which the North Korean leadership said explicitly: "We declare solemnly and confidently that the foolish politicians around the world, including the puppet group in South Korea, should not expect any change from us."

Indeed, for a brief while it appeared as if not much was going to change in North Korea under the new management. Kim Jong Un frequently went to dispense on-the-spot guidance to military units and collective farms across the country. His wisdom and warmth have been enthusiastically extolled by poets, writers, and painters. North Korean TV also hastily produced a documentary where one can see footage of the young Kim getting out of a tank and toying with a rifle. In other words, everything has ostensibly continued much as before.

However, within a few months it became clear that the new North Korean leader was going to seriously deviate from the trajectory once followed by his father. It was almost universally expected that eventually the young leader would get rid of those appointed by his father to supervise him and start running the country as he pleased—but few if any expected that changes would come that soon.

COLLAPSE OF THE OLD GUARD

In December 2011 the North Korean people and the rest of the world witnessed Kim Jong Il's solemn funeral procession. Eight individuals accompanied the hearse of the Marshal, later posthumously promoted to Generalissimo in April 2012. The country's four top military commanders walked to the left of the hearse, with Vice Marshal Yi Yŏng-ho at the front of the line, followed by three other generals. On the right were the country's four top Party leaders and civilian apparatchiks. Significantly, Kim Jong Un, in spite of the militaristic tint of his emerging personality cult, chose to appear at the head of the civilian officials. He was followed by Chang Sŏng-t'aek, widely seen at the time as the most powerful man in the Party.

Many North Korean and foreign media outlets reproduced the solemn images of a black 1976 Lincoln driving through the streets of Pyongyang under heavy snow. However, these images were soon to disappear from the North Korean media. In the two years that followed the funeral, five of the seven top officials who had walked next to his hearse were to be ousted from their posts, disappear, or even be executed.

In a sense, the young leader had little choice. His promotion to power was as sudden as his father's death. This meant that the young leader spent only two years as heir apparent and therefore had little time to create his own team. Things were probably further complicated due to the younger Kim's foreign education, since—unlike his father—he did not spend his formative years among the scions of North Korea's top officials or in the elite schools of Pyongyang.

As a result, the young leader inherited the aging team of his father. His government was to consist of people at least twice his age, whose education, views, and tastes were vastly different from his own. These old officials spent their youths memorizing the works of Stalin, Lenin, and Mao, not watching basketball games in which Michael Jordan and Dennis Rodman demonstrated great athletic prowess. They did not speak foreign languages, and in spite of their (and their wives') occasional shopping trips to major Western capitals, had little in the way of working knowledge about the outside world. Last, but not least, their ideological assumptions were also quite different from that of the young Kim.

In other words, Kim Jong Un would be largely unable to create his own policies unless the entire leadership team of his father were replaced. It was therefore widely expected among Pyongyang watchers that Kim Jong Un would before too long start promoting people of his own generation who shared his worldview—probably, the grandchildren of Manchurian guerrilla fighters who are now in their thirties. It was also assumed that his father's advisers would eventually be retired and/or given ceremonial posts. Nonetheless, it was also widely expected that the young Kim would have to accept the old guard's guidance for a few years and work with them while learning how to properly run his peculiar fiefdom.

Things were to take a rather sudden turn, however. Kim Jong Un began to shed his father's team much more quickly than expected. The dawn of the Kim Jong Un era was marked by purges of a scale and level of severity not seen in North Korea for decades.

The first target of the young leader was the military high command. This was logical enough given the fact that the military is potentially the most dangerous force that Kim Jong Un faces (conspiracies by civilian bureaucracies are not unknown, but it is usually generals who lead coups).

Thus, it was on July 16, 2012, that the North Korean media informed the world that the Politburo had had a special meeting the day before—on a Sunday. The Politburo decided that Vice Marshal Yi Yŏng-ho's health would not allow him to continue with his demanding duties. He was thus relieved of all his official positions, with immediate effect.

For a while, there might have been some room for doubt as to whether this was a purge or just what it appeared—the retirement of an aging soldier (even though Yi Yŏng-ho had shown no signs of health deterioration prior to the meeting in question). Doubts soon disappeared, however: Yi Yŏng-ho's name has not been mentioned in any North Korean publication since his removal from office, and his name and pictures have disappeared from materials published after the removal. In a macabre twist, quite typical for the North Korean media, even documents related to Kim Jong Il's funeral were edited in 2013 to expunge the name of Yi Yŏng-ho from the funeral committee members' list for subsequent official publications.

The other three generals who followed Yi Yŏng-ho in the funeral procession did not fare too well, either. In the procession, Yi Yŏng-ho was followed by Kim Yŏng-ch'un, who at the time was the first deputy Armed Forces minister. He was retired from the military in April 2012 and now works in the civilian bureaucracy. His current job might be a demotion, but he is, at least, alive and in a position of power—unlike the other four generals.

Another of the four generals was Kim Chŏng-kak, who, in December 2011, was the first deputy head of the Korean People's Army (KPA) General Political Department—the top representative of the Party in the military. In November 2012 he was replaced and has not been seen since.

The third in the military escort flanking the hearse was U Tong-ch'ŭk, the first deputy minister of state security. Since at the time there was no minister, he was the acting head of North Korea's security police, intelligence, and counterespionage service. He disappeared in April 2012.

Apart from these unfortunates, a significant number of second-tier generals also lost their positions between 2012 and 2013. It appeared at the time as if top North Korean generals were engaged in a game of musical chairs. In the first two years of the young Kim's rule, from December 2011 to December 2013, North Korea had four ministers of defense and three chiefs of general staff.

Amidst this game of musical chairs, only one person has stood still, remaining for now the de facto chief of North Korea's armed forces. This man's name is Ch'oe Yong-hae, and he is the head of the General Political Bureau of the Korean People's Army (a body in charge of the political indoctrination and Party supervision of the North Korean military). Ch'oe may have the august rank of vice marshal and his father once served as the minister of defense, but he is not a professional soldier. He spent most of his career as a Party bureaucrat, acquiring (if rumor is to be believed) some notoriety for his hyperactive womanizing and luxurious lifestyle. He was given a commission in the military only in 2010, so for career soldiers he is clearly an outsider. In essence, Ch'oe Yong-hae's prominence means that the North Korean military is under the firm (but perhaps not particularly professional) supervision of the Party.

Simultaneously with the decimation of the military command, Kim Jong Un undertook some steps aimed at reducing the economic power of the military. For decades, the North Korean military had been allowed to pursue business ventures, especially through military-controlled foreign trade companies whose profits were theoretically used to pay for the needs of the armed forces but in practice often filled pockets of the top generals. In a curious twist, the General Political Bureau, the Party's eyes and ears in the military, runs its own foreign trade company. Between 2012 and 2013, a significant part of this quasi-military business empire was dismantled and transferred to civilian control.

All of this strongly indicates that during this time, the senior North Korean military leadership suffered a purge without precedent since the late 1960s (removal of the Kapsan group), or even the late 1950s (removal of military officials deemed to have excessively close connection to the Soviet Union and/or China).

The fate of the purged generals remains uncertain at the time of writing, but, if rumors widely circulating in Pyongyang are to be believed, many of them were executed. Some South Korean media outlets, citing unnamed "sources inside North Korea," even claim that the unlucky generals were killed by grenade launchers or were machine-gunned, presumably to ensure that even their physical remains were destroyed as thoroughly as possible. Indeed, these sorts of rumors also circulate in Pyongyang. They cannot be verified, however, and until late 2013, the vast majority of reputable observers were very skeptical. Nonetheless, such skepticism was rattled when in December 2013 the purge and subsequent execution of Chang Sŏng-t'aek demonstrated that the new leader is more willing and able to use violence to a greater extent than anyone had hitherto expected.

At the time of Kim Jong Il's death, Chang Sŏng-t'aek was considered to be the most powerful of all North Korea's top officials, and he ostensibly kept this position for the first year of Kim Jong Un's reign. It is widely believed that Chang was instrumental in arranging the 2012 purge of the military command—at the end of the day, the forced retreat of the generals from power increased the influence of the civilian bureaucrats, of whom Chang himself was most influential.

Chang was born in 1946 in the countryside, obviously in a family with modest revolutionary credentials. The fate of this smart and ambitious man of humble origins changed dramatically when, while studying at Kim Il Sung University in the late 1960s, he met Kim Kyŏng-hŭi—Kim Jong Il's only sister. Kim Kyŏng-hŭi fell in love with Chang, and in spite of Kim Il Sung's initial opposition, she married the young man. His career was full of dramatic twists, but in the last years of Kim Jong Il's rule he was evidently the most trusted lieutenant of the aging dictator. After the suicide of their only child in 2006, Kim Kyŏng-hŭi began to drink heavily and suffered from many health problems, so her political prominence has been largely symbolic. Meanwhile, her husband was not only intimately involved in the running of the North Korean state, but also played an important role in the booming trade with China. Reputedly, Chang was also not particularly faithful to his wife—a circumstance that might have played a certain role in his sudden downfall.

Nonetheless, Chang's influence did not last: in early 2013, it was noticed that the frequency of his joint trips with Kim Jong Un decreased markedly. By late 2013 most observers expected that the once-powerful regent was heading toward a comfortable retirement—though the vast majority of observers thought this would happen after the death of Chang's powerful wife.

However, Kim Jong Un once again decided to move faster than most expected: on December 9 *Rodong Sinmun* published a large report that occupied the entire front page of the newspaper. It told readers of the numerous criminal activities of Chang Sŏng-t'aek who, as readers were told, was arrested the day before. Indeed, on the same afternoon, state TV broadcast photos showing Chang being arrested at the extended Politburo meeting and being dragged away by uniformed police officers. While the arrest itself is reminiscent of Beria's downfall in 1953—Stalin's right-hand

The birth of the regime: Kim Jong Il and General Ivan Chistiakov, 1947.

Voting on the first North Korean elections, 1947.

North Korea in the late 1940s: portrait of young Kim Il Sung, above a slogan "Long live the liberator of small nations Generalissimo Stalin!".

A US air raid, Pyongyang, 1950.

Ruins of Sinuiju, 1951.

Pyongyang street in 1985.

Pyongyang street in 2005.

Anti-American poster on
Pyongyang street (Moravius).

Street vendors on Ongnyu Bridge, Pyongyang (Moravius).

At a bus stop (Moravius).

Building an apartment bloc in Pyongyang (Moravius).

Anglers at Wonsan pier (Moravius).

Construction works at the countryside (Moravius).

Oxcart, the major means of transportation in the countryside (Moravius).

Pyongyang outskirts in winter (Moravius).

Well tended private plots near Nampo (Moravius).

Roadside market—Chongdan county (Moravius).

Road construction works (Moravius).

Ri Sol Ju, the Supreme Leader's wife, helps with the washing up at the house of a model worker.

The Masik Ski Resort, a pet project of the Young Marshal.

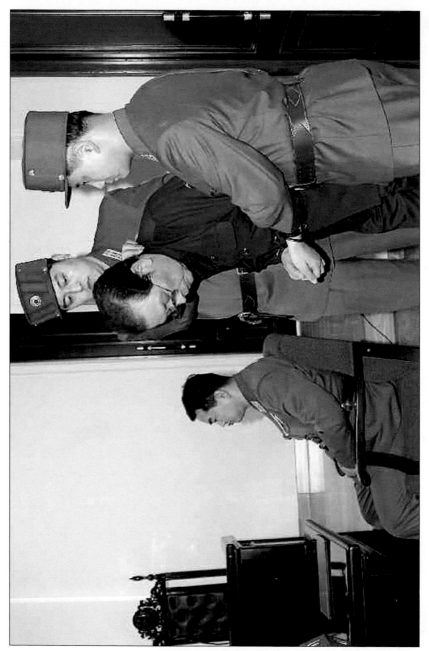

Chang Song Taek on trial.

Kim Jong Un at the Pyongyang Water Park under construction.

Dennis Rodman with Kim Jong Un and his wife.

Kim Jong Un with model octopus.

Kim Jong Un reviewing the master plan for an attack on the continental USA. (The plan itself is visible on the left side of the picture.)

Walking next to Kim Jong Il's hearse: Kim Jong Un and top military and civilian officials at Kim Jong Il's funeral (five out of the seven were purged in the next two years).

man was also arrested at a Politburo meeting—it might be the first incident of this kind to ever be shown on TV.

Subsequent events were all too predictable. In the Soviet Union of 1953, Beria was kept in confinement for a few months, but in North Korea, Kim Jong Un chose to move quicker. A few days after his arrest, the North Korean media informed the world that on December 12th the unmasked "thrice-cursed" traitor Chang Sŏng-t'aek had faced a special tribunal of the Ministry of State Security. Predictably enough, Kim Jong Un's uncle was found guilty and executed. Curiously, one of the crimes he was charged with was terrorism.

The accusations against Chang were both nebulous and voluminous. He was accused of counter-revolutionary factional and anti-state, anti-Party activities. It was said that he had had numerous affairs, used drugs, and was a gambler to boot. It makes sense at this point to provide some of the more colorful material that was to be found in his indictment. What follows are official translations written in North Korea's unique form of English:

> Upon hearing the report on the enlarged meeting of the Political Bureau of the Central Committee of the Workers' Party of Korea, the service personnel and people throughout the country broke into angry shouts that a stern judgment of the revolution should be meted out to the anti-party, counter-revolutionary factional elements. Against the backdrop of these shouts rocking the country, a special military tribunal of the DPRK Ministry of State Security was held on December 12 against traitor for all ages Jang Song Thaek. [...]
>
> The accused Jang brought together undesirable forces and formed a faction as the boss of a modern day factional group for a long time and thus committed such hideous crime as attempting to overthrow the state by all sorts of intrigues and despicable methods with a wild ambition to grab the supreme power of our party and state. [...]
>
> He held higher posts than before and received deeper trust from supreme leader Kim Jong Un, in particular. The political trust and benevolence shown by the peerlessly great men of Mt. Paektu were something he hardly deserved. It is an elementary obligation of a human

being to repay trust with sense of obligation and benevolence with loyalty. However, despicable human scum Jang, who was worse than a dog, perpetrated thrice-cursed acts of treachery in betrayal of such profound trust and warmest paternal love shown by the party and the leader for him. [...]

When [...] the decision that Kim Jong Un was elected vice-chairman of the Central Military Commission of the Workers' Party of Korea [...] was proclaimed, making all participants break into enthusiastic cheers that shook the conference hall, he behaved so arrogantly and insolently as unwillingly standing up from his seat and half-heartedly clapping, touching off towering resentment of our service personnel and people. [...]

He was so imprudent as to prevent the Taedonggang Tile Factory from erecting a mosaic depicting Kim Il Sung and Kim Jong Il and a monument to field guidance given by them. Moreover, Jang turned down the unanimous request of the service personnel of a unit of the Korean People's Internal Security Forces to have the autograph letter sent by Kim Jong Un to the unit carved on a natural granite and erected with good care in front of the building of its command. He was so reckless as to instruct the unit to erect it in a shaded corner. [...]

He let the decadent capitalist lifestyle find its way to our society by distributing all sorts of pornographic pictures among his confidants since 2009. He led a dissolute, depraved life, squandering money wherever he went. He took at least 4.6 million Euro from his secret coffers and squandered it in 2009 alone and enjoyed himself in casino in a foreign country. [...]

All facts go to clearly prove that Jang is a thrice-cursed traitor without an equal in the world as he had desperately worked for years to destabilize and bring down the DPRK and grab the supreme power of the party and state by employing all the most cunning and sinister means and methods, pursuant to the "strategic patience" policy and "waiting strategy" of the U.S. and the south Korean puppet group of traitors.

Some of the accusations leveled against Chang Sŏng-t'aek are more substantial, however. He allegedly did what he could to worsen the economic situation of North Korea with the hope that he could then exploit popular discontent in order to stage a coup and take power. He was even alleged to have sold North Korea's precious natural resources overseas at bargain prices. In addition, he was said to have sold a lease of land in the Rason economic and trade zone to a "foreign country" for a period of five decades. The latter two accusations are particularly important since in both cases they target China, the only foreign country that imports North Korean minerals and also rents port facilities in Rason. This was a very unusual sign: North Korea was implicitly demonstrating dissatisfaction with China.

Remarkably, the disgrace of Chang was followed by major cleanup operations. The online archives of the KCNA, the country's official news agency, and *Rodong Sinmun* (both available only to those outside of North Korea) were shut down. Obviously, this was done in order to destroy all references to his name.

What caused the young North Korean ruler to oust Chang Sŏng-t'aek? On the one hand, it of course made perfect sense to start the large-scale removal of the old guard with a sudden strike at the very top—and Chang was clearly the core person in the North Korean civilian bureaucracy. However, one cannot help but wonder whether the decision was also driven by the wounded pride of the young Kim—both Yi Yŏng-ho and Chang Sŏng-t'aek were clearly meant to be quasi-regents, whose job was to supervise and control the inexperienced young ruler. It is quite possible that Kim Jong Un did not feel himself to be that much in need of supervision and hence was offended by even well-intentioned intrusions from his mentors.

Foreign diplomats witnessed an interesting incident that occurred during one of Dennis Rodman's visits to Pyongyang. Dennis Rodman and Kim Jong Un were sitting with Coca Cola cans on the table in front of them, waiting for journalists to start filming. Just seconds before the cameras began to roll, Chang Sŏng-t'aek stood up and grabbed the can that was on Kim Jong Un's table. Politically, this was wise: this particular type of soda drink has long been vilified as the embodiment of US imperialism, and thus the Supreme Leader should probably refrain from consuming such politically suspicious beverages in front of cameras. However, to the insecure young dictator, this might have appeared to be yet another minor public offense. One can surmise that similar incidents have occurred in the past, and perhaps this was one of the reasons for the dismal fate of Chang Sŏng-t'aek.

The removal of Chang was clearly a political necessity, but did he have to be sent to the execution grounds? In fact, the execution of Chang Sŏng-t'aek was truly unprecedented because he was a top official and a member of the ruling Kim family (albeit through marriage).

It is not widely realized, but under Kim Il Sung's and Kim Jong Il's rule, senior officials enjoyed a relatively high level of personal security. It is true that they did face some risk of being sent to torture chambers and even execution, but compared to the risks faced by their peers in other dictatorships, these people were relatively safe. After the Great Purge of the Chinese and Soviet factions was completed successfully in the early 1960s, Kim Il Sung began to treat his immediate entourage with remarkable leniency. Perhaps this had something to do with their past—most of them were former anti-Japanese guerrillas from Manchuria. Kim Il Sung was seemingly not inclined to shoot the few remaining comrades from the turbulent and heroic days of his youth.

From time to time, some top officials fell from grace and disappeared from public view. However, only rarely were these people actually executed under Kim Il Sung's watch. High officials were seldom physically exterminated. Disgrace usually meant exile to the countryside, where a former party secretary or general would spend time doing physical labor or clerical work. If they did not complain or misbehave during this ordeal, they stood fairly good chances of being pardoned and recalled to Pyongyang, whereupon they were often given some important position once again. This had even been the previous experience of Chang Sŏng-t'aek himself.

There were exceptions to this rule, of course. Sŏ Kwan-hui, the party secretary for agriculture, was executed in 1997 as an American spy who allegedly sabotaged food production in the country. Only mid- to high-level officials were notified about his execution at the time, being told that his alleged treason was one of the main causes of the great famine (a good example of scapegoating tactics so common in dictatorships). Another was the fate of Pak Nam-gi, a senior Party official who was responsible for finance policy and who was scapegoated after the 2009 currency reform. Nonetheless, the execution of high officials has been a rare event.

Chang Sŏng-t'aek's case is even more unusual given the victim's connections with the Kim family. This large family has had its share of issues, and in the course of North Korean history some Kims have faced exile in the countryside or been sent (i.e., de facto exiled) overseas. Nonetheless, until the death of Chang it was thought that a Kim does not kill another Kim.

It appears that this rule does not apply to the third Kim on the throne—especially if persistent rumors about Kim's attempts to kill his half-brother Kim Jong Nam are correct.

It also appears that Kim Jong Un has delivered a serious blow to the old guard, who now understand that nobody is secure under the new system. Nonetheless, the young Kim remains surrounded by the same people whose replacement is politically necessary, but he will probably take a few more years to complete the purging or replacing of all. Only then will we see what policy Kim Jong Un plans to implement. However, one thing is clear already: the young North Korean leader is decisive and ruthless (significantly more so than his late father). It seems that Kim Jong Un is more capricious and given to emotional outbursts.

THE NEW POLICY

So far, it is not entirely clear which path the young North Korean leader will eventually follow. It is not impossible that he will continue his father's nonreformist line. It is also possible, however, that he will steer North Korea in a new direction.

Given this ambiguity, it is not surprising that between 2011 and 2014, the Pyongyang watchers have been searching hard for clues. Aside from personnel matters, other changes have been evident, though these changes have largely been stylistic in nature. For instance, Kim Jong Un is not shy when it comes to talking in public, even though he cannot be described as a great orator. His father, Kim Jong Il, made only one public speech, which lasted about thirty seconds. Meanwhile, Kim Jong Un frequently delivers lengthy, if rather dry and mind-numbing, speeches.

Kim Jong Un has continued the tradition of "on-spot-guidance" in which the leader travels incessantly across the country, visiting schools, factories, and military units. However, unlike his father and grandfather, the young leader often goes to entertainment facilities and public parks, where he tries to interact with the public (it is all but certain, of course, that this "public" is preselected and briefed on how to behave). In a similar vein, he has even visited the house of an exemplary worker, where his beautiful wife helped the mistress of the house with the washing up. In other words, the young ruler has done his best to be seen as approachable and responsive to the demands of the people.

Interestingly enough, Kim Jong Un has paid a peculiar amount of attention to amusement facilities, including a water park in Pyongyang and the Masik ski resort. The latter plays a very prominent role in North Korean propaganda nowadays. The official media presents Masik as a great project where builders performed unprecedented feats of labor heroism while evoking the courageous deeds of their grandfathers who defeated the US imperialists back in the 1950s. It is common for North Korea (or, for that matter, any Communist regime) to have projects that it lavishes such propaganda airtime on. In the past, however, such propaganda accolades have been bestowed upon heavy industry and infrastructure projects. It is unusual and, frankly, comical to see the presentation of a luxurious resort facility, at least partially designed for rich foreign tourists, as a place where battlefield-style selfless heroism is flourishing.

The unusual prominence of the Masik resort might partially be explained by Kim Jong Un's own experiences: as we remember, the young Kim did spend his teenage years in Switzerland. However, this is only a partial explanation. The North Korean government, like many other Leninist governments worldwide, has always been prone to what can be described as "technological fetishism." While quietly realizing that their economies did not perform as hoped, their top decision-makers could not bring themselves to admit that the main problem was their rigid social structure and irrational and/or distorted incentives system. Therefore, they tended to look for wonder technologies to miraculously deliver them from all their economic troubles.

Examples of this trend are numerous. Stalin counted on forest belts and Lysenko's biology to solve chronic Soviet food shortages. Mao believed that the best way to catch up with the West was to build backyard furnaces in every village and behind every kindergarten. North Korea has proven to be no exception; among such "wonder technologies," the terraced field scheme (partially responsible for the agricultural disaster of the 1990s) has been most prominent in North Korean propaganda.

The young Kim has seemingly pinned his hopes on international tourism. In later 2013 he instructed the state tourist agency to increase the annual number of foreign tourists to one million within three years. Right now, roughly, only 200,000 foreign tourists a year visit North Korea, and most of these people are Chinese citizens who come on one-day trips to borderland cities.

It appears, therefore, that Kim Jong Un hopes to make his realm into an East Asian Switzerland, where crowds of rich Westerners will rush with pockets full of cash. This dream is highly unrealistic, especially given the sorry state of tourist infrastructure in the country, as well as a glaring shortage of what is called in professional jargon "tourist resources."

Be that as it may, technological fetishism remains a part of Kim Jong Un's vision of North Korea's future. It is somewhat significant, however, that this time, hopes of a miracle are connected to the outside world. Indeed, there are some signs that Kim Jong Un is not going to entertain his own Western-style tastes in private but will allow his subjects to have glimpses of this other world.

In July 2012 Kim Jong Un visited the first concert of a newly established pop music group named Moranbong (which is also the name of a very famous scenic hill park in downtown Pyongyang). The official media extolled the group and assured the public that their future performances would greatly contribute to "further development and construction in People's Korea." Well, perhaps it will, but the group's first concert was rather unlike anything North Korea had ever seen. To start with, the female performers who comprised the group were dressed rather risquély by North Korean standards. The music performed included the theme from the Hollywood movie *Rocky* and a song by Frank Sinatra. While this politically suspicious music was being performed, actors dressed as Mickey and Minnie Mouse, Winnie the Pooh, and Tigger, too (to quote A. A. Milne), danced on the stage. Disney lawyers even felt obliged to release a statement soon afterward confirming that they had not been involved with the concert.

Kim Jong Un himself was present at the show, and his august presence left little doubt that this combination of risqué dress and Americana had his unconditional approval.

The July performance, however, has thus far proven to be unique. While the Moranbong group is still presented as the pinnacle of North Korea's official pop music, the girls have subsequently begun to appear in more conventional attire, sometimes even donning mock military uniforms. Their repertoire has since come to consist of ideologically healthy songs about the leader and Party, albeit presented in a rather advanced and Western form. Most North Korean electronic ensembles (to use the North Korean term) wear traditional Korean clothing (which is very long and difficult to move rhythmically in) and play very old-fashioned music that resembles (stylistically) music popular in South Korea in the 1960s. Moranbong's players actually dance, their clothes are modern, and their music is quick, too. And we should not forget that the July 2012 concert remains vivid in the memory of North Koreans.

Kim Jong Un was not alone at that concert. A mysterious beautiful woman, dressed impeccably in black, accompanied him. Soon after, the same woman would be seen on a number of other public occasions by the side of the Supreme Leader. Belatedly, in late July of 2012, the North Korean media explained who she was. Her name was Ri Sol Ju, and Kim Jong Un had indeed married her. She has subsequently accompanied her husband quite a few times, talking to kids in a kindergarten, greeting generals at a military meeting, riding a roller coaster, enjoying the company of a young seal in Pyongyang Zoo (often sporting the latest Dior bag), and, as mentioned earlier, helping an exemplary female worker do the dishes. In late 2012 she was visibly pregnant, and in early 2013 the couple had their first child, a girl.

By North Korean standards, the public appearances of Ri Sol Ju are unprecedented. Kim Il Sung's first wife, Kim Jong Suk, was eventually awarded her own personality cult, but she was completely unknown to the general public in her lifetime. Kim Il Sung's second wife, Kim Song Ae, would enjoy a brief spell of political prominence and perhaps had major political ambitions in the 1970s, but she would soon fade into obscurity and only appear in public when her husband met those visiting foreign dignitaries who chose to come to North Korea with their spouses. Kim Jong Il was even stricter in this regard, and none of his numerous wives and live-in girlfriends ever appeared in public in that role. His last mistress, Kim Ok, occasionally accompanied him during overseas trips, but her true standing was never disclosed and she was officially presented just as a member of the delegation.

Both the open endorsement of Western pop culture and the willingness to show off his beautiful wife might be attributable to Kim Jong Un's less than advanced age, as well as his desire to present his country as a less boring place. After all, he had just recently been a Swiss schoolboy, an admirer of electronic gadgets, spectacular sports, and pop music. However, these actions, while seemingly superficial, also indicate that he is at least willing to experiment with new ideas and challenge the existing norms of public behavior in North Korea.

The frequent visits of Dennis Rodman to North Korea can be seen as another proof of Kim Jong Un's interest in things Western—as well as his unwillingness to pursue such interests in private (as his father would definitely have done). Brian Myers has also noted that Rodman's visits to Pyongyang indicate the growing power of Kim Jong Un: only he among North Korea's top elite would have the slightest interest in meeting Rodman, of whom 99.9 percent of North Koreans had never heard of. It is also significant that Rodman's visits have received great publicity in the North

Korean media, making front-page news in *Rodong Sinmun* and, as mentioned before, being accorded significant TV coverage as well.

Rodman has visited North Korea three times, invited by Kim Jong Un, who obviously has used his newly acquired power to meet one of his childhood heroes. As a result of the publicity, the North Korean public has been exposed to the sight of their leader interacting with a very peculiar foreigner.

Tellingly, it was Dennis Rodman who revealed to the world that Kim Jong Un and Ri Sol Ju had just had a daughter. Rodman was also invited to one private residence of the North Korean leader. Later, in an interview with the British tabloid *The Sun*, he compared the residence to a "seven-star resort." One might surmise that it would be difficult to surprise Rodman with luxury, but he was truly impressed by what he saw and the carefree atmosphere he experienced within the carefully guarded compound (the North Korean watchers soon discovered that he was talking about the Wonsan residence of the Supreme Leader):

> It's like going to Hawaii or Ibiza, but he's the only one that lives there. He likes people to be happy around him. [...] If you drink a bottle of tequila, it's the best tequila, everything you want, he has the best.

Kim Jong Un's two-hundred-foot private yacht also did not fail to impress Dennis Rodman, who described the vessel as a "cross between a ferry and a Disney boat."[4]

The irony of the latter description was obviously lost on Rodman himself, who clearly did not see anything shameful about the rich and powerful living in unabashed luxury. He does not seem to have realized that the "seven star resort" exists in a very poor country where the alleged equality of the people and the spartan lives of the leadership are extolled daily by the official media.

It is indeed unusual to see a North Korean leader escorted by his charming wife. It is even more unusual to see songs by Sinatra being publicly sung by young North Korean women clad in risqué attire. The visits of Rodman are stranger still. However, such changes are not all that meaningful and are relatively easy to roll back if the government makes a decision to do so. Nevertheless, the first two years of Kim Jong Un's rule were marked by other, more radical, experiments, which dealt with deadly serious matters of economic policy.

Changes in agriculture began with instructions issued by the Supreme Leader Marshal Kim Jong Un on June 28, 2012. In fact, these instructions have never been published, but the content of the "6.28 instructions" (as they are usually called) has become widely known. This is not surprising since the instructions were delivered to every village cadre in the summer of 2012 and were much discussed. The implementation of the new scheme was postponed until 2013. Officially, the new scheme for agricultural management is considered experimental and in 2013 applied only in some parts of the country. In essence, the "6.28 instructions" constitute a massive shake-up in North Korea's system of agricultural management.

First, the plan envisions that the size of the production teams that toil on North Korea's cooperative state-run farms should be reduced from the current fifteen members to five or six. To many this might appear to be a mere technicality, but actually it is not. The newly introduced teams are equal in size to a normal farming household, and it is widely understood that under the new system, most of the production teams will be family-centered. In other words, North Korean farmers are to be given the right to thinly disguise their family as a production team. This makes much sense in light of the second radical change.

To understand the second change, we should briefly look at the previous status of North Korea's agricultural sector until these transformations. From the late 1950s until the change, North Korean farmers were compelled to surrender their entire harvest to the state. Under the new system, however, things are set to be very different. Production teams will be allowed to keep some 30 percent of the harvest for themselves. It is assumed that they will be able to sell on the private market whatever they do not consume, or otherwise use it in any way they consider beneficial—like, say, in rearing animals for sale and/or personal consumption.

The new system has many potential issues and is fraught with uncertainty. For example, it is not clear how the North Korean state will pay those agricultural workers not directly engaged in crop cultivation—for instance, drivers, vets, and agronomists. Given the rather primitive nature of North Korean agriculture, however, such issues are of lesser importance here than in many other countries: North Korean agriculture is largely based on plowmen who guide oxen. The average farm produces cereals like rice and corn and does not have much in the way of supporting infrastructure.

It seems that the first results of the reforms have been quite encouraging. Chinese experts who recently visited North Korea privately told this author that the reforms have produced an immediate 30 percent increase in output. The 2013 harvest in North Korea was unusually good, and it is possible that the partial introduction of the new system has contributed to the palpable increase in food production.

There is therefore good reason to expect that these reforms will be rolled out nationwide and will become standard in the next year or two.

Objectively speaking, agricultural reforms carry the least political risk of all economic experimentation. Farmers have been known to rebel on occasion, but in general they are the most conservative and least well organized, not to say politically apathetic, social group in most societies. When political discontent erupts, it almost invariably begins in the city, with the urban working class and intellectual groups being the most active elements. Additionally, an outbreak of political discontent in a major city is much more difficult to isolate, control, and suppress than a riot in an isolated village in the countryside.

The partial introduction of family-based agriculture has shown its potential in many countries, above all in China of the late 1970s. Nonetheless, one should keep in mind the limitations of such reforms. North Korea is demographically quite dissimilar to China of the early days of Deng Xiaoping. At that time, 70 percent of mainland Chinese lived in the countryside, whereas only about 40 percent of North Koreans do so today. This means that agricultural reforms alone, however useful, will not be sufficient to kick-start the North Korean economy. The fate of reform in North Korea will be decided by the urban industrial sector. Unfortunately for the North Korean elite, fixing this part of the economy is far more politically dangerous and economically difficult.

So far, it appears that North Korea's leaders have pinned their hopes on three sets of policies. We have already discussed tourism earlier. Additionally, they have sought to provide North Korean industrial enterprises with more managerial freedoms, the assumption being that this will make such enterprises more efficient. Further, Pyongyang clearly wants to emulate the success of Special Economic Zones (SEZs) in China and is currently hard at work trying to establish zones that will be attractive to foreign investors. Unfortunately, both policies have deep flaws.

The policy of giving managers more freedom is very similar to the reforms undertaken in Eastern bloc countries in the 1960s, as well as the early stages of Gorbachev's perestroika in the mid-1980s. In the Soviet Union and Eastern Europe, such reforms were at best partially successful and did not deliver sustainable economic growth. Nonetheless, such attempts show that North Korean decision-makers are now realizing the need for change.

In spring 2013 Kim Jong Un appointed a new prime minister. While in North Korea the power of the prime minister specifically and the cabinet in general is rather limited, nonetheless it still plays a major role in economic management, and hence it is significant that the new job was given to Pak Pong-chu, widely reputed to be the initiator of the 7.1 measures in 2002. While half-baked and generally unsuccessful, the 7.1 measures still constituted the most radical attempts to change North Korean economy ever undertaken from above. During the backlash against these measures and the deepening of marketization in the North, Pak Pong-chu was demoted and sent to the countryside (a Kim Jong Il–era purge par excellence), where he spent a few years as manager of a large factory. He made a comeback in 2013, however, and his presence at the head of North Korea's economic policy apparatus was soon felt.

Starting from October 2013, many factory personnel in export enterprises saw their wages increase a hundredfold. Further, the management of such enterprises now is allowed to use hard currency earnings to reward more efficient workers. This policy will likely create discontent if people doing similar work nearby continue to receive vastly different salaries. Alternatively, if such wage increases also occur in other parts of the state sector, the likely outcome is yet another outburst of hyperinflation. None-theless, attempts to allow managers to do what they consider to be eco-nomically rational constitute a significant first step in the right direction for North Korea's economy.

In November 2013 the North Korean government established thirteen new SEZs (plus reconfirming the SEZ status of the city of Sinuiju). From what little we know, it appears that these zones will be fenced off, with entry rights limited to a select few. Obviously, the latter measure has been put in place in order to minimize the potential negative political impact that these zones could produce for the ideological health of the popula-tion. While North Korea's leadership has in the past toyed with the idea of SEZ-driven growth (a policy again reminiscent of 1970s China), this latest policy attempt appears to be unusually bold and radical by North Korean standards.

In brief, the first moves toward a new and reforming North Korea have been made. Nonetheless, it is not clear whether such changes will continue or whether the North Korean leadership is willing to advance further.

THE NEW LOGIC

A significant part of previous chapters was dedicated to the rationale behind Kim Jong Il's obstinate refusal to initiate market-oriented reforms. Indeed, such reforms are potentially highly dangerous for the North Korean regime, as Kim Jong Il and at least some of his advisers understood perfectly well. However, it is often overlooked that Kim Jong Il and his son differ in one important regard, a difference that might matter enormously: Kim Jong Un is much younger than his father was when he assumed power.

When Kim Jong Il assumed full power in 1994, he was already in his early fifties. He had reasons to hope that the old system had enough strength to hold on for a few more decades, so long as it was left relatively undisturbed. For a man in his mid-fifties with a multitude of health prob-lems, twenty or thirty years is a long time. Kim Jong Il might have realized that the system was gradually withering, but he gambled that it would outlast him. This gamble paid off, as we now know.

Kim Jong Un's situation is very different. He was in his late twenties at the time of the power transfer and can realistically expect to live for another forty or fifty years. Presumably, he would like to spend most of the rest of this time in charge of his country, rather than in exile or, worse, prison—not to mention a possibly even grimmer fate.

He and his advisers surely understand that the system is gradually disintegrating, so they should not seriously count on its ability to last another twenty years—let alone forty or fifty.

In other words, the North Korean elite are trapped between the proverbial rock and a hard place. They can try to change things, transforming North Korea into a peculiar version of "developmental dictatorship" that would combine a market or semi-market economy with authoritarian political control, but Kim Jong Il and his advisers feared that such a transformation would be prohibitively risky and its most likely outcome would be the collapse of the regime. Nonetheless, there is a chance—however slim—that reformers could succeed, thus allowing the elite to stay in power for many years.

The alternative is to continue with the policies of Kim Jong Il: do everything possible to slow down the system's spontaneous disintegration while using nuclear brinkmanship and Machiavellian diplomacy to extract the resources to do so from the outside world. However, while such a risk-averse policy may postpone collapse, it cannot prevent it.

In a sense, Kim Jong Un's choice is akin to a patient who needs very risky but potentially lifesaving surgery on tumors in the brain. The doctor presents two options. The patient can risk surgery that offers a 25-percent chance of surviving, and if the patient does so, a long and normal life is possible. The alternative is chemotherapy, which would slow down the growth of the cancer but would not prevent the patient's death some time within the next decade. The patient has to choose whether to risk life in order to survive long-term or accept fate and prolong death as long as possible.

The choice between the two is largely determined by the age of the person. For a young patient who can hope to live at least a few more decades

if things turn out well, it makes sense to take the risks associated with surgery, even if such risks are very high. For older patients, however, the risk
is prohibitively high and it is better to choose the more conservative option.

Many young people in Kim Jong Un's position would feel very tempted,
given the balance of probabilities, to take a risk and gamble everything for
the slim chance of surviving and living a long and enjoyable life. The alternative for the young dictator is potentially being strung up in the streets of
Pyongyang or spending the rest of his life in exile or prison. Of course, we
cannot be sure whether Kim Jong Un will take the risk, but initial signs are
that he will.

A successfully reforming North Korea is clearly a lesser evil compared
to the status quo, but we should not be under any illusions about the
regime that North Korean reformers will build: it will be brutal, prone to
outbursts of hysterical propaganda, and definitely nuclear.

To start with, as discussed previously, the existence of the prosperous
and attractive South will constitute a great and permanent threat to internal stability in the North. To counter the rather natural inclinations of
its citizenry to look south, the North Korean elite will have to remain quite
brutal and ruthlessly suppress any sign of opposition. North Korea now, in
spite of palpable improvements under Kim Jong Il, still remains the world's
most repressive country, with the highest ratio of political prisoners to
total population. Even if successful reform brings about dramatic economic growth, this sorry human rights record is unlikely to substantially
improve. In fact, it might even worsen.

In order to maintain stability and, thus, control, the reforming North
Korean government will have to rely on propaganda of an unusual intensity and bellicosity. It is possible that nationalist messages in North Korean
propaganda—which have been explored in detail by Brian Myers—will
become even more intense. In order to keep the population compliant, the
elite will have to persuade its people that they all belong to a superior culture under constant external threat.

North Korean elite reformers will not surrender their nuclear deterrent.
They understand that nuclear weapons are their best guarantee against

both an open foreign invasion and a covert intervention in the case of an internal rebellion.

The reforms, if they start in earnest, will have to advance slowly—much slower than reforms in China (which did not face an attractive neighboring alternative). However, North Korea has one important advantage over China: while in China the new entrepreneurial class had to be created from scratch in the 1980s, North Korea already has a powerful entrepreneurial class.

People often assume that the North Korean "new rich" are natural opponents of the regime and supporters of the revolutionary tendencies in North Korea. This indeed might be the case, but reality is probably not that simple and straightforward. As Peter Ward once remarked in his perceptive article, it is often overlooked that black market dealers and Party apparatchiks share one basic common interest: they are the only two major groups who want North Korea to continue as a separate state for the foreseeable future.[5] If the North Korean state turns capitalist, an owner of a few food stalls has a chance of becoming a CEO of a supermarket chain—but only as long as his or her enterprise remains shielded from South Korean retail giants. The best way to achieve this is, of course, to keep the two countries separated as long as possible (or indefinitely).

If a "developmental dictatorship" were to emerge in North Korea, the present author would welcome it enthusiastically—with full understanding that many will accuse him of being cynical and heartless. No system is perfect, and dictatorship, developmental or not, is bound to be nasty. Nonetheless, the lives of the average North Korean will greatly improve under such a regime. In a sense, it might even be preferable to an instant switch to full-scale democracy, which is bound to be very traumatic, as we will see later. However, maintaining such a reformist authoritarian regime will be a permanent exercise in tightrope walking. It is still highly likely that reforms, if attempted in earnest, will merely speed up regime disintegration, so the future North Korean reformer—be it Kim Jong Un or whoever else may succeed him—will likely face not the fate of Deng Xiaoping but rather that of Mikhail Gorbachev.

TENSIONS WITH THE SOUTH

Kim Jong Un inherited power at a time when relations between the two Korean states hit a nadir after the sinking of the *Cheonhan* and the shelling of Yeonpyeong Island, both in 2010. Obviously, the North Korean government had no illusions about the possibility of improving relations with South Korea during Lee Myung Bak's administration. Therefore, the first year of Kim Jong Un's rule was marked by attempts to instead drag the United States to the negotiating table.

At first, they were successful: on February 29, 2012, North Korea signed what became known as the "Leap Day Agreement" with US representatives in Beijing. This agreement was concluded after years of a near-complete breakdown in the lines of communication between Pyongyang and Washington. The agreement gave North Korea 240,000 tons of food aid annually in exchange for assurances that they would refrain from testing nuclear devices and/or missiles.

To the great surprise of all observers, and to the great annoyance of doves in Washington, North Korea almost immediately reneged on the agreement and announced what it called a "peaceful satellite launch." The launch was indeed attempted on April 13. Predictably, the United States saw this as a blatant violation of the agreement and stormed off, while the North Korean side relied on a lame excuse, insisting that what they launched was not a long-range missile but rather a space exploration vehicle.

The Leap Day Agreement should have been ideal from an official North Korean point of view and might have become the forerunner of a more comprehensive compromise agreement that could have become possible a few years later. Nonetheless, the agreement was broken within weeks of it being signed and did not seemingly bring any benefit to Pyongyang—not a single ton of food was delivered.

It is somewhat of a mystery why the North Korean side signed an agreement it planned to break almost immediately. Infighting in the bureaucracy or a lack of communication between different agencies in the North Korean government is one plausible explanation. It is possible that diplomats were pushing for a compromise and aid, while rocket scientists and nuclear physicists (sponsored by the military top brass) demanded additional tests to prove that North Korea is now in possession of an effective missile deterrent. When the top leadership dealt with the transition of power, nobody might have bothered to coordinate, so the result was a diplomatic failure. This is all hypothetical, of course, but at any rate, the agreement's immediate collapse delivered a heavy blow to those in Washington who still wanted to negotiate with North Korea.

The April 2013 missile launch, along with the political fallout following its failure, was rather unusual in and of itself. North Korea announced its intention to launch a satellite into space well in advance and even invited foreign journalists to come and witness these momentous events. However, in spite of the hype, the rocket failed ninety seconds after launch. In an unprecedented move, the North Korean government explicitly and almost immediately admitted the failure.

This was quite remarkable indeed. Three previous launches (1998, 2006, 2009) of long-range missiles had all ended in failure as well, but the North Korean media had insisted that the 1998 and 2009 launches were both successes, while the attempted 2006 launch was never mentioned. By openly admitting that the satellite did not reach orbit, Kim Jong Un took an unprecedented step—in effect acknowledging that technical failures are possible even in his country, blessed with Juche science though it is.

However, fortune was to soon smile on the North Korean rocket scientists who had worked so hard: in December 2012 they finally succeeded in putting a satellite into orbit, even though the satellite obviously did not function as intended. The fifth missile launch was successful and demonstrated to the world that North Korea is closer to developing a long-range missile system than most people had hitherto expected. Of course, there are many technical issues North Korean engineers have not yet addressed—like, say, designing a re-entry vehicle to protect a nuclear warhead when it re-enters the earth's atmosphere from space. Nonetheless, after December 2012, few observers would doubt that the North Korean long-range missile/rocket program was advancing steadily.

From a military point of view, however, long-range missiles make little sense without nuclear warheads. Diplomats also know that for best diplomatic results, missile launches should be accompanied by nuclear tests. Kim Jong Un's personal ambitions might also have played a role: the young leader would probably have liked to include a successful nuclear test under his rule.

Indeed, the third nuclear test took place in February 2013, in spite of stern warnings from the international community, including China. Official media hinted that this time the North Koreans had tested a potential warhead—a nuclear device small and strong enough to be mounted on a long-range missile. However, we should keep in mind that there is no way to verify such assertions.

Soon after Kim Jong Un's sudden ascension to power, a change of guard also occurred in Seoul. In spite of the ardent efforts of South Korean "progressives," the so-called "conservatives" (the common but rather misleading descriptions of these two political groups) again won the presidency, and Park Geun Hye, the daughter of General Park Chung Hee, was elected the first female president of South Korea in 2012. Her victory created a rather peculiar situation: in both Korean states, the highest respective position was occupied by the offspring of former leaders.

Soon after the 2012 election in South Korea, an experienced Russian diplomat remarked to the author that in the near future the North Koreans would test the strength of Park's administration by manufacturing another crisis. His predictions proved to be correct. This is exactly what happened, but I do not think that he or anyone else could have anticipated the intensity of the (manufactured) crisis that struck on the Korean peninsula in March 2013.

Ostensibly, there were two reasons that gave rise to the North Korean government's feigned anger. First, in March 2013, the UN Security Council adopted Resolution 2094, sternly condemning North Korea's nuclear test and somewhat tightening existing sanctions. Simultaneously, South Korean and US forces conducted their annual joint military exercises.

The North Korean media and government spokespeople were united in their hyperbole: they presented US-ROK military exercises as preparation for a large-scale invasion of their country, although such exercises have taken place most years for decades, and an invasion has yet to be attempted by the two militaries. They also stated that the UN Security Council, at the behest of the United States (no reference to Russia or China was made, even though these two countries also voted for the resolution), was conspiring to deprive North Korea of its nuclear deterrent. They presented such acts as grave offenses, little different from acts of war.

While it is not unusual for the North Korean government to assure their people and the outside world that a US invasion is imminent, North Korea's propaganda machine has probably never reached such a crescendo as it did in March and April of 2013. While most of the statements and actions (symbolic and otherwise) have parallels in the country's past, the intensity was very unusual.

The verbal offensive commenced on March 13 via a spokesperson of the North Korean Ministry of Defense, who invalidated the 1953 Armistice agreement: the DPRK's enemies "would be well advised to keep in mind that the armistice agreement is no longer valid and [North Korea] is not restrained by the North-South declaration on non-aggression."[6] Technically, this was tantamount to a declaration of war with the United States, but few people in Washington bothered to notice. This indifference is understandable; the North Koreans have made such "Armistice withdrawal statements" a couple of times before (in 1994 and 2009), so this menacing-sounding statement was (correctly) seen as merely another exercise in empty belligerence. However, this time North Korean leaders decided to raise the belligerent tone of their rhetoric to a hitherto-unheard pitch. On March 27 the telephone "hotline" between the North and South Korean governments was unilaterally cut by the North Korean military. The North Korean representative made it clear: "Under the situation where a war may break out any moment, there is no need to keep North-South military communications."[7] On March 30 North Korea formally declared that it is in a "state of war" with the United States: "The prevailing grim situation more clearly proves that the Supreme Command of the KPA was just when it made the judgment and decision to decisively settle accounts with the U.S. imperialists and south Korean puppets by dint of the arms of Songun [army-first policy], because the time when words could work has passed." The statement also briefly described what to expect: "This war [...] will be a blitz war through which the KPA will occupy all areas of south Korea including Jeju Island at one strike, not giving the U.S. and the puppet warmongers time to come to their senses."[8]

This tension-building hysteria reached its apex in early April. The North Korean government officially approached a number of embassies in Pyongyang, urging that they immediately evacuate their personnel. The safety of diplomats was said to be endangered by the war that was sure to break out in the next few days. The evacuation deadline was set for April 10. The Russians ignored the "warning" quietly while the British issued a statement where Her Majesty's government made clear that British diplomatic personnel saw no reasons to leave.[9] A few days later, the North Korean government extended an official warning to foreigners living in South Korea. Pyongyang urged foreigners to leave South Korea immediately, lest they become collateral damage of a mighty counterstrike that North Korea was set to deliver in the near future: "Once a war is ignited on the peninsula, it will be an all-out war, i.e., a merciless sacred retaliatory war to be waged by the DPRK. It does not want to see foreigners in south Korea fall victim to the war. […] All foreign institutions and enterprises and foreigners […] are requested to take measures for shelter and evacuation in advance for their safety."[10]

North Korean propagandists probably outdid themselves in late March, when state TV broadcast images of a deadly serious looking Kim Jong Un sitting in front of a map at a military headquarters. The map's caption, large enough to be legible on a TV screen, explained that this was a map of North Korea's planned nuclear retaliation strike targeting the continental United States. The cities that were to suffer a nuclear holocaust included not only the obvious Washington, D.C., and New York, but also Austin, Texas. One day, the present author hopes to ask a North Korean propagandist why they decided to single out the Live Music Capital of the World. At any rate, soon afterward a history professor from the doomed city of Austin published an op-ed in *The New York Times* with the headline "Bomb North Korea, Before It's Too Late."[11]

North Korea's agitprop shock brigades also reminded South Koreans to watch their step. It was said that Seoul was soon to become a sea of fire—presumably because of the shells of the invincible Korean People's Army.

On April 9 the North took the unprecedented step of unilaterally closing the Kaesong Industrial Zone, whose operations had remained undisturbed in the past (even at the height of the 2010 crisis, neither side touched the flagship of North-South cooperation). Having been given a day's notice, the 53,000 North Korean workers did not show up at work. After a few weeks, the South Korean government reciprocated and withdrew all South Korean personnel from the zone, which remained idle for a few months. This was one of the cases when the new administration of Park Geun Hye actually reacted to the ongoing crisis. Such reactions were rare, but not always helpful, to put it mildly: after the North Koreans began their tension-building campaign, the US-South Korean joint military exercises were scaled up, with B-52 and B-2 stealth bombers flying over Korea. Their participation in the exercise was quite unusual. This act can be seen as a tough response to provocations, or as an unnecessary provocation in itself—of course, it depends on the way you look at it, but such actions certainly served to exacerbate tensions.

On the other hand, in mid-April, the South Korean police prevented an anti-Pyongyang activist group from launching balloons with leaflets from the border. Such launches had been staged regularly, but in early April the North said that the South would face a "catastrophic situation" if such balloons were launched on the eve of Kim Il Sung's birthday, as activists initially planned.

The length and intensity of this North Korean exercise in belligerence had a massive impact on the international media, even while diplomats in Seoul and Washington remained largely unimpressed.

In late March the world media started reporting that "tensions between the two Korean states have reached a critical point" and therefore "North and South Korea are on the brink of war." For a few weeks, news from Korea dominated front pages worldwide. Dozens of journalists descended on Seoul to report on the ongoing "crisis."

Most of these people were surprised to see a scene of remarkable tranquility in Seoul and spent much time looking for a Seoulite who exhibited even the slightest unease about all this noise from the North. Once upon a time, in the early 1990s, similar campaigns did have some impact on the minds of South Koreans. In 1994, when the North Koreans promised to transform Seoul into a "sea of fire," some worried Seoulites ran to shops to stock up on canned food, rice, and batteries. However, after so many reruns, such political shows have ceased to have much impact on the people of South Korea. As a result, foreign journalists were surprised to find Seoulites sipping their coffee and munching their kimchi, oblivious to the war that was allegedly just about to erupt "at any moment."

Professional Korea watchers showed the same lack of concern over the "crisis." No serious observer actually expected the two Korean states to come to blows, and even the risk of escalation was seen as relatively minor. Most observers assumed that the North Korean leadership had staged the ongoing show in order to gain some political and economic concessions from the outside world (especially South Korea), as well as to strengthen the power of the regime at home.

This seems to have indeed been the case. Obviously, North Korea's leadership wanted to show Seoul that it should not be ignored. While their intentions were not quite clear, they obviously hoped that the international media panic would damage South Korea's international standing by discouraging trade, economic cooperation, and investment. They probably also hoped to capitalize on divisions within South Korean society—perhaps they even hoped that the 386s and their sympathizers would launch a political campaign to put the South Korean government under pressure (forcing it to make concessions to the North). However, it is also possible that the real reasons behind such an unusual display of bellicosity were related to North Korea's domestic politics; it has been suggested that the young Supreme Leader might have wished to demonstrate his toughness to the world and also to his own entourage and his subjects.

However, the theatrics failed to produce much impact on the new administration in Seoul. Therefore, as widely predicted, the noisy campaign suddenly ceased on April 15. This happened suddenly, as if some switch had just been turned off. From late April, threats were suddenly replaced by offers to deepen cooperation (with the South). Within a few months, the two sides had reached an agreement to reopen the Kaesong Industrial Zone (it had suffered significantly from the forced halt in its operation), and by autumn of 2013 it was business as usual.

The Park Geun Hye government has proven to be relatively tough and unwilling to dance to North Korea's tune. With a change at the top, the tune may have changed, too. This outburst in spring 2013 might be seen as a sign that North Korea under Kim Jong Un is more prone to violent and potentially dangerous acts—this, however, does not mean that the young Kim is suicidal (he is unlikely to ever contemplate starting a war). That said, under Kim Jong Un, the old balance of power still holds. The North is well aware that it will lose a full-scale war with the South and the South knows that it will win such conflict but only at a prohibitively high cost. Thus, both sides keep their belligerence to the realms of diplomatic rhetoric and gestures (most of the time).

THE CITY OF MONUMENTS

Pyongyang is usually presented as an ancient city. And this, in a sense, is the case. The area has been the site of a major settlement for nearly two millennia. However, the present Pyongyang was built almost from scratch in the mid-1950s.

This was largely the result of a major US bombing campaign that reached its height in 1952. The US command had hoped to bomb the North Korean government into submission—by the end of the war, some 90 percent of the city ceased to exist, and most of its population had fled to the countryside.

Reconstruction began in the 1950s. From the very beginning, the new government wanted to build an exemplary Communist city free from reactionary traces of the feudal and imperialist past (Kim Il Sung was quite explicit when he said, "There were many defects in Pyongyang because it was built in an uncultured and lopsided way, under Japanese imperial rule"). The skyline that emerged owed much to the late Stalin's Soviet Union. Indeed, many parts of the 1950s' and 1960s' Pyongyang look exactly like a Soviet provincial city of the same period. At the time, many important positions in the construction industry were occupied by Soviet Koreans who would later be purged and accused of "wrecking."

(continued)

The center of 1960s' Pyongyang was called Stalin Street (eventually renamed Victory Street). However, a new round of major construction began in Pyongyang in the 1970s. This was a time when most of the major landmarks of modern North Korea were erected. On the hill overlooking the Taedong River, a great statue of Kim Il Sung was put up. Behind that, the museum of the Korean Revolution was built. Not far from there one could see the Mansudae Theater, where the exemplary revolutionary operas were performed in the 1970s. The large central square, predictably named after Kim Il Sung, was topped off with a mammoth People's Study House. Most of these structures broke with earlier Soviet heritage and were built in a mock traditional style (but still with a touch of characteristic megalomania).

On the opposite side of the Taedong River, a Tower to the Juche Idea was erected in 1982. The general shape of the Chuch'e Tower duplicates that of the Washington monument in the US capital, but exceeds it in size. The tower is 150 meters high and is crowned with a 20-meter-high torch that is illuminated at night. The tower includes 25,550 granite blocks—one for each day Kim Il Sung had lived by the time the monument was unveiled.

And, of course, there were a great many high-rise apartment buildings constructed in the 1970s and 1980s. Some of these high-rise quarters are actually off-limits for normal Pyongyangites, including a large district near the thirty-five-story Koryo Hotel. This is where Central Committee officials live behind high fences.

The construction boom ended abruptly in the late 1980s, when Soviet subsidies dried up. The sad, if somewhat comical, history of the Ryugyong Hotel is a reminder of it. This 110-story, as yet unfinished, hotel was meant to be the largest hotel in East Asia. Initially it was meant to be completed in 1989, but due to the economic crisis, work stopped, and for two decades the skyline of Pyongyang was dominated by a gigantic concrete pyramid (official photographers worked overtime to ensure it was never seen in official photographs).

Very recently, however, a new construction boom has been underway in Pyongyang. New high-rise buildings and monuments started to appear after 2007, and even the ugly Ryugyong Hotel was finally glassed—thanks to a deal with an Egyptian mobile phone company. However, it remains to be seen whether the Ryugyong will ever be opened to the public. It might just be for show, like much of Pyongyang.

The city of Pyongyang was built to be a visual representation of paradise as imagined by Kim Il Sung and his fellow guerrilla partisans. They have probably achieved what they wanted, but one cannot be sure whether outsiders are sufficiently impressed by the results of their efforts.

CHAPTER 5

Survival Diplomacy

The North Korean elite of today finds itself in a peculiar and unenviable position. It cannot reform itself because, in a divided nation, Chinese-style reforms are likely to trigger regime collapse, which in turn will bring ruin to many (but not all, as we shall see) members of the current elite. North Korea is therefore stuck with an outdated economic system that cannot generate growth and sometimes cannot even provide for the very physical survival of the country's people. Hence, the North Korean government has no choice but to seek outside aid just to stay afloat.

This has proven problematic, since such aid cannot be sought through channels usually utilized by poorer countries—that is, by lobbying international organizations and NGOs. "Normal" aid is not of much help to North Korea's rulers because such aid always comes with strings attached that are seldom compatible with their policy goals.

North Korean leaders know that they are unlikely to attract enough aid with politically acceptable conditions if they follow the established explicit and implicit rules of aid-seeking. They have thus decided to bend the rules, playing myriad games and using a variety of techniques to get aid on their own terms. While the outside world tends to concentrate on the nuclear issue, one should not forget that while the nuclear card is the best known and most powerful of these diplomatic tools, it is by no means the only one. The game of diplomatic cat-and-mouse is played by the North Korean elite with admirable skill, but also with remarkable disregard for actual humanitarian concerns—even as they do their utmost to obtain as much humanitarian assistance as possible.

PLAYING THE NUCLEAR CARD

A discussion of North Korea's foreign policy should start with the nuclear issue, which has dominated Western discourse about North Korea for more than two decades. Former Deputy Assistant Secretary of Defense Gregory Schulte recently described this attitude as a "fixation with nuclear diplomacy."[1] A Vietnamese diplomat, posted to the United States, once joked that he would have to work hard to explain to Americans that Vietnam is not a war. Whether or not he has succeeded as yet remains to be seen, but it is certain that for the vast majority of Americans and Europeans, North Korea is a nuclear device.

This overemphasis on the nuclear issue has obscured the reality that for North Korea's leadership, its nuclear weapons program is not an end in itself but rather one of many strategies they deploy to achieve the overriding goal of regime survival. Their costly decision to go nuclear is anything but irrational—rather, it is deeply intertwined with the peculiarities of DPRK's domestic and international situation and is therefore unlikely to ever be reconsidered.

The United States and other major Western countries have good reason to worry about the North Korean nuclear program. But contrary to what North Korean propagandists now tell their domestic audience, US leaders do not lose sleep in fear of a North Korean nuclear attack on the United States. The North Korean nuclear potential is small, and its delivery systems are, as yet, unreliable at best. Thus, at least in the foreseeable future, the chances of an attack are very low, and the chances of the attack itself being successful are lower still.

Admittedly, the North Korean military can be very creative and could compensate for its technological shortcomings through ingenious tricks—for example, a nuclear device could be hidden in an ordinary-looking fishing boat and then detonated somewhere in San Francisco Bay.

It might be argued that in the event of a war between the United States and North Korea, the trawler in question would probably arrive at its destination long after hostilities are over and the North Korean regime has ceased to exist. This is true, but a device might be detonated closer, like in

Tokyo Bay or Incheon, a couple of dozen miles away from Seoul. Such a (relatively) low-tech revenge operation will not merely kill tens of thousands of people but also close down these important transportation hubs, creating an economic shockwave of global proportions.

Nonetheless, the probability of such a doomsday scenario is not high, so the North Korean threat is largely indirect—but still serious. North Korea's audacious defiance of the international non-proliferation regimes sets a very dangerous precedent. If North Korea were to get away with its nuclear program, it would likely be followed by other rogue states.

Another worry for Washington is the threat of nuclear technology and/ or fissile materials being sold to the highest bidder. Nuclear proliferation and cooperation between Pakistan and North Korea is a well-known fact, and seemingly reliable intelligence indicates that North Korean nuclear weapons experts have maintained links with Iran, Burma, and Syria.[2]

Consequently, for the United States, DPRK denuclearization is an overwhelming priority, while all other issues are seen as marginal. Had North Korea had no nuclear weapons, few in Washington would care about this faraway country. Pyongyang decision-makers rightly assume that nuclear weapons are their major leverage in dealing with the developed world— and they have made great use of this leverage during the last two decades.

The North Korean nuclear program has a long history: as early as 1959, the Soviet Union and North Korea signed their first agreement on cooperation in nuclear research. A similar agreement was soon concluded with China as well (Pyongyang always tries to avoid putting all of its eggs in one basket).

In the 1960s the North Korean version of Los Alamos began to take shape in the city of Yongbyon, some ninety kilometers north of Pyongyang. For reasons of great secrecy, the nuclear research facility was called the Yongbyon Furniture Factory, although the equipment being used in this "furniture factory" was not a sawmill but a small Soviet-designed research reactor, the IRT-2000, completed in 1965. In the 1970s North Korean scientists independently modernized the reactor, increasing its output.

There are few doubts that from the earliest stages, North Korea's elite were interested in the military applications of their nuclear program, but it seems that the decisive turn occurred in the 1970s. At that time, South Korea was working hard to develop nuclear weapons of its own—and came quite close to success.[3] For the North, which has always had good intelligence about its archenemy, Seoul's nuclear ambitions were well known. As a result, around 1975, the leadership decided to accelerate the DPRK's military nuclear program.

The chief obstacle was the position of the USSR, at the time the major supplier of nuclear know-how. Moscow took non-proliferation seriously and had no intention of seeing its nuclear monopoly eroded—let alone creating conditions where its rogue and unruly quasi-allies would be able to provoke serious trouble. Sensing the true intentions of Pyongyang, the Soviet Union made nuclear cooperation conditional on a number of measures that would seriously hinder the development of nuclear weapons. Incidentally, Washington treated South Korea's nuclear plans in much the same manner and eventually ended the nuclear ambitions of Seoul. China also did not want a nuclear power across its border, so the usual North Korean strategy of playing Beijing against Moscow didn't work as it normally did.

Nonetheless, Pyongyang persevered. As Walter Clemens writes in his research on the history of the North Korean nuclear program:

> [S]everal features of its diplomatic behavior are of more than historical interest. First, Pyongyang was aggressive and insistent in seeking foreign aid and assistance for nuclear purposes [....] Second, [...] North Korea's leadership consistently evaded commitments to allies on nuclear matters, particularly constraints on its nuclear ambitions or even the provision of information. Third, North Korea's words and deeds evoked substantial concerns in Moscow and other Communist capitals.[4]

The Soviets made their continuing cooperation conditional on North Korea's participation in the international non-proliferation regime. In exchange for compliance, North Korea was promised technical assistance in building a nuclear power station of its own. Pyongyang bowed to Soviet pressure and in 1985 formally joined the Nuclear Non-Proliferation Treaty (NPT).[5]

But the world was soon to change. The Communist bloc that both controlled Pyongyang's nuclear ambitions and provided it with aid collapsed, and the North Korean economy nose-dived immediately. North Korea also ceased to be a part of the uncomfortable but sometimes reassuring Cold War alliance system, so it had to take security far more seriously. To meet the new challenges, the nuclear program had to be sped up.

When promoting their nuclear program, North Korean leaders essentially had two main goals in mind.

First, the North Korean nuclear program serves military purposes. Nuclear weapons are the ultimate deterrent, and, with a credible nuclear potential, North Korea is unlikely to be attacked by any foreign power. Theoretically, it could be argued that the alliance with China would provide North Korea with a measure of security. However, Pyongyang's leadership may be reluctant to depend on China's willingness to get into a major confrontation in order to save the Kim family from annihilation—the world has changed much since 1950, when Chinese forces had crossed the Yalu.

Needless to say, this fear of being attacked was amplified by the experiences of the 1990s and 2000s, when a number of states were the subject of US military actions. Following the outbreak of the Iraq War, North Korean diplomats and politicians have frequently observed to foreigners that "If Saddam Hussein had really had nukes, he would probably still be in his palace." This opinion was further reinforced by events in Libya—after all, Colonel Gadaffi's willingness to surrender nukes did not prevent the West from intervening militarily when Gadaffi's regime was challenged by the local opposition forces.

Second, Pyongyang requires nuclear weapons for diplomatic purposes—as an efficient tool for diplomatic blackmail. On balance, this seems to be even more important than the need for a strategic deterrent.

If we look at the geographic situation and macroeconomic indicators, the country that resembles North Korea most closely is Ghana. If the CIA Factbook is to be believed, in 2010 North Korea's and Ghana's populations were 24.4 and 24.7 million, respectively, while their per capita GDPs were

$1,800 and $1,700, respectively. Still, North Korea is light years ahead of Ghana when it comes to international attention and ability to manipulate the external environment. In terms of aid volume, North Korea punches above its weight.

Aid-monitoring in North Korea is remarkably lax by any international standard because it has to be. North Korea does not merely need foreign aid: it needs aid that comes without too many conditions, and whose distribution donors will not monitor too closely. Contrary to what some extreme critics of the regime assert, it does not want to starve its population. Kim Jong Il and his son, Kim Jong Un, as well as their advisers, would probably much prefer to see North Korean farmers alive and well (and extolling the leadership's wisdom and benevolence), but their survival is not very high on the regime's political agenda. Thus, uncontrolled aid is distributed to select groups whose support or, at least, docility is vital for political stability—above all, to the military, police, officials, and the populations of Pyongyang and other major cities. Therefore, the irritating presence of foreign monitors is not welcomed. Needless to say, the political demands of donors—like, say, to reform the economy—are not acceptable, either.

So far, North Korean diplomats have been remarkably successful in getting aid on conditions that would be unimaginable for almost any other country—and there is little doubt that the nuclear program has played a key role in this success.

AID-MAXIMIZING DIPLOMACY

The first nuclear blackmail campaign (aka, "the first nuclear crisis") was launched around 1990. Evidence of Pyongyang's nuclear weapons program began to surface, despite the fact that North Korean officials denied the very existence of such a program officially, while at the same time secretly arranging media leaks. As tensions mounted, North Korea threatened to withdraw from the NPT, and at one point Pyongyang diplomats even promised to turn Seoul into a "sea of fire" if the necessary concessions were not made—a threat that has since become de rigueur in North Korea's arsenal of verbal bellicosity.

Blackmail brought success. After much saber-rattling and diplomatic maneuvering, in 1994 the oddly named "Agreed Framework" treaty was signed in Geneva. According to agreement, North Korea promised to freeze its nuclear weapons program and accept international monitoring of its nuclear facilities. It also agreed to suspend construction of two additional nuclear reactors and ship some spent nuclear fuel rods out of the country.

In exchange, Pyongyang got a hefty payoff. As a mechanism to implement the Agreed Framework, an international consortium known as KEDO (Korean Energy Development Organization) was created. The chief donors to the KEDO budget were South Korea, Japan, and the United States (between 1995 and 2005 they provided $1,450, $498, and $405 million, respectively).[6] KEDO was to build two light water reactors in North Korea. Such reactors are good for power generation but not particularly useful for production of weapons-grade plutonium. It was also promised that until the completion of the reactors, KEDO would regularly ship significant quantities of heavy fuel oil to North Korea, free of charge.[7]

It is widely rumored that the US negotiators were prepared to be quite generous because at that time they assumed the North Korean regime would not last long and thus the promised aid and concessions would not need to be delivered. In 1994 Jeffrey Smith of the *Washington Post* quoted unnamed US officials who assured him that the implementation period of the Agreed Framework "is almost certainly a sufficient period of time for their regime to have collapsed."[8]

Apart from the light water reactors and fuel oil, North Korea also received much additional foreign aid without many strings attached. To a large extent this reflected the mood at the time, which remained dominant during the Clinton administration. During this period, a number of US policy-makers believed that by providing aid and pursuing the KEDO agreement, the United States might eventually build enough trust to persuade North Korea's leadership to surrender its nuclear program completely—or at least keep the situation under control until the collapse of the Kim family regime, which they thought would happen soon.

Most of the aid was presented as purely humanitarian in nature and unrelated to the ongoing crisis, but there are good reasons to think that North Korean officials saw the aid as a kind of tribute, an additional reward for their willingness to ostensibly freeze their nuclear weapons program. This might be a cynical view, but a look at the statistics confirms that North Korean officials might have been right in their hard-nosed assessment. As will be seen later, as soon as relations with the United States deteriorated in 2002, American aid all but disappeared. The same happened to Japanese aid after a crisis in relations caused by revelations about the abduction of Japanese citizens. This hardly supports the view that aid was given exclusively because of lofty humanitarian considerations.

Throughout the period between 1996 and 2001 (when the food crisis was most acute), North Korea received a total of 5.94 million metric tons of food aid. Most of this aid came from countries described by Pyongyang's official propaganda as the "mortal enemies of Korean people"—the United States, South Korea, and Japan. The United States provided 1.7 million metric tons (28.6 percent of the total), South Korea provided 0.67 million metric tons (11 percent), and Japan provided 0.81 million metric tons (13.6 percent). Of ostensibly "friendly" countries, only China was a major provider of aid throughout this period, shipping 1.3 million metric tons of food to the North.[9] The food shipments played a major role in mitigating this humanitarian disaster.

North Korean diplomats have not merely succeeded in acquiring a large amount of aid, but also have ensured that this aid has come with minimal oversight and hence has been channeled to those social sectors whose compliance and support are vital for the regime's survival. Foreign monitors have been denied any access to a significant part of the country, including areas hit hardest by the 1996–1999 famine. Even in the most permissive period, around 2004, foreign monitors were allowed to supervise distribution in only 167 of the North's 201 counties.

No Korean speakers were initially allowed into the country, and until 2004 the authorities even banned World Food Program (WFP) personnel from attending Korean-language classes. Monitoring teams were always accompanied by government-assigned interpreters who filtered all questions and answers. North Koreans have often assumed—probably correctly—that these people were spooks by default, so they were unlikely to say anything dangerous in this menacing atmosphere. The number of WFP monitors was kept small, and their inspection trips had to be approved by authorities well in advance. This way, everything could be arranged to ensure monitors saw only what their handlers wanted them to see.[10]

Things changed after the so-called second nuclear crisis, which erupted in October 2002. At the time, US Assistant Secretary of State James Kelly was visiting Pyongyang. The US government had recently acquired intelligence indicating that North Korea was cheating on the Agreed Framework and that Pyongyang was secretly pursuing a uranium enrichment program (its earlier program was plutonium-based). In Pyongyang, Kelly confronted his North Korean opposite number, whereupon, according to Kelly, the North Korean deputy foreign minister admitted the existence of the highly enriched uranium (HEU) program. The North Koreans later denied that such an admission had ever taken place, instead asserting that the North Korean diplomat in question had merely said that North Korea was entitled to have an HEU program since it was facing a hostile superpower—implying that the entitlement was more or less theoretical. At any rate, this exchange was taken as proof of a clandestine HEU program.

With the wisdom of hindsight, it seems very likely that Kelly's version of events was correct, since in 2009, after years of denial, Pyongyang admitted that it had an HEU program. In November 2010 North Korean officials proudly showed off a huge uranium enrichment facility to visiting US nuclear scientists.

It is possible that in 2002, North Korea hoped to acquire an additional source of income by negotiating a buyout of their HEU program for another hefty payoff—a scheme rather similar to the buyout of the plutonium program in 1994. If this had been the initial plan, it did not work as hoped. With George W. Bush and his neoconservative advisers in the White House, things took a rather different turn. Instead of bargaining for another buyout, the United States cited the HEU program as proof that North Koreans should not be trusted, and large-scale aid was discontinued.

In 2003 North Korea formally withdrew from the NPT, becoming the first state to ever do so (creating a dangerous precedent). Subsequently, the KEDO project was closed down, with all personnel being withdrawn from the construction sites between 2005 and 2006.

Obviously some Washington hard-liners assumed that without US aid, North Korea would soon collapse. However, North Korean diplomats have been successful in finding substitutes for US aid, namely, South Korea (prior to 2008) and, later, China. Such shipments have compensated for the sudden halt of the US food and economic assistance. Indeed, the North Korean economy actually began its partial recovery right around the time when US aid was halted. At any rate, until 2006, the Bush administration was not in any mood to talk to Kim Jong Il, whom Bush despised and once even dismissed as a "pigmy" (North Korea itself was described as a part of the "axis of evil").

As an important part of efforts aimed at pressing the North Korean regime and driving it to denuclearization and/or collapse, the US government used Section 311 of the Patriot Act to target financial institutions it knew handled accounts of the North Korean government and Kim family. They were accused of money laundering—an accusation not completely unfounded but perhaps exaggerated, as only a relatively small part of Pyongyang revenue comes from illegal activities. In September 2005 a small bank in Macao, Banco Delta Asia (BDA), was singled out as a "money laundering outlet"—indeed, it was very involved in dubious transactions with Pyongyang. As a result, $25 million of North Korean funds were frozen, and US banking institutions ended operations with BDA.

Clearly, the US government wanted to set a precedent by issuing a warning to all banks that might wish to become too cozy with the North Korean regime. When it comes to state finances, $25 million is not a large sum of money even for a poor state like North Korea, but the decision produced a surprisingly strong reaction from Pyongyang—apparently because the funds were part of the Kim family's personal treasury. For a brief while, international bankers avoided any interaction with their North Korean peers, and in some cases large transactions had to be conducted in cash. It was argued that such measures interrupted the supply of perks to the Kim family and top North Korean bureaucrats, whose appreciation for Swiss cheese and French cognac is well known.

Another byproduct of the "second nuclear crisis" was the launch of the six-party talks, which began in 2003 with the stated goal of laying the groundwork for the eventual denuclearization of the Korean peninsula. The talks were attended by the six powers involved in the ongoing nuclear crisis—the United States, China (the host of the talks), South Korea, Russia, Japan, and, of course, North Korea. From the very beginning there was little doubt that the talks were not going to achieve their stated goal, since the Kim family regime has never had the slightest intention to surrender its nuclear program. Nonetheless, the six-party talks were not useless: negotiations helped to ameliorate tensions and created a useful forum where Korea-related security issues could be discussed freely.

In 2006 North Korean leaders decided that it was time to dramatically raise the stakes. By that time North Korea had amassed enough plutonium to produce a few crude nuclear devices. In early 2010 it was estimated that North Korea had manufactured forty to sixty kilograms of weapons-grade plutonium, of which twenty-four to forty-two kilograms was available for weapons production. Siegfried Hecker believes that North Korea is "most likely to possess a nuclear arsenal of four to eight primitive weapons," even though it still "appears a long way from developing both a missile and a warhead to launch a nuclear weapon to great distance."[11]

What followed was yet another exercise of Pyongyang's favorite tactic. When North Korean strategists are not happy about the situation and suspect that more aid and concessions can (and therefore should) be squeezed from the outside world, they follow this pattern. First, they manufacture a crisis and drive tensions as high as they can. They do this by launching missiles, testing a nuclear device, dispatching commandos, and/or dropping an assortment of threatening hints. When tensions are sufficiently high, with newspaper headlines across the globe telling readers that the "Korean peninsula is on the brink of war" and foreign diplomats feeling a bit uneasy, the North Korean government suggests negotiations. The offer is, of course, accepted with a sigh of relief, giving North Korean diplomats the leverage to squeeze maximum concessions out of their negotiating partners as a reward for Pyongyang's willingness to restore the pre-crisis status quo. Such a routine has been very successful.

A similar policy was applied to the Soviet Union and China during the 1960s and 1970s (without missile launches, of course), though different and subtler ways were used to manipulate Moscow and Beijing.

During October 2006 North Korean leaders decided that this was the time to begin such a routine, by conducting their first nuclear test. The yield was surprisingly low and it seems almost certain that the nuclear device did not work as intended. Nevertheless, the underground explosion in the remote northern mountains was enough to demonstrate that North Korea was indeed moving toward creating an effective nuclear weapons capability.

After the test, the UN Security Council immediately passed the appropriately stern Resolution 1718, which was supported by all permanent members (including Russia and China). At the time, optimists cheered the news and began to persuade themselves and everybody around that China had finally done the right thing and from now on would work in concert with the United States and other interested parties. This was not the case, of course: China was not in the same boat as the United States on matters related to Pyongyang—and never will be. While unhappy about nuclear proliferation, China is not going to do anything that might trigger an acute domestic crisis in North Korea. Even though they profess to participate in the sanctions regime, the Chinese have not let it influence their position. On the contrary, 2006, the year of the first nuclear test, also marked an upsurge in the scale of Chinese aid to and economic cooperation with Pyongyang—and this scale increased until the first half of 2013 (and probably continued to fall after the execution of Chang Sŏng-t'aek for selling out to the Chinese, among his other multifarious "crimes").

As we will see later, South Korea, with left-leaning administrations in control from 1998 to 2008, was even more willing to shower North Korea with aid without asking too many awkward questions.

The Bush administration belatedly realized that sanctions and pressure were not achieving the desired result. On February 13, 2007, a joint statement was produced during another round of the six-party talks. The joint statement promised the resumption of US and foreign aid in exchange for North Korea's theoretical commitment to eventual denuclearization. Around the same time, the State Department effectively halted measures aimed at Banco Delta Asia and scaled down operations that dealt with real or alleged money laundering by the North Korean regime.

The present author learned about the 2007 joint statement while in Moscow, eating lunch with a group of Russian diplomats. An ambassador who was sitting next to the author read the faxed text of the statement and said: "Well, the North Koreans will know what to do when they run out of money again." This was a really perceptive remark: the return to talks might have been a correct (or, at least, an unavoidable) decision on the part of the United States, but the timing of the February 2007 joint statement was most inappropriate. Indeed, from the North Korean point of view, it did not merely confirm that blackmail works but also that it works wonders. One could hardly find a better confirmation of the efficiency of Pyongyang's usual tactics—first generate a crisis, then escalate tensions, and, finally, extract payments and concessions for the restoration of the status quo.

MEANWHILE, IN SOUTH KOREA . . . (THE RISE OF 386ERS AND ITS CONSEQUENCES)

Under the George W. Bush administration, Washington discovered that the US approach to North Korean issues seriously differed from that of the South Korean government, hitherto the United States' most reliable ally in East Asia. Some people even argued that the US-led sanctions were derailed by a soft-line policy that dominated the South Korean approach in the years between 1998 and 2008. This is probably not the case, since the hard-line stance was likely to fail anyway, but the discord between Seoul and Washington was nonetheless all too open and real. Needless to say, North Korean diplomats have made the most of these disagreements.

This discord has primarily domestic roots, being brought about by slow but important changes within South Korean society. It makes sense to look at these changes—not least because they are likely to influence Korea and Korean-US relations for years to come.

From the end of the Korean War until around 1980, South Korean politics and ideology were almost completely dominated by the right. South Korean rightists were hard-line anti-Communists and thus favored a long-term alliance with the United States as the cornerstone of their nation's foreign policy. Naturally, the right saw the eventual unification of Korea under a capitalist and liberal regime as Korea's primary long-term goal (although as time went on, South Korea's commitment to and interest in unification began to wane). These views were predominant among the political and intellectual elite and were widely shared by the broader South Korean population. There were dissenters, of course, who favored democratization of their own country and a more conciliatory approach to the North. There were also some individuals, especially in academia, who held leftist views to the point of being orthodox Leninists. However, the latter had almost no impact on the general political climate—living under a repressive and militantly anti-Communist regime, they had to keep much of what they thought to themselves.

Things began to change in the late 1970s, following a generational shift. The new generation of Koreans did not have firsthand memories of the Korean War and the destitution of the 1950s. They did not survive on cans of US food aid and came to see three daily meals of rice (an unattainable dream for their parents' generation) as a natural and unexciting part of daily life. They also were the first generation in Korean history that had almost universal access to secondary education—and many of them proceeded to college as well. Much later, in the 1990s, this group was nicknamed the "386 generation," since they were born in the 1960s, attended universities in the 1980s, and were in their thirties in the 1990s when this term was coined.

This 386 generation took spectacular economic growth for granted—they largely saw this as the natural fruits of their nation's intrinsic greatness. They despised the military dictatorships and were skeptical about the market economy. They were a generation that managed to live through one of the greatest success stories in the history of capitalism without even noticing it. Where their once-starving parents saw growth, prosperity, and security, they saw inequality, social injustice, and subservience to foreign powers. This new generation of young Koreans—or rather its politically active minority—was passionately anti-authoritarian, anti-American, vigorously nationalist, and left-wing.

This trademark combination of nationalism and hard-core leftism, as well as a deep disgust with the military regimes in Seoul, initially made a significant number of the 386ers into North Korean sympathizers. The early 1980s was an era when the works of Marx and Lenin were much perused by aspiring young South Korean intellectuals. Some of them went further, reading treatises on Juche thought and exchanging smuggled North Korean publications and transcripts of North Korean radio broadcasts. The more radical of these young dissenters began to imagine the North as a land of social justice, unspoiled Koreanness, and, somehow, democracy.

Leftist activists—many without sympathy for Pyongyang—played a major role in the pro-democracy movement that in 1987 brought an end to decades of authoritarianism in South Korea. However, soon after this triumph, the more radical faction of the nascent South Korean radical left suffered two major blows.

First, between 1989 and 1990, the Communist bloc disintegrated. It instantly became clear that neither the Soviet Union nor Eastern Europe was what South Korean student radicals somehow believed them to be, namely, a paradise of workers' rights, general well-being, and true democracy—lands where happy peoples enjoyed the eternal bliss of a near-perfect social system.

Second, in the mid-1990s, dramatic increases in contacts and interactions with North Korea (both direct and indirect, via China) made it impossible to dismiss reports of North Korea's destitution as "fabrications of the reactionary forces" and "lies of CIA-paid hacks." It began to dawn on South Korean leftists that North Korea was a very poor Third World country run by an authoritarian government (many still often cannot make themselves utter the word "dictatorship" when talking about the Kim dynasty). Even now, many of South Korea's self-styled "progressive intellectuals" have remained remarkably willing to ignore even the most repulsive features of the Pyongyang regime, while being unforgiving when it comes to abuses committed by the South Korean military dictators. Nonetheless, their initial enthusiasm for a Juche utopia vanished by the mid-1990s.

Unification played a major role in the worldview of the 386 generation. In the heyday of South Korean student radicalism during the late 1980s, a vocal minority of activists believed that the country should be unified under some version of Leninist Socialism, more or less similar to the then-current North Korean system. The majority, however, preferred a less radical solution and talked of a confederate state where both parts of Korea would keep their peculiarities whilst moving toward a compromise in social and political terms.

Meanwhile, the mainstream of South Korean society also moved far away from the anti-Communism of former times and discovered important reasons to be skeptical about the prospect of unification. Since the mid-1990s, a growing number of younger South Koreans have begun to quietly entertain doubts as to whether unification is such a good idea after all.

This ongoing shift of opinions reflects changes in South Korean society. The number of people in the South who have ever had a direct personal connection with the North is dwindling. As of 2014, people born before 1944 constituted merely 8.4 percent of South Korea's population.[12] They are the only people, however, who might possibly have some firsthand memories of the North or North Korean relatives and family members.

The bitter German experience has also played a major role in the reassessment of a once rosy attitude toward unification. News from Germany has made Seoul decision-makers and the general public realize that the unification of the two Koreas would be vastly more expensive than anybody had hitherto imagined. The difference in per capita income between East and West Germany was 1:2 or 1:3, while in Korea, even if one believes the most optimistic estimate, the ratio is 1:15 (pessimists think it is closer to 1:40). The ratio of the population (roughly 1:2) is also less favorable than in Germany—a larger minority of a united Korean population will be Northerners. Given how expensive and protracted the unification process was in Germany, many in Seoul have become very skeptical about unification.

The generational shift in South Korea has also contributed to other changes as well. The politically active youngsters of the 1980s (now in their forties or even early fifties) wanted unification because they were both leftist and nationalist. Their parents (now in their sixties and older) wanted unification because they were anti-Communist and nationalist. However, the young generation of today—the 386ers' children and younger siblings— are different. Born in the 1980s and 1990s, they are less nationalistic, less anti-American, more accepting of markets, and, most significantly, they do not really see North Korea as a part of their national community. They also tend to associate unification exclusively with economic hardship, not with the realization of some lofty national dream.

This slow-motion decline of the once-universal enthusiasm for unifica- tion is reflected by public opinion polls. In 1994, 91.6 percent of South Koreans said they considered unification "necessary." In 2007, according to a poll conducted by Seoul National University, the number of such people shrank to 63.8 percent.

Age is highly significant in these matters: the younger a South Korean is, the less likely he or she is to express enthusiasm for unification. A 2010 Seoul National University study of attitudes toward unification indicated that 48.8 percent of South Koreans in their twenties perceived that "unifi- cation is necessary." The youngest constituted the only age group in which the idea of unification was supported only by a minority. Among people in their thirties, 55.4 percent of the participants agreed that "unification is necessary," and among those over fifty, 67.3 percent favored it.[13] This should not come as a surprise—anyone who interacts with younger South Koreans is aware that serious doubts about unification are pervasive and, indeed, almost universal in this milieu.

Even older people are now having doubts. A Korean businessman in his early seventies, himself born in what is now North Korea and with a long experience of interacting with Northerners because of his manifold business projects, recently described his feeling about unification to the present author: "Well, the Northerners say they are so happy under the wise guidance of their Dear General. Let them be happy there, if they like it so much. They are so different from us now. Even their physical appearance is different, they are so short! So, the later we unify, the better. In a hundred years, perhaps."

It is remarkable that nowadays even supporters of unification seldom rely on nationalist or other emotive sentiments—obviously on the assumption that such idealism is unlikely to be shared by their compatriots. Instead, they talk about the supposed economic advantages of unification, such as access to the "cheap labor and rich mineral resources" of the North. Regardless of whether such statements are true, they clearly reek of a quasi-colonial attitude toward their supposed "brethren"—and this attitude does not bode well for North Koreans' post-unification future.

There is one interesting peculiarity to take note of, however: these changes in public opinion are seldom reflected in the public discourse. This silence is understandable. All "ideological packages" that exist in South Korea include ethnic nationalism as a key ingredient, and the idea of unification is an inseparable part of all varieties of Korean nationalism. For any Korean public figure, it would be politically suicidal to openly question the imperative for eventual unification. Any good Korean citizen, regardless of his/her views on any other issue, is expected to believe in the shared historic destiny of North and South. This contradiction between professed beliefs and actual feelings makes many look for excuses that would justify postponing unification into a distant, undetermined future—but without falling into the heresy of openly challenging the need for unification as such.

A DECADE OF SUNSHINE

Against such a backdrop, in late 1997, Kim Dae Jung, a lifelong dissenter and pro-democracy activist, was elected president of South Korea. His campaign was based on a critique of the old right-leaning establishment. Kim Dae Jung promised more social security, a softer policy in dealing with North Korea, and a harsher approach to big business. Aging Kim Dae Jung was old enough to belong to the generation of the 386ers' parents, but the 386 generation embraced his candidacy with much enthusiasm. The next elections in 2002 were won by another candidate who clearly associated himself with the South Korean nationalist left—Roh Moo Hyun, a former human rights lawyer and pro-democracy activist.

The conservative South Korean media sometimes made it sound like both presidents were closet Communists. This was clearly not the case, and their opinions on the economy or welfare were not much different from those of German Social Democrats or the British Labour Party (even though they and their supporters were remarkably nationalist by the current standards of the European left). However, in dealing with the North, the left-leaning administrations were more than prepared to jettison the old hard line. To an extent, their approach reflected the ideological biases of the 386ers, some of whom held important jobs in both administrations. At the same time, this softer approach reflected the gradual demise of anti-Communism, as well as echoing the increasingly strong doubts the average South Korean had with regard to a German-style unification-by-absorption.

This is the context to how the Sunshine Policy came to be launched by Kim Dae Jung's government in 1997 and continued by Roh throughout his term of 2003–2008. The stated goal of the Sunshine Policy was to encourage the gradual evolution of North Korea through unilateral aid and political concessions. The policy's name refers to one of Aesop's fables, "The North Wind and the Sun." In the fable, the North Wind and the Sun argue about who is able to remove a cloak from a traveler. The North Wind blows hard but fails to succeed, since the traveler wraps his cloak even more tightly to protect himself. The Sun, however, warms the air, thus enticing the traveler to remove the unnecessary cloak.

The policy was based on the belief that a soft approach would persuade the North to institute large-scale reforms, more or less similar to those undertaken in China and Vietnam. The hope was that this would open the way to a gradual and manageable form of unification, perhaps through some form of confederation. An important aspect of this policy was a belief (in all probability, erroneous) that reform would prolong the existence of the North Korean state and make possible the gradual elimination of the huge economic and social gap between the two Koreas. As Korea expert

Aidan Foster-Carter has noted, "Despite the rhetoric of unification, the immediate aim [of the 'Sunshine' policy] was to retain two states, but encourage them to get on better."[14]

After 1997 the South began to provide the starving North with considerable amounts of aid, but the breakthrough in relations between the two Koreas was achieved in September 2000, when President Kim Dae Jung went to Pyongyang to meet Kim Jong Il in the first-ever inter-Korean summit. Kim Dae Jung had to pay a political as well as financial price to achieve this success—it was later discovered that North Korea demanded a payment of $500 million as a preliminary condition for accepting the proposed summit. The payment was promptly delivered, and only then did the summit take place.

These concessions annoyed South Korean rightists, who often claim that "Kim Dae Jung paid $500 million in order to purchase a Nobel Peace Prize for himself." Indeed, the South Korean president became the Nobel Peace Prize winner in 2000, "for his work for democracy and human rights in South Korea and in East Asia in general, and for peace and reconciliation with North Korea in particular." There might be a kernel of truth in these accusations since Kim Dae Jung, being a lifelong politician, never overlooked self-promotion. At the same time, however, the 2000 summit did open channels for a truly astonishing increase in inter-Korean exchanges.

Keep in mind that between 1996 and 2001, the United States and Japan were among the main suppliers of food aid to North Korea. In 2002, however, the United States dramatically reduced its aid after the "second nuclear crisis." The South stepped resolutely into the breach, significantly increasing its aid to the North. During the period between 2002 and 2007, the North received 5.1 million metric tons of outside food aid—some 850,000 tons in an average year. Of this, South Korea supplied 2.41 million metric tons of food aid (nearly half of the total—47.1 percent). During the period, China provided 1.60 million metric tons (31.3 percent of the total), while the United States supplied 0.57 million metric tons (11.2 percent).[15] The combined contribution of all other countries was marginal—yet another reminder of the essentially policy-motivated nature of the "humanitarian" aid to North Korea. Actually, the South Korean contribution was even larger than the figures suggest, since in the years of sunshine it also shipped huge quantities of chemical fertilizer (between 200,000 and 350,000 tons a year throughout 2000–2007, or some 35–45 percent of all fertilizer used in North Korean agriculture). Without these shipments, North Korean harvests would have been much lower.[16]

A great number of North-South economic projects, large and small, were launched from 1998 through 2008. Most of them were officially described as "cooperative projects," but they tended to take the form of a rather lopsided form of "cooperation." Most South Korean companies that dealt with the North were directly and indirectly subsidized by the South Korean government.

Among these projects, three were of especial importance—the Kŭmgang Mountain Tourist Region, the Kaesŏng Industrial Zone, and the Kaesŏng City Tours. All these projects were politically acceptable for Pyongyang, whose leaders are always cautious about the possible political consequences of unrestricted interaction between Northerners and Southerners. From the North's perspective, the Kŭmgang Mountain Tourist Region, the first of the "Big Three" projects, can be seen as an ideal undertaking. It was, essentially, a fenced-off ghetto for South Korean tourists.

The project was conceived of as early as 1989, when Chung Ju-yung, the founding chairman of Hyundai Group, the largest South Korean business conglomerate at the time, first met Kim Il Sung. Chung Ju-yung was born in what is now North Korea, and in the last years of his long and eventful life he demonstrated a sentimental attachment to his native land. This seems to be the impetus behind his Hyundai Group (or, to be more exact, its Asan subsidiary) taking on all three major inter-Korean projects.

Chung Ju-yung's proposal envisioned the establishment of a South Korean resort in North Korea. The resort was to be located in the Kŭmgang ("Diamond") Mountains, which for centuries have been seen in Korean culture as the embodiment of scenic beauty. The mountains conveniently lay near the DMZ.

In November 1998 the Kŭmgang project commenced operations. As with the majority of North-South "cooperation" projects, the South did most of the work, while the North received the lion's share of the project's benefits. For the South Korean side, the project could hardly be called a financial success story. In January 1999 Hyundai predicted that by the end of 2004, there would have been a cumulative 4.9 million visits to the resort. The actual figure was merely 900,000. Hyundai Asan also projected in 1999 that by 2004, some 1.2 million South Korean tourists would visit the project annually. Yet the actual number of visits in 2004 was 274,000— four times lower than initial expectations. In 2007 the number of visitors peaked at 350,000—an impressive figure, but still well below the rosy expectations of the late 1990s.[17] Between 2001 and 2002, the project nearly went bankrupt, and only a massive infusion of South Korean government funds saved it from capsizing.

South Koreans did not rush to the new resort. This lack of enthusiasm was easy to explain, since the trips were not cheap: a tour to Kŭmgang would cost almost as much as cheaper tours to China or Southeast Asia. At the same time, the allure of North Korea, once clearly a "forbidden fruit," was fast diminishing in the South.

At the resort, South Korean visitors were not allowed to venture outside the fenced area. The local population was removed from this area completely, and only a few hundred North Korean minders and plainclothes "guides" were present there. Most of the semi-skilled personnel at the project were ethnic Koreans recruited from China—they were willing to work for low wages, and they were politically safe for the North Korean authorities (like the tourists themselves, Chinese-Korean personnel were not allowed to leave the resort).

Nonetheless, some "ideological damage" is possible even in such circumstances. A North Korean refugee whom the author has met was sent to work on a construction site at the resort during a labor mobilization in the early 2000s. During his stay, he had no contact with South Korean tourists whatsoever and did not see them even from afar, but later, after his defection to the South, he mentioned this trip as a turning point in his ideas about the South. He could see some South Korean equipment and also some buildings erected by the Southerners, and this was enough. In his words, "I knew that the South was ahead of the North, but only after my trip to Kŭmgang Tourist Region did I realize how far ahead they actually were."

Much in line with the Kŭmgang Tourist Region was the decision to start tours to the ancient city of Kaesŏng, located near the DMZ and of great historic significance to all Koreans. Compared to the Kŭmgang tourist zone, Kaesŏng city tours were potentially politically more dangerous for Pyongyang. Every day, the inhabitants of Kaesŏng could see a dozen or so large, shiny South Korean buses crisscrossing the small historical downtown of Kaesŏng. Each bus, apart from a driver, had two or three minders whose job was to make sure that visitors did not take photos of everyday life in the city. Pictures could be taken only at designated stops. Upon departure, all digital cameras (only digital cameras were allowed on tours) had to be checked frame by frame, and those visitors who dared to take politically incorrect pictures—of, say, an ox-cart on a city street—would have to pay a fine.

Nevertheless, the North Korean authorities obviously were not able to completely segregate South Korean tourists. The police did not allow North Koreans to get within a few dozen yards of tourists, but even from such a distance Northerners could see that Southerners were well dressed and unusually tall by Northerner standards.

Interaction with minders was also allowed and even frequently initiated by the minders themselves. Obviously, these young police and intelligence officers were supposed to do their job—that is, gain intelligence. Nonetheless, there is no doubt that in the process they also discovered many interesting things about actual life in the South. One might argue that the secret police personnel would have known the truth anyway, but this was hardly the case: normally, such people would be far too low in the pecking order of the North Korean bureaucracy to be allowed that much access to subversive knowledge about the "other Korea."

Of all three projects, the Kaesŏng Industrial Zone (KIZ) is by far the most significant, both economically and politically. The idea of the KIZ is based on the increasingly common assumption that the interests of both Koreas can be served by the unification of Southern capital and technology with Northern cheap labor. In an industrial park in the vicinity of the

DMZ (to minimize South Korean ideological penetration), South Korean companies would employ North Korean workers who, laboring under the supervision of South Korean managers, would produce cheap items for sale in South Korea and beyond.

KIZ construction began in 2003, and by late 2004 the first production lines came online. Big business did not show much interest in the idea, so only small- and medium-sized South Korean companies chose to move into the KIZ. The South Korean government provided generous inducements, including, among other things, subsidized loans and guarantees. The guarantees were especially important, since even in the early days of the Roh administration, when North-South relations were going through a short honeymoon, South Korean businessmen were afraid that overinvesting in the KIZ would one day make them hostages to the policies of both Seoul and Pyongyang.

Contrary to earlier worries, the KIZ was remarkably successful. Admittedly, as was the case with the Kŭmgang tours, the initial estimates proved to be overly optimistic: in 2003 it was projected that as early as 2007 approximately 100,000 North Korean workers would be employed by some 250–300 South Korean companies in the area. The actual results were less impressive: by late 2010, some 120 South Korean companies operated in the KIZ, with 47,000 North Korean workers employed. Over half of the companies (seventy-one, to be exact) dealt with clothing and textiles. In 2010 KIZ-based companies produced goods worth $323.3 million (again, slightly over half consisted of textiles and clothing). For the mammoth South Korean economy, this is small change, but for the North this income is significant enough.[18]

The KIZ is located some ten kilometers away from the DMZ, so South Korean personnel commute daily, but some stay overnight (thus creating the ever-present possibility of a hostage situation in case of a crisis). As of 2013 there were between eight and nine hundred South Korean technicians and managers supervising the North Korean workers.

Theoretically, South Korean companies pay their North Korean workers the agreed basic monthly wages of $61 (as of 2010), but this figure does not include overtime premiums and special incentives, so the actual monthly payment seems to be close to $90–100 per worker. However, this salary is paid to a North Korean government agency that makes a number of deductions, so only a fraction of the total—less than 35 percent—reaches the workers' pockets. Indeed, the KIZ is a major cash cow for the North Korean state, providing an estimated annual revenue of $25–40 million. This has allowed the numerous critics of the project to describe it as a "slave labor camp." The description is grossly unfair: even after deductions, KIZ jobs are by far the best-paid regular jobs in North Korea, and locals vie to get employment there.

Interaction between North Korean workers and South Korean managers is discouraged. In one incident, a South Korean manager was arrested and held for several months, allegedly for criticizing North Korea and encouraging a female North Korean worker to defect. The specifics of the affair have never been made public because both the North and South wanted to avoid potential complications.

Nonetheless, one should not underestimate the impact that the KIZ has had on the city of Kaesŏng and the surrounding area. A significant part of the local population is employed in the KIZ. It looks like an average South Korean industrial district and, as such, would probably be best described as monotonous and faceless by visiting aesthetes from other parts of the world. But for the North Koreans themselves, the area looks stunningly unusual and beautiful. The streets are lined with trees, roads are paved, and bright electric lights are on every night. Standard prefabricated buildings are clean and brightly colored. This is not what average North Koreans have seen in a typical industrial district in their country. As a matter of fact, first-time visiting North Korean officials cannot hide their surprise—even though such improper reactions might be politically dangerous.

North Korean workers in the KIZ need not talk to South Koreans to get an idea of what life in South Korea looks like. The South Koreans are tall, well dressed, and their skin testifies to the fact that they do not spend much time on labor mobilization, neither planting rice with bare hands nor pushing cement blocks around. Even small talk might not be that innocent, since hints about daily life in the South—both intentional and incidental—are bound to be dropped and North Koreans will certainly take notice. No amount of police surveillance will prevent this from happening.

Smuggling from the KIZ has also had a remarkable impact on the hearts and minds of the people living in the surrounding area. For snacks, many North Koreans are given Choco Pies, a seriously unhealthy, sugar-rich but delicious snack that is popular in the South. It is known that most of them get Choco Pies from the KIZ to share with their families. These Choco Pies have become carriers of highly subversive messages about South Korea's sophistication and prosperity—like pretty much everything that is taken from the KIZ, legally or otherwise (and theft is a big problem there).

The KIZ does fill the regime's coffers, no doubt, but it also serves as a conduit for new and uncensored knowledge about the outside world. We can be sure that, thanks to the KIZ, an overwhelming majority of some quarter-million people who live in its vicinity have come to understand that most of what they read about South Korea in the official media is completely false. Even minders and political police agents are not immune from the effects of these discoveries.

IN SEARCH OF A GULLIBLE INVESTOR

In 1991 the North Korean government established a special economic zone (SEZ) in the remote northwestern corner of the country. The Rason SEZ, as it later became known, was to be located where the borders of China, Russia, and North Korea meet and become a business hub of the region.

News of the establishment of North Korea's first SEZ produced much enthusiasm in the international media. As usual, there was no shortage of pundits who saw the decision as a sure sign that Chinese-style reforms soon would be launched in North Korea. After all, in China of the early 1980s, similar SEZs—islands of the market economy in an ocean of state Socialism and central planning—played a major role in the early stages of the reform. Surely, the optimists claimed, the introduction of the SEZ was a sign that North Korea would soon emulate China.

As subsequent developments demonstrated quite well, the Rason SEZ was not a sign of reform. Neither was it a success. By 2000, the total volume of foreign investment in the area was a paltry US$35 million. Yet again, there were some very rosy forecasts in 1991–92 of the possibility of $1–2 billion of investment.

The major problem was the location. The Rason area is underdeveloped even by North Korean standards. The only paved road in the area connects Rajin and Sonbong, and even this is only a single lane. The bridge that connects the area with China has remained unchanged since colonial days. Obviously, Pyongyang expected that rich foreign investors would pay for the upgrading of the infrastructure. They did, but only on a very limited scale.

Thus, for two decades the Rason SEZ has largely remained dormant, becoming essentially a large marketplace where North Korean merchants can buy Chinese goods for further resale in the inner regions of North Korea. (The merchants needed a special pass to get in since the area is fenced off and off-limits to ordinary North Koreans, but nowadays a small bribe can solve this problem with ease.) For a brief time it also served as a gambling enclave for rich Chinese, but after some ugly embezzlement incidents, the Chinese demanded the closure of the local casino.

The zone became much more active around 2010, when the Russian and Chinese companies began to use its port facilities. For Russia, Rason presents a wonderful opportunity to relieve the burden of Vladivostok, a major port of the Russian Far East. The Chinese were attracted by the prospect of large savings on the transportation costs. For factories and mines in the adjacent parts of China, it is much cheaper to export their produce via the North Korean seaports than to pay for slow land transportation to the nearest Chinese port, which is located some thousand miles to the south.

In 2002 the North Korean government made another, more radical, plan to launch an SEZ—this time in the border city of Sinuiju. It was stated that the entire population of Sinuiju, some 350,000 people, would be relocated to other areas, to be replaced by 200,000 model workers, handpicked by the authorities for their skill and perceived political reliability. The most unusual decision was the appointment of a foreigner as the SEZ governor—Yang Bin, a Chinese entrepreneur with Dutch citizenship and reputedly the second richest man in China. He was thirty-nine years old at the time.

(continued)

On September 12, 2002, the Supreme People's Assembly, the North Korean rubber-stamp parliament, adopted the Basic Law of the Sinuiju Special Administrative Region. The Law consisted of six chapters (government, economy, culture, fundamental rights and duties of residents, structure, and the emblem and flag of the region), with an impressive 101 articles. The Basic Law proclaimed that the legal system would remain unchanged for fifty years and that foreigners would enjoy the same rights as North Koreans in the area. Foreign judges were to be invited to solve disputes and oversee the enforcement of the laws.

It looked too good to be true, and for a while there was a great deal of media hype about a "breakthrough." The North Korean vice minister for foreign trade called the SEZ "a new historical miracle." However, "new historical miracle" Sinuiju hardly lasted fifty weeks, let alone the promised fifty years.

It was probably the Chinese who sank the project. Beijing was not amused by the turn of events. Yang Bin wanted to transform the city into a gambling center, a "Macao of the North." This was not welcome. It is also likely that China did not want competition between Sinuiju and its northeastern cities. It did not help that the North Koreans, following their modus operandi, did not bother to liaise with the Chinese beforehand. Yang Bin was already under investigation at that time. He was soon arrested for fraud and sentenced to eighteen years in prison. No one heard about the Sinuiju SEZ for another decade.

In 2011 an announcement about a new SEZ in the vicinity of Sinuiju was made—largely on the assumption that it would attract Chinese businesses. However, by early 2014 it has become clear that the new attempt to revive the Sinuiju dream had again failed.

THE SUN SETS

By late 2007 North Korea's strategists had good reason to feel happy about the results of their diplomacy and brinkmanship. The US administration had caved in and resumed aid, and even the revival of KEDO seemed likely after the February 13 declaration. Aid from the South helped to make up for the innate inefficiencies in the North Korean economy. In the long run, the Sunshine Policy might not have been as good for the North Korean regime as Kim Jong Il and his lieutenants seemingly assumed, but its potential destabilizing effects were unlikely to be noticed until much later. In addition, China had become increasingly involved in the North Korean situation, so North Korean diplomats could and obviously did hope to resume their old game of skillfully manipulating rival sponsors. But then things suddenly took an ugly turn.

Between 2005 and 2006, the South Korean public became increasingly dissatisfied with the Roh Moo Hyun administration. Rightly or wrongly, Roh's government was seen as responsible for an economic slowdown. It also became clear that the noble past of pro-democracy fighters did not shield them from the scent of corruption. The political right, at the same time, acquired charismatic leadership in the shape of the former Seoul Mayor Lee Myung Bak (nicknamed "the bulldozer," due to his passion for demolition and construction). By late 2007 few doubted that the right was destined to win the next elections in a landslide. In a last-ditch attempt to save his legacy and the Sunshine Policy, President Roh rushed to have his own inter-Korean summit, which took place in Pyongyang in October 2007. Among other things, he promised to open another industrial zone along the lines of Kaesŏng. But it was too late. The right triumphed in the elections as expected, and in February 2008 Lee Myung Bak became the new president of the Republic of Korea. Tellingly, the domestic North Korean media did not report the results of the elections for some two months.

The issue of North Korea remained marginal during the campaign. The foreign media usually only bother to mention Korea in relation to some North Korea–induced crisis, so people outside the Korean peninsula tend to assume that South Koreans see the North Korean issue as a defining or at least very important part of their country's political agenda. This has long ceased to be the case. A poll taken before the 2007 presidential elections encapsulates this spirit quite well. In the poll, potential South Korean voters were asked to name "the most important task of the next president." Of the participants, 36.1 percent cited "economic development and the creation of jobs"; 27.4 percent advocated "closing the income gap and improving welfare"; 22.4 percent wanted "political and social unity"; 11.2 percent wanted "political reform and leadership"; and only a meager 2.4 percent said that the next president should, first of all, concentrate on "improving inter-Korean relations."[19]

Though the issue was not central to Lee's election campaign, Lee Myung Bak and his administration had rather different ideas about how to deal with the North. He accused the two previous administrations of propping up the North Korean regime and making it even more dangerous. He also emphasized the need for strict reciprocity in dealing with North Korea—aid should be conditioned on meaningful political concessions from the North.

These views were epitomized in the "Vision 3000" plan, officially known as "Vision 3000, Denuclearization, Openness." Vision 3000 sets out a plan to develop a denuclearized North Korea. With North Korea's disarmament, the South promised, the North would be flooded with aid on a hitherto unthinkable scale. Within merely a decade, South Korean aid would help to increase per-capita annual income to some US$3,000, approximately three times the current level (which, by the way, would be achievable only with annual growth rates exceeding 20 percent—hardly a realistic assumption). As the name itself suggested, the North Korean government was expected to improve economic efficiency by initiating Chinese-style reforms.

Needless to say, this proposal was clearly a nonstarter and was rejected outright. On May 30, 2008, the official North Korean wire agency, KCNA, described the "No nukes, opening and 3,000 dollars" (this is how the official name of the "Vision 3000" plan is rendered into North Korean English newspeak) in its highly idiosyncratic English:

> No nukes, opening and 3,000 dollars peddled by traitor Lee Myung-bak as a policy toward the north suffices to prove that he is desperately pursuing the confrontation between the north and the south in ideology. [...] Lee's pragmatism is little short of a hideous act of treachery as it is intended to sell off the national interests to the

outsiders and make the dignity and sovereignty of the nation their plaything.

Soon afterward, President Barack Obama took office. It was initially assumed that Obama would pay little attention to the North—and this was bad news for Pyongyang.

Faced with this new and unfavorable situation, the North Koreans resorted to the tactics they had used in the past with so much success. Obviously, North Korean strategists decided that it was high time to manufacture a new crisis—as usual, to squeeze necessary concessions from their adversaries/donors.

The first incident took place in July 2008, when a South Korean housewife was shot dead in the early morning while walking on the beach in the Kŭmgang tourist zone. It remains an open question as to whether the shooting was indeed an accident or a part of a North Korean tension-building strategy. At any rate, the North Koreans took an unusually tough stance when it came to investigating the incident, and the Kŭmgang resort's operations were halted.

In November 2008 it was the turn of the Kaesŏng city tours. At the time, anti-Pyongyang activist groups had begun to send balloons with leaflets into North Korean territory. The North Korean government demanded the immediate cessation of such activities, and when Seoul refused, the North Korean authorities halted tours to Kaesŏng. In order to further increase the pressure on Seoul, they also introduced measures that greatly restricted activities in the KIZ.

North Korean strategists seemingly assumed that the deterioration in North-South relations would make the South Korean public uneasy and thus force the Lee administration into adopting a softer approach. This was a miscalculation. None of the tourist projects were of economic importance to the South, and the average South Korean voter cared much less about the North than North Korean policymakers assumed. Hints of the possible closure of the Kaesŏng Industrial Zone failed to produce the desired result as well, since the project was (and remains) very marginal to the South Korean economy.

At the same time, North Korean strategists began to raise the stakes in their relations with the United States. In April 2009 they again launched a long-distance missile that could theoretically hit targets in Alaska and Hawaii—that is, if it worked properly. Instead, the launch, like the previous long-range missile tests, was a failure. Nonetheless, the North Korean media told the public that Juche science had again succeeded in putting a satellite into space. To further emphasize the message, the North went one step further and in May 2009 conducted a second nuclear test. Unlike the 2006 test, the second nuclear test was a technical success and demonstrated to the world that North Korea had indeed developed a workable nuclear device.

The UN Security Council produced another stern resolution (Resolution 1874), once again duly supported by the Chinese. However, merely a few months later, Chinese Prime Minister Wen Jiabao visited Pyongyang, and Chinese aid to the North was increased further. After the nuclear test, the volume of trade between China and North Korea began to grow with remarkable speed, tripling between 2006 and 2012 (before falling in the first half of 2013).

As was expected by those accustomed to North Korea's negotiating style, the barrage of threats and bellicosity was followed by a charm offensive. In July 2009 the flood of macabre abuse aimed at Seoul and Washington suddenly ceased, and, all of a sudden, the North Korean media started to express their goodwill toward both South Korea and the United States.

As one sign of goodwill, Pyongyang agreed to release two US journalists who in the spring of 2009 had crossed the Sino-Korean border. They had spent a few months under arrest before an "unofficial" US delegation led by former President Clinton flew to Pyongyang and negotiated their release. The Hyundai Asan chairwoman also came back from Pyongyang with the Hyundai employee who had allegedly plotted the defection of a North Korean female worker.

This "crisis manufacturing strategy" had worked well in the past, but by 2008–2009 both Washington and Seoul had had enough. This time, neither was going to reward North Korea merely for its willingness to reduce tension and return to the status quo.

To a very large extent, earlier US willingness to give concessions was based on the assumption that the North Korean nuclear issue could be resolved through diplomacy. In other words, it was assumed by many in Washington that the North Korean government could be convinced and/or bribed into surrendering its nuclear weapons. This was (and still is) a misconception, of course, since the North Korean government never had either the intention or, frankly, a valid reason to surrender its nuclear weapons. However, for a while this illusion was shared by many in Washington, making negotiations and concessions possible. Such hopes disappeared, however, by 2008.

The United States has more recently taken an approach often described as "strategic patience" (also known as "benign neglect"). The term implies that the United States will not do anything of significance until the North demonstrates its sincere commitment to denuclearization by taking certain measures that will clearly and irreversibly diminish its nuclear capabilities. The approach of Seoul has been even harsher.

By early 2010, the North found itself in a new and unfavorable situation, with both major adversaries-cum-donors suddenly becoming unreceptive to the customary mixture of threats, tension-building provocations, charm offensives, and minor concessions. Pyongyang's strategists therefore decided to increase pressure by reminding the world of their ability to create additional problems for the United States and the ROK.

This might seem illogical, but such an approach is rational, since North Korea does not risk too much by driving tensions higher. Certainly, North Korean policymakers know that if a war were to break out, they would lose it quickly. But they also know that war would be prohibitively costly for democratically elected politicians in Seoul and Washington.

At the same time, North Korea might actually have advantages over the South at the level of border skirmishes and small-scale raids. The North is aware that the South is incapable of inflicting damage on anything of value to the North Korean regime. If a major exchange of fire were to occur in the DMZ or the NLL (the disputed Northern Limit Line maritime border that divides the two Koreas in the Yellow Sea), the South Korean military might be perfectly capable of sinking a few North Korean patrol boats or wiping out a coastal defense battery or two or perhaps even destroying a command headquarters, complete with a few dozen unlucky colonels and a couple of one-star generals. However, neither the rusty vessels of World War II vintage nor the lives of humble colonels are of much significance to Pyongyang. The domestic political impact of such a military misadventure is also not going to be large, since the government-controlled media will either hide news of any disaster or even present a humiliating defeat as a great triumph.

At the same time, such an exchange of strikes and counterstrikes might have a significant political impact on South Korea. First, South Korean voters are not fond of tension, and they might, in the long run, penalize their government for its inability to keep North Korea quiet and non-threatening. Second, the South Korean economy is very dependent on foreign markets and foreign businessmen, who do not take well to media reports of a war that is, allegedly, "likely to erupt in Korea next week." Such reports are gross exaggerations, to be sure, but overseas car importers are not supposed to understand the intricacies of the inter-Korean politics better than your average journalist.

This asymmetry means that North Korea can raise the stakes with relative impunity when it chooses to do so—as long as the risk of skirmishes escalating to a full-scale war remains low.

With this in mind, Pyongyang simultaneously pursued two tension-building programs in 2010, one directed at Seoul and the other at Washington. The message they intended to deliver was still the same, however: Pyongyang wanted to show that it could not just be ignored and neglected, and that it would be cheaper and safer to pay North Korea off than suffer the trouble it was (and is) capable of creating.

In order to drive this message home in Seoul, the North Korean military undertook two important and somewhat unprecedented operations. In March 2010 North Korean submariners torpedoed the South Korean naval corvette, the *Cheonan,* in a bold raid. It sank immediately, taking forty-six lives, roughly half of its crew. A few months later in November, North Korean artillery shelled the island of Yeongpyeong, located in disputed waters near the NLL (South Korea's claim to the island itself is not disputed by the North). It was the first major artillery attack on South Korean territory in decades.

In dealing with the United States, Pyongyang chose to target Washington's usual weak spot—that is, fear of nuclear proliferation. In 2002 accusations of uranium enrichment led to the repudiation of previous US-NK agreements. Until 2009 North Korea vehemently denied the very existence of a highly enriched uranium (HEU) program. In 2009, however, the existence of the HEU program was acknowledged, and in November 2010 Pyongyang extended an invitation to Dr. Hecker, former director of the US Department of Energy nuclear research site at Los Alamos, to visit their nuclear facilities. They showed him around a modern, fully operational (and very large) uranium enrichment facility. Of course, this once again demonstrated that North Korean diplomats had been lying all those years. Hardly anyone was surprised by such a discovery, however.

THE ENTRY OF CHINA

Another important change of the last decade was the re-emergence of China in North Korean politics. In the early 1990s China obviously wrote Pyongyang off and perhaps did not expect the Kim family regime to last for more than a few years. But from around 2001, trade and general economic interactions between North Korea and China began to grow, and this growth accelerated around 2006, when the first nuclear test led to a tightening of the sanctions regime. Chinese dignitaries began to frequent Pyongyang, and in the last years of his life, Kim Jong Il visited China at least once a year. By 2010 annual trade between North Korea and China had for the first time exceeded North Korea's trade with all other countries combined—and then continued its growth.

China is often described in the media as "North Korea's ally." This is not truly the case, since in reality the Chinese—general public and officials alike—tend to look at North Korea with bemused disdain. It reminds them of parts of their own past that few if any Chinese people want to return to. The Chinese are often annoyed by North Korea's provocative behavior that jeopardizes stability in the region. Most Chinese scholars and scholar-officials behind closed doors agree that *in the long run* unification of Korea under Seoul's control appears to be likely, almost inevitable (this position was confirmed by WikiLeaks cables, but this was hardly a revelation for those who interact with the Chinese frequently). However, China would prefer this long run to be very long indeed—and with good reason. For Chinese policymakers, all things considered, a nuclear-armed North Korea seems to be a lesser evil than an unstable or collapsing North Korea (and, perhaps, even less an evil than a Korea unified under a US-friendly Seoul government).

Chinese goals on the Korean peninsula form a hierarchy. To simplify things a bit, first, China needs stability in and around Korea. Second, China would prefer to see the Korean peninsula divided. The desire to stop North Korea from developing nukes comes as a rather distant third.

Beijing's greatest fear seems to be the instability that would be caused by North Korea's implosion. China sees such a prospect as dangerous because it will have to deal with refugee flows, the threat of WMD proliferation, and geopolitical uncertainties of different kinds—like, say, the smuggling of nuclear material to (or through) Chinese territory.

The Chinese government also has valid domestic reasons to prefer the status quo. Chinese leaders are well aware that the domestic support for their own regime overwhelmingly depends on their ability to maintain a very high level of economic growth. Any disturbances in adjacent areas might divert resources and, in the worst case scenario, might even trigger some unrest in China itself.

The second most important concern of Beijing's policymakers is to keep Korea divided (if not forever, at least for the longest possible time). North Korea constitutes a buffer zone on the borders of China and, official pro-unification rhetoric notwithstanding, the emergence of a unified Korean state would not serve Beijing's long-term interests. There is little, if any, doubt that such a unified state would be dominated by South Korea. Unification, therefore, will produce a democratic and strongly nationalist state, likely to be a US ally, on China's borders.

The continued division of Korea also provides China with manifold economic advantages. The dire economic situation of the North Korean state allows Chinese companies to get access to North Korean mineral resources and transport infrastructure at minimal cost. It is also possible that over the next decade, China will begin to make use of North Korea's cheap but relatively skilled labor force. Needless to say, in a unified Korea, labor will not remain cheap, and it will be much more difficult for Chinese businesses to acquire mining rights.

Last but not least, China also worries about the influence such a unified Korean state would exercise on the ethnic Korean minority in China—and the quasi-official territorial claims frequently voiced in Seoul[20] do not help to alleviate these worries, either. One should remember that a significant number of South Koreans, including several politicians, have openly expressed reservations about the 1909 treaty between Korea (then under Japanese domination) and China that defines the current border between the two countries. They claim that a large area of Kando (Jiandao in Chinese) in Northeast China should rightfully belong to Korea, although the area is currently home to millions of Chinese citizens. In 2004 up to a dozen ROK National Assembly members established a group solely dedicated to the promotion of the Kando claims.[21] More radical nationalist Korean groups continue to make loud territorial claims to even greater parts of Manchuria and Russia's Maritime Provinces.[22]

The third strategic aim of China is denuclearization. Admittedly, the nuclear issue is less important to China than to the United States. Nonetheless, it is still significant. According to the Nuclear Non-Proliferation Treaty of 1968, China is one of five recognized nuclear-weapon-possessing states. This makes China a member of a small and highly exclusive international club, giving it little reason to welcome dilution of the power accorded by nuclear weapon possession. More troubling is that North Korea's nuclear ambitions could potentially trigger a nuclear arms race in East Asia, with South Korea and Japan developing nuclear weapons as well—a prospect that would not be welcomed by Beijing.

Additionally, economic considerations are often discussed when it comes to Chinese goals in Korea. Indeed, China dominates North Korea's foreign trade almost completely. In 1995 the trade volume between the two countries was $0.55 billion. By 2000 it had decreased slightly, to $0.49 billion. From there it steadily grew. By 2005 the volume had tripled, reaching $1.6 billion; over the next five years it tripled again, reaching the level of $5.6 billion by 2011, increasing from $3.4 billion in 2010.[23]

Currently, it is difficult to know to what extent such growth is driven by strategic considerations in Beijing, and to what extent it comes "naturally," as a byproduct of China's own unstoppable growth and its appetite for natural resources. It seems that both the strategic considerations of the Chinese state and the purely economic interests of Chinese businesses have conspired to bring about this growth.

However, in spite of this impressive growth in trade volume, in purely economic terms North Korea is of secondary importance to China. Loud talk of a Chinese "economic takeover of North Korea" should not obscure the fact that the volume of trade between the North and China in 2013 was a paltry $6.45 billion, while the volume of trade between South Korea and China is in excess of $250 billion—an impressive fortyfold difference.[24] To put things in a more global perspective, China's trade with Chile ($35 billion in 2013) is roughly five times larger than its trade with North Korea, even though Chile has a smaller population and, needless to say, is far more distant both politically and geographically.

To the extent that China's economic interests exist, they can be divided into three groups. First, Chinese companies are interested in North Korea's mineral resources. North Korean deposits of coal, iron ore, and copper might not be exceptionally rich by world standards, but nonetheless are of considerable value to the resource-hungry China. Thus, over the last decade, Chinese companies have negotiated a number of mining concessions.

Second, China is interested in the use of North Korea's transportation infrastructure. The three northeastern provinces of China are landlocked, so if a Chinese company in the vast and populous area wants to ship goods overseas, the nearest port is either Dandong or Dalian, about a thousand kilometers away. China recently obtained the right to use the port of Rason, potentially leading to big savings for nearby Chinese businesses.

Third, Chinese small businesses are increasingly interested in outsourcing to North Korea, where wages are well below what would be acceptable for unskilled and semi-skilled workers in China. In North Korea, local girls are willing to work at a Chinese-operated sweatshop for $20–25 a month. In China, an entrepreneur would have to pay some $100 a month for the same job.[25]

With this in mind, it is not surprising that this growing economic dependency on China worries Pyongyang. For decades, the North Korean government has been very good at avoiding exclusive dependence on just one donor, since Pyongyang politicians have demonstrable adroitness at using donor country rivalries to North Korea's advantage.

Therefore, one should not be surprised that China is not treated too favorably by internal North Korean propaganda (this was also the case for the Soviet Union when it was the major donor to North Korea in the 1980s), and North Korean minders even express their dislike for the Chinese to (sort of) trusted foreign visitors. The North Korean public and, especially, North Korean officials are frequently reminded by their superiors that they should not get too cozy with the Chinese. In 2007 North Korea's state media reported on alleged spies of an unnamed foreign country being unmasked by the North Korean security service. No details were given at the time, but hints indicated that these real or alleged spies were working for China.

The North Korean elite has good reason to be cautious. It is true that China would prefer to see Korea divided and hence favors a separate regime in Pyongyang, but this does not mean China has to maintain the Kim family in power. China seems to be the only power that has the potential to intervene in North Korean domestic affairs when and if it sees some serious need to do so. The North Korean leadership seems to take seriously the probability of another Chinese-backed conspiracy, somewhat similar to the August conspiracy of 1956. Currently, it appears that China is not eager to intervene directly in the internal politics of Pyongyang, since it has no reason to jeopardize the status quo that, on balance, serves China's interests reasonably well. But things may very well change eventually.

As we will see later, there might be situations in which the North Korean elite shifts its attitude toward China. Still, this will most likely be a last resort—if, for instance, an acute domestic crisis arises. For the time being, however, Pyongyang clearly prefers to keep Beijing at arm's length.

The degree of not-so-hidden mistrust between Pyongyang and Beijing is well demonstrated by what David Straub once aptly described as "the strategic partnership fantasy," quite widespread in North Korean ruling circles. In spite of all the anti-American rhetoric, frequently of almost comical bellicosity, in confidential talks North Korean dignitaries often suggest that North Korea does not really mind becoming an ally of the United States, thus helping Washington to deter China (for a hefty reward, needless to say). When the author himself first heard such remarks from a North Korean official, he was taken aback, but then it became clear that such hopes are regularly expressed to foreigners, including influential Western diplomats or ex-diplomats (of whom David Straub is one). This dramatic reorientation is not going to happen, to be sure, but the existence of such unrealistic expectations speaks volumes about the actual attitude toward China in Pyongyang's ruling circles.

Many in the United States, especially during the last few years, have expressed a hope that China could use its alleged influence in Pyongyang in order to somehow press North Korea into denuclearization. Alas, this hope is unfounded since China has very limited leverage when it comes to dealing with North Korea. As all major partners of North Korea (including Seoul, Moscow, and Washington) have learned to their dismay over the decades that it has existed, significant economic involvement with and assistance to North Korea does not translate into comparable political leverage.

Theoretically, China could inflict significant economic pain on North Korea by halting aid and putting severe restrictions on cross-border trade. If China wished to do so, it could plunge North Korea into another economic disaster that might even exceed the famine of the late 1990s. However, China cannot fine-tune North Korean politics and squeeze concessions on the issues North Korean leaders see as vital for their survival. A senior South Korean diplomat once told the present author, "China doesn't have leverage when it comes to dealing with North Korea. What it has is not a lever, but rather a hammer. China can knock North Korea unconscious if it wishes, but it cannot really manipulate its behavior."

Contrary to the expectations of some optimists in Washington and Seoul, China has little reason to use this "hammer." The problems created by North Korea's risky behavior and its nuclear program are seen in Beijing as less significant than the problems likely to be created by a serious domestic crisis in North Korea and/or by the emergence of a unified Korean state on China's border. China prefers to maintain a status quo, which has many downsides, but on balance seems to be better than any of the likely alternatives.

The Contours of a Future: What Might Happen to North Korea in the Next Two Decades

Let us be frank: predicting the future makes fools of us all. History has a very long (and still growing) list of prophets whose confident predictions have proven to be completely wrong. Many widely anticipated events never happened, while a number of pivotal changes came absolutely out of the blue. The collapse of the Soviet Union took most by complete surprise, while perennial predictions of the impending collapse of Western capitalism have thus far proven to be false.

Having covered his back with these necessary preliminaries, the author nonetheless intends to engage in some speculations on the possible future (or rather futures) of North Korea. Of course, the reader should not forget that this discussion is speculative, so expect the author to make generous use of such adverbs as "plausibly," "probably," and "perhaps," as well as such verbs as "might" and "seem."

It appears that the future development of North Korea will consist of three stages. The first stage is the present stage of stability. However, the current system is unsustainable in the long run, while reforms are very risky, so this stability is likely to end in a dramatic crisis.

There are a number of triggers that might unleash this crisis, as well as a number of ways in which it may unfold. However, North Korea will probably not remain unstable for any length of time. There are good reasons to believe that the crisis period, as chaotic and dangerous and violent as it might be, will be relatively short, so some sort of new and relatively stable political and economic regime will emerge.

Perhaps many members of the North Korean leadership would like to see the complete revival of Kim Il Sung's North Korea. However, such wishes will never be realized, as no amount of government effort can possibly roll the situation back to what it used to be under Kim Il Sung in the 1960s and 1970s. In those days, North Korea's version of "national Stalinism" was viable because, at that time, many North Koreans were willing to accept and even support the system and also because Korea still had a lot of untapped resources that could be mobilized for the needs of the industrial economy. The international environment was also very different half a century ago. In the 1950s North Korea boasted the most advanced economy of continental East Asia and was surrounded by poor and dictatorial regimes. Last but not least, it was so much easier to keep people isolated and ill-informed before the advent of the digital age. However, things are different now. Thus, as stated earlier, the North Korean leadership finds itself at a crossroads. It can continue along the same path, postponing a collapse that is likely to happen before too long. Alternatively, and more likely, it can take a new path, attempting reforms. The latter may ensure the regime's viability, but more likely will hasten its demise.

But how will the regime collapse in a country without civil movements or organized opposition?

Currently, it seems that there are three likely scenarios that might trigger a dramatic crisis. These scenarios are as follows: (1) factional clashes in the leadership; (2) spontaneous uprisings; (3) the contagion of unrest in China. Of course, a combination of all of the above or some other unforeseen development is also possible.

The outbreak of serious factional infighting within the top leadership might become a trigger for the disintegration of the regime. Such an outbreak might take the form of a purge of prominent officials, or it might lead to an attempted coup (successful or not—does not really matter). The purge and execution of Chang Sŏng-t'aek has shown that such a possibility is real.

So far, North Korean leaders have understood the need to maintain unity and not rock the boat. However, nothing is eternal and the next generation of leaders might lack an understanding of how dangerous an open feud could become. Alternatively, a loser in a factional clash might decide to go down fighting and make the conflict quite public and even violent. Understandably, if a general believes that he will face an execution squad tomorrow, he is not going to care a great deal about the regime's long-term stability—and the Chang Sŏng-t'aek affair has shown that purged officials can indeed be put to death. In another twist of the same scenario, some foreign power (in all likelihood, China—nobody else is in a position to stage such an operation) might decide to encourage a group of ambitious rising stars to challenge the old guard.

Whatever the reason, such an open clash might jeopardize the regime's stability. A lack of unity at the top will be perceived by the North Korean people as a sign of the elite's inability to keep the situation under control. In this situation, people who would otherwise remain docile will start expressing their grievances—with predictably dangerous consequences for the regime's future.

The second possible scenario for the regime's endgame is a spontaneous outbreak of popular discontent—a local riot quickly developing into a nationwide revolutionary movement, somewhat similar to what we saw in 2011 in the Arab world. The public suicide of an unsuccessful fruit peddler in a countryside Tunisian town sparked a revolt that in no time wiped out many Arab dictatorships and seriously damaged others. Similarly, the Ceaușescu regime in Romania, arguably the most repressive of all the Communist regimes of the late 1980s in Eastern Europe, was doomed when the security police attempted to arrest a popular priest in the small town of Timisoara.

At present, North Koreans appear to be too terrified, isolated, and distrustful of one another to emulate the Tunisians of 2011 or the Romanians of 1989. Nonetheless, control is steadily getting weaker, fear is dying, and knowledge of available alternatives is spreading, so in the longer run, such an endgame is possible.

The third scenario is the spread of some unrest in China—the only country where an outbreak of civil disobedience or a riot might produce some impact on North Korea. Right now, the Chinese "developmental dictatorship" appears to be stable, but if a major challenge to the regime arises (due to a financial crisis, for instance), it is likely to produce a deep impact on North Korea as well.

Of course, these scenarios could easily blur into one, and the present author is not sufficiently vain to believe that he has listed all of the possibilities in this short sketch. On top of that, neighboring powers might be entangled with such developments as well, even though, at present, outside players would prefer to steer clear of North Korean perils. Nonetheless, one thing appears to be certain: due to the peculiarities of North Korea's domestic and international situation, neither a gradual and manageable transformation of the regime nor its perpetual survival appears to be a likely outcome. Eventually, it will go down in crisis—in all probability, suddenly and, alas, violently.

There are at least two pieces of bad news that relate to the previously outlined possibilities.

First, unfortunately for us outside observers, North Korea will probably look perfectly stable on one Monday morning, only to become a chaotic mess by the Friday afternoon of the same week.

Second, the coming collapse might become quite violent—there is little reason to expect a North Korean revolution to be bloodless. The major factor is the difference between the interests of the ruling elite and a majority of the population. It is likely that in the event of a crisis, a majority of North Koreans will demand unification with the prosperous and free South. They will probably act not so much out of democratic or nationalist idealism (even though both are likely to be present), but out of material considerations. Since the gap in living standards between South Korea and the North is at least the same as the current gap between the United States and Vietnam—and perhaps much larger—the pull of glittering South Korean prosperity will be irresistible.

Conversely, the North Korean elite is likely to have very different opinions about the subject. As has been mentioned previously, these people understand that in case of regime collapse, they will not be able to maintain their privileges. Many of them are afraid that if unification happens, they will be persecuted by victorious Southerners or perhaps even lynched by angry mobs of their own compatriots. These fears might be exaggerated, but they are not completely groundless.

Therefore, the elite might choose to fight, under the assumption that they will be fighting for their lives and the lives of their loved ones. The elite constitute only a small part of the population—if we include the security police, elite units of the military, and mid- to high-level party functionaries as well as their families, the total is likely to be one to two million people or some 5 percent to 7 percent of the entire population. However, these people know how to handle arms, are organized, and are also better informed and have more social skills than humble commoners. There is also good reason to suspect that they have already made some preparations for guerrilla war, and a fair amount of arms are at their ready disposal.

The elite's initial instinct will be to put down riots and unrest, butcher the ringleaders, and attempt to restore what the Kim family regime defines as "law and order." If unsuccessful, they will beg for Chinese help. And if all else fails, they will literally fight to the death, with all the troops they can summon to their side and all the arms they can get.

However, there is good news: instability in North Korea, while highly probable in the long run, is unlikely to last for long. For a while, the country might even look a bit like Somalia, where rival cliques wage a violent struggle for control over a few remaining objects of economic or strategic value. However, even if that were to be North Korea's fate, it would not last long.

North Korea is no Somalia. It is located in the middle of a highly developed region, and the combination of its small size and long coastline make the projection of force relatively easy. It has considerable nuclear stockpiles and a large WMD arsenal that no major international player would like to see left unattended. In other words, it seems that a major crisis in North Korea will be seen as a clear and present danger by the international community, as well as major regional players. Therefore, an international or unilateral peacekeeping operation of some kind appears to be likely—even though currently none of the potential "pacifiers" is too happy about such a prospect.

In the current situation, there are three different kinds of peacekeeping operation that are possible. First, a South Korea operation, launched unilaterally (probably with some US involvement). Second, a unilateral Chinese action is possible—though many powers in the region and the wider world would probably not see it as a "peacekeeping operation." Finally, an international one is also possible, perhaps mandated by the UN.

A South Korean intervention seems to be the logical place for us to start our discussion. Few people outside the Korean peninsula realize this, but from Seoul's official point of view, no North Korean state has ever existed. According to Article 3 of the ROK Constitution, "the territory of the Republic of Korea shall consist of the Korean peninsula and its adjacent islands." Therefore, the northern part of the Korean peninsula is legally the sovereign territory of the ROK (at least so far as the South Korean constitutional court is concerned anyway), with the Democratic People's Republic of Korea (North Korea's official name) a breakaway regime without a shred of legal standing. Officially, South Korea goes to great lengths to emphasize that North Korea is not actually another state, but merely a special region within the borders of ROK (North Korea does the same in regard to the South). Suffice it to say, even economic exchanges between the two Korean states are not officially described as "exports" and "imports"—a special word had to be coined, to emphasize that such exchanges are not, really, international in nature.

This sounds fine on paper, but it may become convoluted if North Korea collapses—not least because of the profound changes that have happened within South Korean society over the last couple of decades. The South Korean public is still committed to unification, but this commitment is increasingly theoretical. There is little doubt that the South Korean public will approve a unilateral action if a mild and nonviolent "velvet revolution" erupts in Pyongyang, so the people of the North will welcome South Korean tanks waving ROK national flags and showering them with azaleas.

However, such a rosy outcome is unlikely to occur. Indeed, South Korean forces might have to fight their way to Pyongyang against the determined resistance of Kim loyalists. This will not look pretty, and given the current mood in South Korean society, one cannot help but doubt whether a South Korean government will have the political will to dispatch troops to Pyongyang if the threat of large numbers of causalities looms. The present author has privately asked a number of South Korean officials and military officers whether, in their opinion, a unilateral operation would be possible under such circumstances. Nearly all of them think that the chances are at best relatively low.

Chinese unilateral intervention is another possibility. So far, Chinese policy on the Korean peninsula has been largely aimed at keeping the North afloat (at moderate cost). However, if the situation in the North were to destabilize, China would have to decide whether it is willing to get the North out of trouble by committing many more resources and perhaps even military force. As we have seen earlier, if a crisis were to occur, a very significant part of the current North Korean elite is bound to side with China, begging the Chinese government for help. They would much prefer a Chinese-controlled satellite regime to the alternative of unification under South Korean aegis.

Will China meet such demands? Chinese intervention will restore stability in North Korea, thus preventing a refugee crisis and greatly curtailing the likelihood of uncontrolled nuclear proliferation. It will also ensure that North Korea continues to exist as a strategically useful buffer zone and that Chinese corporations are able to maintain their privileged access to North Korea's resources.

However, for China, these geopolitical gains come with a large price tag. Chinese analysts themselves have explicitly described the possible sources of complications to the present author.

To start with, a Chinese takeover of the North and the emergence of a Beijing-controlled regime there will produce a tidal wave of anti-Chinese sentiment in South Korea. Even as the South Korean public demonstrate little actual enthusiasm for unification, they are still likely to be outraged by a Chinese intervention in the North. China may instantly become the major target of Korea's nationalist passions, and the ROK-US alliance will be strengthened dramatically.

Inside North Korea, nationalism will emerge as well. It is almost certain that a China-controlled satellite regime will embark on a path of market-oriented reforms. Being backed by Chinese subsidies (and tanks), such a regime can afford to take the political risks that are prohibitively high for the present North Korean government. Reforms will likely lead to an economic revival of the country and a dramatic improvement of living standards for the North Korean population. Nonetheless, such new wealth and individual freedoms—however considerable—will not transform the majority of North Koreans into supporters of the regime, let alone admirers of their Chinese overlords.

The Soviet experience in Eastern Europe serves as a subject lesson. In 1956 Soviet tanks crushed a popular rebellion and installed a pro-Soviet client regime in Hungary. This regime was more successful than anyone had anticipated and soon made Hungary, according to a popular joke of the time, "the merriest barracks of the Soviet camp." Soviet subsidies played a major role in the consumerist boom there, but this did not make either the Soviet Union or its Hungarian clients popular with the Hungarian people. Common Hungarians still despised their government and blamed the Russians for more or less everything that did not go right there. A similar, albeit less pronounced, picture could be found in other parts of Soviet-controlled Eastern Europe. We have little reason to believe that Chinese intervention in North Korea will prove to be any more popular (more so since the average North Korean will be looking to the free, prosperous, and "purely national" South with admiration—and the gap between the two Koreas will remain huge for a couple of decades at least).

Last but not least, an open intervention into a North Korean domestic crisis will deliver a heavy blow to the myth of the "peaceful rise of China"— a myth that plays a pivotal role in Beijing's global image-building efforts. All of China's neighbors will be very concerned by the news of Chinese intervention, since they will see themselves as possibly the next victims of China's rediscovered "imperial ambitions." This will lead many of them to improve their relations with the United States. They will take measures to ensure that the Chinese will not have leverage over their domestic political situations. Beijing will, of course, not welcome such developments.

Problems like these might cause Beijing to embrace the third option— an international peacekeeping operation in what is now North Korea. The

United Nations could authorize such an operation, but in practice the slow and unwieldy UN bureaucracy is hardly able to handle the unpredictable situation fast enough. Therefore, for all practical purposes, such an operation would probably be best handled by the Six-Party Talks mechanism—in other words, by coordinated efforts by South Korea, China, the United States, Russia, and Japan (a UN mandate might still be a good way to make the operation sufficiently legitimate).

Such an international peacekeeping operation will probably be acceptable to all major players, since it will help to address the major concerns of all parties involved. The political damage will be mitigated, too: even if China is clearly in the driver's seat, the UN mandate will largely protect it from accusations of "neo-imperialist designs."

For South Korea, an international peacekeeping operation might be acceptable as well. The mandate of the peacekeeping forces is likely to be explicitly restricted, so that after a certain period, the forces would be withdrawn. At this point (given current circumstances), one can be almost certain that North Koreans will overwhelmingly support unification with the South (or, at least, for some kind of Korean federation). In other words, a UN-mandated operation will ensure that Chinese forces, in due time, will leave the peninsula.

For the United States, an international operation would also be preferable to a unilateral Chinese intervention. It would deliver both outcomes that the United States wants most in Northeast Asia: first, it will denuclearize the North; second, it will eventually lead to the emergence of a Seoul-dominated Korean state.

For both the long-term strategic interests of South Korea and the United States, as well as for the majority of the North Korean population, the emergence of a pro-Chinese satellite regime in North Korea will still be better than indefinite continuation of the status quo. Nonetheless, the unification of Korea should still be seen as the most preferable outcome. Therefore, one should be ready to consider measures that will persuade China that a unified Korea is more acceptable than intervention.

First, China should be assured that a unified Korea would not become a strategic bridgehead for the US military in continental Northeast Asia.

For example, if the ROK and United States made a joint statement promising that, upon unification, no US forces and/or US military installations would ever be located north of the present-day DMZ area, it would help to ameliorate Chinese strategic concerns.

The United States will probably find such concessions acceptable. On balance, Washington will gain much from Seoul-led unification of the Korean peninsula. The emergence of a unified democratic (and nationalist) state on China's border will also be conducive to US national interests. Therefore, relatively minor concessions concerning troops' number and location are likely to be seen as an acceptable price to pay.

We should also not forget that another problem must be taken care of in case of a "unification crisis." Recurrent support of irredentism in Northeastern China and semi-official claims about alleged Korean territorial rights to large chunks of Chinese territory do not escape the notice of Beijing—and strengthen their suspicion that a unified Korea would strive to ferment discontent in the borderland areas of China. It would therefore help if the ROK government explicitly stated that earlier agreements pertaining to Sino-Korean borders will be respected by a unified Korea.

It will also be necessary to explicitly assure Beijing that the government of a unified Korea will respect and honor all Chinese concessions and mining rights that were granted by the North Korean state. Many of these deals were signed under dubious circumstances and might appear redolent of the unequal treaties of the nineteenth century. Nonetheless, it remains an important step toward winning Chinese support—and this support is vital for Korean unification.

CHAPTER 6

What to Do about the North?

Let us begin with the bad news: the North Korean problem has no simple or quick solutions. Negotiations and concessions will not help much, while pressure and sanctions will be even less useful. We should therefore brace ourselves for a long, winding, and, occasionally, dangerous ride.

This does not mean that the situation is beyond hope. North Korea's leaders are fighting a losing battle, trying to preserve what is, essentially, unsustainable. Eventually, they will lose, and the outside world (well, those in the outside world who want North Korea to change) can do something to facilitate developments and make sure that unavoidable changes will be less rough and violent. Many measures are simple, cheap, and useful but will require a great deal of long-term commitment and a touch of counter-intuitive thinking. Alas, both qualities are somewhat lacking in modern-day democracies.

WHY STICKS ARE NOT BIG ENOUGH

Throughout the past two decades, since the emergence of the North Korean nuclear issue, US strategy has oscillated between two positions.

There are soft-liners who believe that if the Pyongyang regime is given sufficient monetary rewards, political concessions, and security guarantees, it will ultimately abandon its nuclear ambitions and perhaps revive its economy through Chinese-style reforms—thus becoming a "normal state." They insist that Pyongyang should be treated gently and given concessions and monetary rewards. According to this logic, Pyongyang should be persuaded that compromise will serve its own best interests. In the aftermath of the second and third nuclear tests as well as other events during the time period between 2009 and 2013, the number of doves in Washington and Seoul has shrunk dramatically, but the soft-line option still remains on the sidelines and might eventually regain popularity.

Their opponents are hard-line hawkish believers in the power of sanctions and pressure (these beliefs are often strengthened by the recurrent hope that the Pyongyang regime is on the brink of collapse). They assume that pressure will eventually either cause Pyongyang to denuclearize or push it to extinction (or both). They believe that economic hardship and perhaps even fear of military reprisals will make North Korea surrender its nuclear program.

Given the nature of democratic politics, which regularly puts new (and not necessarily experienced) people into important jobs, there is little doubt that both approaches will keep competing in the foreseeable future. Consequently, US policy (and, for that matter, the policy of Seoul) will continue to oscillate between these two extremes. This is not good news since experience demonstrates that neither approach is going to work. Neither pressure nor concessions will accelerate the delivery of the desired outcome—a nonnuclear and developing North Korea.

Regardless of what hawks say, threats or use of military force against North Korea is not credible—even if one forgets the legal niceties that any such action would clearly be defined as an act of aggression. Surgical strikes and air raids against nuclear installations (akin to the Israeli strikes on Iraq's nuclear research center in 1981) will not work. It is too late for this now. The weapons-grade plutonium and nuclear devices have already been made and surely by now are safely hidden in underground facilities, for which North Korea is so famous. It is virtually impossible to locate all of the North's nuclear devices, and even if, by some miracle, reliable intelligence is obtained, it would be difficult to destroy these massive, heavily fortified underground facilities.

For a number of reasons, a large-scale invasion by ground forces is also a nonstarter. North Korea is a rugged, mountainous country with a large, if poorly equipped, army. It has no chances of winning such a war, but it is

perfectly capable of making its adversaries pay a very high price for ultimate victory.

An additional—and very important—problem is the vulnerability of
Greater Seoul. This metropolitan area is home to nearly half of the ROK's
population (some 24 million out of 50 million) and is located a mere
twenty-five to thirty kilometers away from the DMZ. To make the most of
this strategic advantage, the North Korean military built heavily fortified
artillery positions, with some 250–300 long-range artillery pieces that can
hit targets within the entire city. In case of war, North Korean artillery will
inflict potentially devastating damage to the South Korean capital. A fast
evacuation of the mammoth city is virtually impossible. This ensures that
war, regardless of its outcome, is bound to be bloody and will bring with it
massive destruction to South Korea's major city.

North Korean strategic planners know that they will lose a full-scale
war, and this is why they will never start one. However, they also realize
that Seoul will not start such a war unless seriously provoked. In spite of
the expected outbursts of rhetoric, losing a passenger airliner to a North
Korean bomb or a naval warship to a torpedo attack is not seen in Seoul as
a sufficiently serious provocation.

With its impressive technological superiority, the South Korean military
could probably sink half the North Korean navy or wipe out a number of
their artillery positions within a few hours. In most places, that sort of defeat
would have serious political consequences—but not in North Korea.

The lives of North Korean soldiers and sailors are of no value to the
Pyongyang decision-makers: their scions do not serve in the military but
shop in Paris instead. The death of a few hundred soldiers will be seen as
an annoying but fully acceptable price—and will not deter Pyongyang
from planning a new round of provocations.

Some argue that such a military disaster would damage the regime's
credentials, which are primarily based on a "military first" policy for the
defense of the Juche motherland. However, Kim's regime controls the
media so completely that even the most humiliating defeat could be spun
as a great victory and spectacular triumph of North Korean arms. Only a
handful of generals would know the ugly truth. As these generals understand

that they would have no future without the current regime, they would be unlikely to reveal the man behind the curtain.

The more reasonable hard-liners in Washington and Seoul understand this peculiar situation well and thus are left only with sanctions. However, the efficiency of such sanctions is dubious at best. First, strict and comprehensive sanctions are difficult to impose, since China, and to a lesser degree Russia, will be unwilling to be party to a truly rigorous (read: efficient) sanctions regime. Neither Russia nor China wants North Korea to go nuclear, but both have other issues on their respective agendas, and some of those issues are more pressing than the Korean nuclear question.

The use of financial sanctions—such as a ban on the activity of North Korean banks, more or less along the lines of the Banco Delta Asia (BDA) incident—is an option to which North Korea would appear to be relatively vulnerable. However, the efficiency of such sanctions has never really been tested. To make things worse, North Korean society is designed in such a way as to make even efficient sanctions politically irrelevant.

Normally, sanctions work in an indirect way. In most cases, sanctions affect the populations of the target country, making their lives less comfortable (or even sustainable) and more stressful. This theoretically leads to a growing discontent as the public begins to blame their government for their declining living standards and other associated problems. The strategy of economic sanctions is based on the assumption that a dissatisfied populace will press for change in the policy, or even remove their government via popular revolution (or, in the case of a more democratic and tolerant regime, at the ballot box). This is seemingly what happened in Iran in 2013.

Alternatively, dissatisfied and/or ambitious members of the ruling elite might also use the crisis as an opportunity to overthrow the regime, peacefully or not. Once these dissatisfied elite members take power, they might make the necessary concessions to have the sanctions removed.

However, none of these mechanisms is likely to work in North Korea. Despite the relaxation of the past two decades, North Korea is not liberal enough for its people to have any influence in matters of governance. North Koreans do not vote (well, they do vote with a predictable 100-percent

approval rate for a single government-appointed candidate). They are terrified and isolated, do not have the rudimentary self-organization necessary
for creating a resistance movement, and are still to a large extent unaware
of any alternative to their mode of life. A popular revolt, Tunisia-style,
might be possible in the end but is unlikely to happen any time soon.

At times, it has been suggested that sanctions (especially financial sanctions)
will deprive the regime of the funds that it uses to reward the top brass with
small perks, like bottles of Hennessy cognac and Mercedes. It is often assumed
that, as a result of such deprivations, North Korean generals and dignitaries will
become restive and exercise some pressure on the government, such as demanding the surrender of nuclear weapons and/or reforms. This is an unrealistic expectation. The entire upper crust of the North Korean elite is likely to
share the belief that regime stability is a basic condition for their survival.
Therefore, we might presume that they would be willing to put up with locally
produced liquors and used Toyotas if the alternative is regime disintegration
and thus (or so they believe) imprisonment or even an exit from this world by
being hanged from lampposts. In other words, in the highly unlikely case that
China sincerely cooperated with a sanctions regime (the only way such sanctions would really have any teeth), the sanctions would merely help to starve to
death another few hundred thousand North Korean commoners.

WHY THE CARROTS ARE NOT SWEET ENOUGH (AND WHY "STRATEGIC PATIENCE" IS NOT A GREAT IDEA, EITHER)

Thus, a hard-line approach will not have much impact on North Korea.
Alas, the same is applicable to the major alternative, a policy of engagement.
Washington's soft-liners usually cite three major incentives that can be put
on the table as a reward for denuclearization: aid, security guarantees, and
normalization of relations with the United States. To borrow the expres-
sion of Wade Huntley, an influential soft-liner, US administrations should
just "sit down and talk" in order to resolve the nuclear issue.[1] The roots of
the current problems, soft-liners insist, is both America's unwillingness to

be flexible and generous enough and its adherence to an approach that is too militant and/or excessively idealistic. This approach is what Huntley describes as "emancipatory militant idealism"—the belief that the United States might and must use force to achieve the benevolent goal of emancipation of oppressed peoples worldwide.[2]

The aid that soft-liners would most likely send would, of course, be most welcome in Pyongyang. However, even a large lump sum is not a long-term solution. Once the money is spent (and it will be spent quite quickly), a nonnuclear Pyongyang regime would have great difficulties in obtaining additional aid. Without nuclear weapons, North Korea would become just another impoverished country that must compete for donor attention with such places as Sudan and Zimbabwe. Even though some aid would probably come its way, it would be on a smaller scale than what the North can currently get. It also would be strictly conditional and its distribution carefully monitored.

In order to survive, the Kim family regime needs to be able to distribute its foreign aid according to its own priorities, without excessive interference from donors. The North Korean leadership needs money, but only the kind it can control. They prefer payments and giveaways to investment, since the latter implies a great deal of interaction between foreign investors and North Koreans. Additionally, it cannot be directly channeled to programs the regime considers necessary for its own survival. It is the existence of the nuclear program that allows Pyongyang's politicians to determine the conditions on which aid should be delivered and distributed.

The promises of US security guarantees—even if such promises are to be believed—are also not sufficiently attractive to change Pyongyang's behavior. Few people would doubt that North Korea's leaders are sincerely afraid of a large-scale US-led invasion, and this fear is justified, as the fate of Iraq, a fellow member of the "axis of evil," has demonstrated. There are at least two reasons why such security guarantees might be irrelevant.

First, North Koreans deeply distrust Americans (and, more broadly speaking, all foreigners), and they do not believe in the value of foreign promises, especially when such promises are extended by democratic guarantors where leaders and policies are bound to change every few years and where the moral outrage of the public might easily render such guarantees null and void.

Second, North Korea's leadership knows that in the final analysis, their major security threat is internal, not external. They are afraid of a US-led invasion, Iraq-style, but they are even more afraid of a domestic coup or revolution. Needless to say, neither the United States nor any other outside player can provide them with a guarantee against such an outcome—indeed, as events in Libya have demonstrated, they are likely to actively encourage such a consequence. One cannot imagine a US president sending US Marines to suppress a pro-democracy rebellion in Pyongyang, but one can easily imagine a president dispatching marines—or, more likely, jets—to save the rebels from slaughter by the Kim loyalists. At the same time, their nuclear status at least increases Pyongyang leaders' ability to fend off unwanted intervention in the event of a domestic crisis, as well as their ability to extract foreign aid under conditions they can control.

As if to further underline this point, on March 22, 2011, the Korean Central News Agency (KCNA)—the official wire agency of North Korea—quoted a spokesman for the DPRK Foreign Ministry as saying:

> The present Libyan crisis teaches the international community a se-rious lesson. It was fully exposed before the world that "Libya's nu-clear dismantlement" much touted by the US in the past turned out to be a mode of aggression whereby the latter coaxed the former with such sweet words as "guarantee of security" and "improvement of relations" to disarm itself and then swallowed it up by force. It proved once again the truth of history that peace can be preserved only when one builds up one's own strength as long as high-handed and arbitrary practices go on in the world.

The present author believes that this particular KCNA statement is abso-lutely reasonable. Indeed, in 2003, Colonel Gaddafi did exactly what North Korean rulers have stubbornly refused to consider—he surrendered his country's nuclear materials in exchange for better relations with the United States and other Western nations. When his own people decided to get rid of him, however, the rebels found willing military support in the West, and the eccentric dictator had nothing to deter mighty NATO from intervening in the domestic politics of his country. The North Korean leadership must have thought that had Gaddafi not surrendered his nuclear program in 2003, the West could not have intervened in Libya.

The North Korean regime is thus not going to respond to either pressure or rewards, and this is increasingly obvious to interested parties. There is therefore a great—and growing—temptation to say that North Korea is better off forgotten and left alone. This is the essence of the "strategic patience" strategy, which has quietly become the mainstream of the US foreign policy establishment after 2009. This doctrine dictates that the United States should be willing to talk to North Korea, and maybe even "reward" it with some monetary and political concessions, only if North Korea does what the United States wants it to do—that is, start dismantling its nuclear program. If it does not do so, the United States should, as strategic patience promoters insist, ignore North Korea's antics, since North Korea will do little harm anyway.

This reasoning might be attractive, but it seems to be unrealistic. North Korea does not have the slightest desire to be left alone. Indeed, the Kim family regime cannot afford to be left alone. In order to compensate for the innate inefficiency of its economy, it needs outside help that is delivered according to their specific conditions. So far, the best way to squeeze this aid has been to appear dangerous, unpredictable, and irrational. Therefore, they will continue to appear thus, attempting to cause more trouble for countries from whom they think they can squeeze resources. The alternative is not attractive—either survive on the meager returns of their nonfunctioning economy or become excessively dependent on just one sponsor (China).

The supporters of strategic patience (aka, benign neglect) should understand that whilst being benignly neglected, North Korean leaders will work hard to improve their nuclear and missile arsenal, simultaneously undertaking to proliferate (to sell nuclear material and technology at a profit and also raise tensions, thus making aid more likely to be forthcoming).

Like it or not, the strategic patience of Washington is limited. Eventually, the United States is likely to give in and rejoin the game that is initiated and stage-managed by Pyongyang. It appears that Seoul, having followed a similar line under the Lee Myung Bak administration, has, under Park Geun Hye's government, given in and gone back to the negotiating table. The price for Seoul not doing so is too costly. An endless cycle of confrontation and ever-growing tension does not serve South Korea's interests (nor that of the United States).

It therefore makes sense to be prepared to rejoin the game on conditions that are—in the long run, at least—more favorable for Seoul, Washington, and, in the final count, the majority of the North Korean population. The North Korean problem has no quick fixes, but this does not mean that it has no solution whatsoever.

THINKING LONG TERM

When we discuss the North Korean problem, it is important to keep in mind that it has three different, if interconnected, dimensions.

For the United States, the major problem is North Korea's willingness to develop and maintain (perhaps, even proliferate) nuclear weapons and other WMD, as well as Pyongyang's inclination to engage in seemingly reckless provocative behavior.

For South Korea, the major issue is North Korea's refusal to initiate any kind of reforms that would bring about economic growth and a political transformation, thus creating better conditions for a manageable unification. The ceaseless brinkmanship of Pyongyang also constitutes a serious problem for Seoul (actually, a significantly greater problem than for the United States, which is lucky to be located thousands of miles away).

There is also another, often unmentioned, dimension to the problem: that of the average North Korean. For them, the continued existence of the North Korean system in its present ossified form means that North Koreans are doomed to live lives that are both materially and spiritually impoverished (and full of fear, too). Unable to enjoy the fruits of economic growth that the luckier people in all neighboring countries have experienced, their lives are, essentially, struggles for physical survival. They are deprived of even the theoretical opportunity to become acquainted with more refined forms of culture. In addition, they are also aware that any political deviations can get them into very serious trouble indeed. It is this waste of human lives and energy that constitutes the greatest consequence of the Kim family's dictatorial rule.

As we have seen, all of Pyongyang's policies—the nuclear and WMD programs, unwillingness to reform, determined efforts to maintain a police state, a penchant for creating regional tensions—are closely connected to the nature of the North Korean regime. Without these strategies, the regime and the ruling elite would be in serious trouble, and so they persist with these policies, no matter what the cost to their own population, to outsiders, and even to the long-term future of their country. The only way to alter North Korea's behavior is to change the nature of North Korea's regime. But how?

To answer this question, it makes sense to have a closer look at the not-so-distant past. How did Communism in Eastern Europe and the Soviet Union end? It was the ingrained inefficiency of the centrally planned economy and thus its inability to provide the population with a Western standard of living that ultimately doomed the system. This is not to deny that the desire for national independence among ethnic minorities, as well as a longing for democracy and political freedoms among the better educated sections of the population, also played a significant role in the demise of Communism. However, on balance, the fate of the Communist regimes of Eastern Europe and the Soviet Union was sealed by their economic inefficiency, not their political repressiveness. The author himself was witness to this transformation and hence can assure readers that the decisive impact on the Soviet imagination in the final decades of Communism was produced by the sight of shelves at American supermarkets rather than by the sight of vote counting at American polling stations.

The less dramatic transformation of China was also the result of similar changes. By the 1970s, Beijing's leaders were aware that China, in spite (or rather because) of the mad experiments of Chairman Mao, was increasingly lagging behind its neighbors, and that its state-planned economy had failed to deliver. They concluded that reform was necessary.

However, in order to become a political factor, this economic inefficiency had to first become known to and acknowledged by the majority of the population—at least by the majority of the political elite, as was the case in China. Had the Soviet leadership been willing and able to maintain a North Korean level of isolation and repressiveness, the Soviet Union might still be in existence today. But the regimes of Eastern Europe and the Soviet Union were comparatively soft on their population (in the post-Stalin era, that is) and did not maintain the level of isolation required. Consequently, the average Soviet and Eastern European citizen gradually became aware that the peoples of the developed West were living lives that were both more affluent and free. The same is applicable to Chinese decision-makers of the 1970s. They knew that China was lagging behind, and this knowledge prompted them to act.

If anything, North Korea is even more vulnerable to outside information than the Soviet Union and Eastern European countries ever were. After all, it is the success of South Korea, a country on the same peninsula with the same culture and language, and not that of other nations, that now threatens the very existence of North Korea. For a long time, Soviet agitprop tried to cushion the impact of news about Western prosperity by insisting that it was the cruelty of fate, not problems intrinsic to the system, that prevented the Soviet people from enjoying the same standard of living as Americans. In the 1960s and 1970s, the Soviet media argued that the Soviet people should not compare themselves with the lucky inhabitants of North America, who had never suffered a foreign invasion and could exploit the entire world for their selfish purposes (references to the slave trade and genocide of American Indians were frequently made). The majority of the Soviet population did not buy the argument, but, for a while at least, it helped to some extent.

North Korean propagandists face an unenviable situation. They have to explain the stunning prosperity of an area that at the time of the division was an agricultural backwater and whose population are members of the same ethnic group. As the information blockade has become more difficult to maintain, North Korean propaganda does its best to justify South Korean success as the fruits of shamelessly selling out to US imperialism. The ruse might work to some extent, but this explanation has less chance of succeeding than the elaborate but plausible constructs of 1960s Soviet propaganda.

Another peculiarity makes the North Korean regime particularly vulnerable to the spread of information about the outside world. The personality cult of the Kims has some similarities to a religious cult, but on balance, the North Korean ideology is secular, with roots going back to Marxism and further back to the European Enlightenment. Unlike fundamentalist ideologues in some other parts of the world, North Korean propagandists do not promise that the faithful shall enjoy eternal happiness in the afterlife in the company of seventy-two virgins. Instead, they claim that North Korean official ideology knows how to best arrange the economic and political life of the country and how to provide economic growth and general well-being. However, unfortunately for the North Korean elite, their system has failed to deliver the promised goods, and this failure has become abundantly clear by the remarkable success of South Korea.

The existence of the rich and free South is the major challenge for North Korean leaders, so the spread of knowledge about South Korea is bound to make the status quo untenable.

In order to initiate changes in North Korea, it is necessary to put North Korea's rulers under pressure from their people in general and from the lower echelons of the elite in particular. Only the North Koreans themselves can change North Korea. They are not only the major victims of the current unfortunate morass, but will also become the major beneficiaries of change.

The only long-term solution, therefore, is to increase internal pressure for regime transformation. The primary way to achieve this is to increase North Koreans' awareness of the outside world. If North Koreans learn about the existence of attractive and available alternatives to their regimented and impoverished existence, the almost unavoidable result will be a growth of popular dissatisfaction. This will create domestic pressure for change, and the North Korean government will discover that its legitimacy has begun to wane even among a considerable part of the elite.

This process might end in regime collapse, but it is also possible that, in the face of such pressure, the leadership might attempt some reforms that it would not otherwise contemplate. Reforms could theoretically end in success—that is, in the emergence of a developmental dictatorship, North Korean–style. However, due to the reasons outlined earlier, it seems far more probable that attempts at reforms will simply hasten the collapse of the regime. Either way, the outcome will be an improvement for both a majority of the North Korean people and those beyond.

One of the earlier-mentioned scenarios is almost certain to happen eventually. As history has shown countless times, in the modern era an economically inept regime always falls sooner or later. Information about the outside world is spreading anyway, whatever the government does—largely thanks to new technologies (like DVD players), but also due to the slow-motion disintegration of domestic surveillance and control. The measures discussed later will *not* change the course of history, but will merely accelerate events to a certain (perhaps quite small) extent—and will also make the coming crisis more manageable.

This outside support for information dissemination will also serve another important purpose that is not well understood. The half-century rule of the Kim dynasty has been a social and economic disaster, but its collapse might initially trigger a disaster of comparable proportions. It is already time to start thinking about a post-Kim future and undertaking measures that will make the eventual transformation of North Korea less painful.

This policy is unlikely to bear fruit in the short-term, so we need serious strategic patience in dealing with North Korea—as long as strategic patience does not mean merely doing nothing. This policy—or, rather, set of policies—can be implemented by a number of actors. The bureaucracies of the different states that have a stake in the issue can carry out efforts aimed at changing North Korea. However, there is also a great deal of space for NGOs, private foundations, and even individuals. Any effort that increases North Koreans' exposure to the outside world should be welcomed. All interpersonal exchanges should work toward the same goal.

Currently, three channels can provide the North Korean populace with unauthorized information about the outside world. First, officially approved academic, cultural, and other interpersonal exchanges endorsed by the North Korean authorities will unavoidably introduce potentially dangerous information to the country. Second, radio broadcasts and digital media might deliver news beyond the control of the North Korean regime. Third, the small but growing community of North Korean refugees—currently residing in South Korea but maintaining relations with families and friends in the North—might play a major and important role in disseminating information.

THE HIDDEN BENEFITS OF ENGAGEMENT

Of all the three channels mentioned earlier, official exchanges between North Korea and the outside world are especially significant. Since such exchanges have to be approved by the North Korean authorities, nearly all participants will necessarily come from the country's current elite.

One can expect conservatives in Washington, Seoul, and elsewhere to question the value of such exchanges. They may say that such exchanges in effect reward the North Korean leadership and its cronies. There is a kernel of truth (actually a rather large kernel) to this argument. There is no doubt that top functionaries in Pyongyang and their offspring princelings in Pyongyang government sinecures will be the first to take advantage of international student exchanges or overseas study trips. However, to be frank, they are exactly the type of people who matter most. Changes to North Korea might start from below, but it is more likely that well-informed and disillusioned members of the elite will initiate the transformation.

There is a historic precedent that shows the potential power of seemingly controlled and limited exchanges. In 1958 an academic exchange agreement was signed between the Soviet Union and the United States. In the United States, diehard conservatives insisted that the agreement would merely provide the Soviets with another opportunity to send spies or educate propaganda-mongers. In addition, the critics continued, this would all be done on American taxpayer money.

The first group of exchange students included exactly the people the conservatives were not eager to welcome onto US soil. There were merely four Soviet students selected by Moscow to go to Columbia University for a year of study. One of them, as we now know, was a rising KGB operative whose job was indeed to spy on the United States. He was good at his job and eventually had a brilliant career in Soviet foreign intelligence. His fellow student was a young but promising veteran of the then-still-recent Second World War. After studies in the United States, he was elevated to the Communist Party central bureaucracy, where it took him just ten years to become the first deputy head of the propaganda department—in essence, a second-in-command among Soviet professional ideologues.

Skeptics seemed to have been proven right—until the 1980s, that is. The KGB operative's name was Oleg Kalugin, and he was to become the first KGB officer to openly challenge the organization, criticizing the KGB's role as a party watchdog and initiating a campaign aimed at its transformation into a regular intelligence and counterespionage service.

Alexandr Yakovlev, another member of the same group, in the late 1950s was a young party propagandist. In due time, he was to become a Central Committee secretary, the closest associate of Mikhail Gorbachev. Yakovlev made a remarkable contribution to the collapse of the Communist regime in Moscow (some people even insist that it was Yakovlev rather than Gorbachev himself who was the real architect of perestroika).

Eventually, both men said it was their experiences in the United States that changed the way they saw the world, even though they were prudent enough to keep their mouths shut until the time was right.

Indeed, academic and personal exchanges seem to be the most efficient way to promote the spread of subversive information. By their nature, such exchanges imply a great deal of immersion in the host society. North Koreans will see many things that they will know could not possibly be staged and come to understand how rich many other countries in the world are, as well as why these countries are rich.

Such a program will target people who tend to belong to the elite and who, upon their return, will quietly share their impressions with those who really matter. We should also not forget that interpersonal exchanges will help introduce North Koreans to the knowledge and technology that will be so necessary when the decades-long North Korean stagnation finally ends.

It is unlikely that the North Korean authorities will agree to send a significant number of their students, scientists, and officials to the United States (let alone South Korea). Therefore, in most cases, education programs should be conducted by other countries, including those that are seen as more or less friendly toward North Korea. South Korean and American hard-liners may take issue with this, but *all* exchanges with the outside world are good for promoting North Korea's transformation.

Naturally, these programs are not going to be paid for by the North Korean government itself. To paraphrase a remark by veteran North Korea expert Aidan Foster-Carter, North Korean leaders never do anything so vulgar as pay their bills. There is therefore a need to financially support academic and interpersonal exchange programs, and this is a place where both official agencies of third-party countries and perhaps private foundations will have a role.

This issue might be somewhat difficult politically. From personal experience, the present author knows that diplomats from some developed countries are reluctant to support exchanges with North Korea out of a fear that such exchanges might be perceived in Washington as a breach of international solidarity with the South and as rewarding a brutal and disgusting regime. Given the conservatives' approach to the issue, these fears might be quite justified. This is unfortunate, however, since exchanges will not just reward the North Korean elite but also change North Korean society, thus undermining the elite's grip on power.

Apart from academic exchanges, one should encourage all activities that create an environment conducive to contact between North Koreans and foreigners (and especially between North and South Koreans). This is the major reason why the Kaesong Industrial Zone is actually a very good idea. Projects where North and South Koreans work together are bound to produce many situations where uncontrolled and unscripted exchanges between them take place.

From the regime's point of view, Kim Jong Il's decision to tolerate and even encourage the Kaesong Industrial Zone was a grave mistake—perhaps even the greatest mistake ever made by North Korea's oligarchs, as their survival depends on their ability to keep their people ignorant about the outside world. The Kaesong Industrial Zone might generate a significant income for the North Korean authorities, but it has also produced a dramatic transformation of the worldview of the 150,000 to 200,000 North Koreans who live in Kaesong and whose family members or friends work in the industrial park.

Regarding the political consequences that are likely to result from such apolitical interactions at the workplace, the present author would like to relate an incident that happened a few years ago, when he was flying from Seoul to Moscow. While on the plane, he sat next to a Russian couple in their late fifties. Given their dress and behavior, the man appeared to be a moderately successful businessman who had begun his career in Soviet times as an engineer in the author's native Leningrad. He related to the author an episode when, in the mid-1970s, a team of French engineers came to his plant to assist in the installation of newly purchased French equipment. The factory's First Department (that is, the resident KGB bureau) told the Russians that it would be okay to talk to the French about anything as long as politics was avoided. For their part, the French engineers did not touch upon dangerous topics.

One night, the French equipment stopped working. It was too late to go home, so the French and Russian engineers ended up staying all night, drinking tea, talking, and waiting for a repair team. In the middle of their conversation, a French engineer said, "You are so happy here!" Sincerely or not, the Russian engineers gave a patriotic answer: "Thanks to our Socialist System we are happy!" The French engineer, however, did not leave it at that: "Your life is so shitty but you have no clue how awful it really is and this is why you are so happy!" This exchange was obviously not a life-changing experience for my fellow traveler—but sudden life-changing experiences are more common in B-movies than in real life. Nevertheless, this short exchange had a real impact—the man sitting next to me still remembered it some thirty-five years later.

From this perspective, it is unfortunate that in 2008 the Seoul adminis-tration postponed and, for all practical purposes, canceled plans for a second industrial park that had been proposed by the Roh administration in 2007. The more industrial parks in the North, the better!

An added—but very important!—advantage of industrial parks and other forms of joint North-South enterprise is the role they play in introduc-ing North Koreans to the modern industrial environment and modern technologies. In effect, they can teach North Korean workers some practical manufacturing skills. These skills are not particularly sophisticated, but in the future, even these moderate competences might make a difference.

Hence, if one wants to change North Korea, all exchanges between the North and the outside world, especially exchanges between North and South Korea, should be actively encouraged—even if ostensibly such ex-changes enrich the regime by providing it with money or benefiting members of the current elite. This is why the Sunshine Policy, so much criticized and even vilified by the South Korean and American right, was probably not a bad idea. It is true that it was not based on reciprocity. However, one cannot expect reciprocity when dealing with such an im-poverished country, anyway (and, of course, the goal remains to change North Korea, not make economic gains through cooperation with it).

THE FLOWER OF UNIFICATION

In the summer of 1989 Pyongyang hosted a lavish international festival—the thirteenth World Festival of Youth and Students, to be precise. Such events are essentially gatherings of young left-leaning intellectuals and artists, and used to be heavily subsidized by the Soviet Union and the Communist bloc. The Pyongyang festival was meant to be a symbolic response to the 1988 Olympic Games, uncoincidentally held in Seoul. (At the time, North Korea still did its best to compete with the South.)

That summer, North Koreans were exposed to a great number of happenings and personalities, but none left as much an impression as a girl named Im Su-gyong, a student of Hankook University of Foreign Studies and also an activist from the National Council of Student Representatives, a left-leaning, nationalistic, and generally pro-Northern students' organization in Seoul.

At the time, North Korean sympathizers played an important and perhaps even decisive role in the South Korean students' movement, so one should not be surprised that a powerful South Korean students' organization would decide to dispatch a delegation to Pyongyang. The South Korean government, then still dominated by hard-line anti-Communists from the then recently deposed military regime, banned the trip, but Im Su-gyong and some other activists ignored the ban. Only Im herself managed to get to Pyongyang.

Upon arrival in North Korea, Im Su-gyong was met with the greatest pomp imaginable. North Korean propagandists saw the girl as a gift from heaven: she was beautiful, charming, charismatic, and full of enthusiastic belief in the glories of Stalinism with North Korean characteristics. They did their best to present her as representative of South Korean youths in general, who if the North Korean official media was to be believed, spent their days and nights secretly studying the works of Kim Il Sung and Kim Jong Il and planning demonstrations in front of US army bases.

There is no doubt that many South Korean students, at that stage at least, sincerely believed that North Korea was a viable alternative to the capitalist South. Many "progressive intellectuals" in the South saw their own country as the "underdeveloped victim of US neo-colonialism." Thus, Im herself did not say anything to embarrass her handlers and duly delivered the politically correct statements the authorities wanted to hear.

However, more than twenty years later, one can see that Im Su-gyong's visit to North Korea was a major blunder by the North Korean authorities. Regardless of the beliefs of Im herself and the calculations of her handlers, her trip to Pyongyang dramatically contradicted the then officially approved image of South Korea in the North Korean media. South Korea was allegedly a place of destitution and poverty. In

(continued)

this image, South Korean workers were starving, whilst their kids made a miserable living by working in sweatshops, begging, or polishing the shoes of sadistic American soldiers.

It would have been difficult *not* to believe these stories, since the North Korean public was cut off from the outside world to an extent that would have been inconceivable in any other Communist country, including the Soviet Union of the Stalin era.

This image, however, was a fantasy of North Korean propaganda. Through the 1970s and 1980s, as North Korea stagnated, South Korea went through an economic miracle, transforming itself into a developed industrial society. Yet North Koreans knew none of what was happening just a few hundred miles from their villages, towns, and cities.

We should probably describe what happened as "Im Su-gyong mania." The girl was known in official propaganda as "the flower of unification"—the epithet is still remembered by virtually all in the country. North Koreans noticed that the girl looked healthy and optimistic and was very well dressed. For a while, she became a trendsetter in the world of North Korean fashion—North Korean women wanted to wear "Im Su-gyong–style trousers" (even though North Korean women at the time were discouraged from wearing trousers outside the workplace) and imitate her short, straight haircut. North Koreans also noted—with some shock—that she often did not wear a bra.

People were also surprised by her willingness to deliver unscripted speeches—something that was quite unusual for North Koreans, who took it for granted that all political statements had to be carefully prepared and rehearsed. Even though she did not say anything to contradict the official North Korean line, her apparent sincerity and the ease with which she spoke were striking and so very different from what the North Korean public was used to.

After a month and a half spent in North Korea, Im Su-gyong and Mun Kyu-Hyon, another South Korean leftist/nationalist dissident, went back to the South. As a way to protest the division of Korea, on the 15th of August, 1989, on the anniversary of Korea's liberation from the Japanese colonial regime, they chose to cross the DMZ at Panmunjom, even though such a move was against South Korean law.

The duo crossed the border, whereupon they were immediately arrested. The North Korean public assumed that Im Su-gyong made a great sacrifice. It was widely believed that she would spend the rest of her life in the terrible dungeons of the South Korean dictators.

Im Su-gyong indeed stood trial after her return to the South. The anachronistic and nondemocratic National Security Law, then and now still in operation in South Korea, criminalizes any kind of unauthorized visit to the North. As a result, Im Su-gyong was sentenced to five years in prison (she was released after three-and-a-half years). Needless to say, this was a shameful decision, but it is not the focus of our story.

North Korean propaganda then miscalculated again. Trying to capitalize on Im Su-gyong's tremendous popularity, they aired an interview with her parents, who lived in Seoul. This interview is widely remembered by North Koreans, since it produced an explosive impact on their thinking about the South.

North Koreans were surprised to discover that the family members of a political criminal were allowed to stay in their home in the capital city, keep their jobs, and talk freely to journalists—even entertaining them with beer, a very precious commodity in the North. Having seen the interview, North Koreans began to suspect that South Korea was far more affluent than they were told. They also came to the conclusion that the "ruling Fascist clique" in Seoul was unusually soft when dealing with internal opposition.

I think they would be much more surprised to learn that in 2012, Im Su-gyong—whose views have not changed that much—became a member of the South Korean National Assembly. However, from the late 1990s, her exploits ceased to be reported by the North Korean media.

Im Su-gyong's trip was the beginning of major changes. A few years later in the late 1990s, unauthorized information about the outside world began to filter into North Korea.

However, the first breaches in the information blockade were inflicted by North Korean authorities themselves. They wanted to show how popular their regime was in the South, but they ended up unwittingly providing proof of South Korean economic success and political freedom.

REACHING THE PEOPLE

Personal exchanges seem to be the best way to put information about the outside world within the reach of North Koreans. However, apart from such officially approved activities, other channels might be used to reach the same goal—and not all such channels need be to the North Korean government's liking.

Until recently, there was good reason to be skeptical about attempts to reach the North Korean people over the heads of their masters. In Kim Il Sung's North Korea, all possible channels of uncensored interaction were controlled by the regime. However, in recent decades, the situation has changed measurably. DVD players are common now, and even computers are not unheard of. Tunable radios, while still technically illegal, are smuggled into the country in growing quantities, together with banned South Korean DVDs. Additionally, North Korean denizens are less afraid to talk amongst themselves and sometimes even raise politically dangerous topics. Authorities are less willing to enforce old regulations that still remain on the books.

These changes mean that nowadays, for the first time in decades, it is becoming possible to deliver unauthorized knowledge directly to North Koreans. The information blockade can be bypassed, and the North Korean public seems to be more receptive to critical messages than it has been since the end of the Korean War.

Of the various ways to break through, the first is radio broadcasts. Dissidents and the general population in post-Communist countries now widely acknowledge the momentous role that radio broadcasts played during the Cold War. When Lech Wałęsa, leader of the Polish democracy movement Solidarity, was asked about the degree of influence Radio Free Europe had on the Polish opposition, he famously replied: "The degree cannot even be described. Would there be Earth without the Sun?"[3]

Fortunately, recent years have been marked by a dramatic increase in broadcasts targeting North Korea. According to a study conducted in the summer of 2009 by the InterMedia Group, at that time there were five radio stations that specifically targeted North Korea—not counting the government-run KBS and some Christian stations in South Korea. The total broadcast time amounted to 20.5 hours a day (once again, excluding KBS). Given that a few years ago the total broadcast time did not exceed four to five hours, this is a remarkable breakthrough.[4] The size of the audience is difficult to appraise, but a variety of sources indicate that it is not insignificant. For example, in early 2010 Peter Beck estimated that the number of listeners might have reached one million (or some 5 percent of the total population).[5]

The North Korean audience is currently targeted by large Korean and US government-owned stations, of which KBS (Korean), Radio Free Asia, and Voice of America are the most important. There are also a number of smaller refugee-run stations. They are understaffed and underfunded, but are not short of enthusiasm and often maintain clandestine networks that collect valuable information from inside North Korea. These stations—both large and small—need more active support.

Another traditional medium is leaflets, which are now delivered exclusively by the refugees' NGOs (as a government program was halted a decade ago). This author is somewhat skeptical of the efficacy of the balloon program. The occasional encounter with a short piece of information provided by a printed text is unlikely to seriously change the worldview of a North Korean. Nonetheless, such efforts might still serve to jar the minds of those who pick the leaflets up.

The digital age has brought an array of new opportunities that have never been utilized. For example, the continuing spread of VCR/DVD players inside North Korea creates manifold opportunities for introducing information about the outside world. It is now possible to produce visual material—essentially documentaries—specifically designed for North Korean audiences. Such documentaries can rely on the obvious advantage of visual appeal and thus have the potential to be more effective than radio broadcasts.

Digital technologies also have simplified the process of dissemination of textual material. During the Cold War, broadcasts reached a far larger audience than text and had a much greater impact, since printed books were unwieldy and difficult to smuggle and copy. In Communist countries, photocopying machines were closely monitored by the secret police, so in most cases copying had to be done via a typewriter. It took about a week to make four or five copies of the average book. This is the reason why *sam-izdat*, secretly published materials so much discussed in the West, were widely accessible only to a handful of opposition-minded intellectuals.

Things have now changed, however, thanks to the advent of digital technology. A book can now be easily scanned and/or converted into a text file. Hundreds of such files can easily fit on one USB drive or DVD disk. In the 1970s it would take years of typewriting (or days of photocopy-ing) to reproduce such a large volume of text, but now the job can be done within minutes. A digital book is also easier to hide or destroy than its paper equivalent. The efficiency of digital technologies means that even one copy of a book (or rather a collection of books, a "digital library") once smuggled across the border could easily spread inside North Korea.

By its very nature, text will be more appealing to intellectuals and the lower reaches of the elite. Such scanned materials might include textbooks on the humanities, as well as purely technical material (special attention should be given to textbooks and manuals dealing with computers). It is important to introduce books that have different, even mutually exclusive, opinions—as long as the books are well-written and the arguments sound. North Kore-ans should not be treated with syrupy propaganda and anti-Communist harangues. Instead, they should become accustomed to intellectual differ-ences and arguments. They should read what is written by the left and right, zealous anti-globalists and stubborn libertarians alike. They should be ex-posed to the modern world, with all its complexity and uncertainty.

WHY THEY MATTER: WORKING WITH THE REFUGEES IN SOUTH KOREA

When, in the 1970s, Václav Havel, the future president of Czechoslovakia and later the Czech Republic, was talking about the future of his country, he specifically emphasized the special role that might be played by "the second society." He admitted that the Communist regime in Czechoslovakia

(ridiculously permissive and liberal by North Korean standards) was repressive to the degree that made organized resistance impossible. Thus,
Havel reasoned, the only way to resist was to minimize and avoid popular
involvement with the regime. People could not (and hence should not)
protest openly, but instead should live their lives as if the Central Committee, Party Youth, and political study sessions simply did not exist.

What Havel described was already in existence in the Soviet Union and
Eastern Europe by the 1970s. Only a tiny minority was directly involved in
dissent, but many more lived lives that were completely disconnected
from the official worldview. By the late 1970s, among the intellectuals of
Moscow (let alone Warsaw and Prague), it became almost suspicious if
someone professed sincere support for the existing political system. In
this milieu, party rhetoric and party politics were treated as something
akin to bad weather. It was tacitly admitted that nothing could be done
about it, but rain outside was not a reason to stop one's daily routine or to
deprive oneself of the small pleasures of life.

This milieu of nonpolitical (or slightly opposition-minded) intellectuals
was the environment that produced active dissenters. It also played an important role when Communism began to crumble in the late 1980s. Many
of these people eventually became political activists, journalists, educators,
and even industrial managers. They were a group from which a significant
part of the post-Communist elite emerged. These were people possessing
the knowledge, experience, and, in some cases, nationwide fame and moral
authority. They were also people who were not compromised by a track
record of collaboration with the overthrown Communist governments.

As a rule, the stronger and more influential a "second society" was in a
particular Communist country, the less painful and more successful the
post-Communist transition tended to be. Among other things, it produced a sad paradox—countries where former Communist apparatchiks
fared worst after the Communist collapse were usually the very same
countries where Communism itself was least repressive (Hungary, Poland,
and Czechoslovakia).

Unfortunately, the North Korean regime has always been exceptionally
thorough in its control over its population. As a result, no second society

has been able to emerge. More or less every North Korean with education and experience can be plausibly described as a lifelong regime collaborator. The Kim dynasty does not give its subjects any chance of living lives that would be autonomous from the state—or at least this is the case with socially prominent individuals. Closet opponents of the regime exist amongst educated North Koreans, but they are usually too terrified to share their doubts even among themselves (if indeed they can even recognize other dissenters).

This absence of a second society does not merely strengthen the Kim family's regime. It is also bound to create many problems in the future when the regime loses power. Everyone who is someone has skeletons in their closet.

It is therefore important to encourage the emergence of an alternative elite. Such an elite is unlikely to emerge inside North Korea, however, even though broadcast and proliferation of digital materials might play a role in bringing modern knowledge within the reach of some educated North Koreans. Hopes, therefore, should be pinned on the refugee community in South Korea.

North Korean refugees are very different from the Eastern Europeans who fled West during the Cold War. As discussed earlier, they cannot be plausibly described as "defectors" since most of them were driven away from the North by starvation and/or other nonpolitical reasons. Furthermore, Eastern European and Soviet defectors were well educated, while North Korean refugees are largely farmers and manual workers. At first glance, it seems unlikely that from such a group an alternative society can emerge.

However, the situation is not that hopeless. First, there is a small but not insignificant number of well-educated refugees. Contrary to what is often assumed outside South Korea, they are not actively supported by the South Korean state, so one should not be much surprised by the sight of a former North Korean engineer who makes a living through pizza delivery (well, more likely he will be working at a Chinese eatery, far more common in Seoul). Support systems and jobs for such people are crucial.

Second, there are younger defectors who still see themselves as North Koreans but who can and should be educated. There is an urgent need to introduce scholarships that would specifically target this group.

Scholarships for MA and PhD studies are of special importance. Currently, refugees who are accepted to a university can study for free, but this important privilege is granted only to undergraduates. Nowadays, a bachelor's degree alone does not mean much in South Korea, where some 80 percent of high school graduates proceed to tertiary-level educational institutions. It is advanced degrees that matter, but so far there is no systematic support for aspiring MA and PhD refugee students.

One might expect that such support would be forthcoming from the South Korean government. However, due to reasons largely related to the domestic situation, the South Korean government is not enthusiastic about providing such support. Among other things, such preferential treatment might provoke outrage from South Korean MA and PhD candidates and their families. Therefore, such scholarships must be provided by overseas donors.

There is, of course, a need to support the political and cultural undertakings of the small but growing refugee community—radio stations, newspapers, and artists. We need more North Koreans to become journalists, policy analysts, and painters in South Korea. However, there is an even greater need for North Korean professionals—construction engineers, accountants, scientists, water-treatment specialists, and doctors.

These people will play at least three roles in future developments. First, refugees will make an additional—and highly efficient—channel for efforts to reach the average North Korean. As we discussed earlier, refugees stay in touch with their families and friends back at home—thanks to Chinese cell phones and a network of "brokers" who deal with the movement of people, money transfers, and letter exchanges. It is understandable that a refugee who has become, say, an accountant will channel back to the North information of much greater importance and impact than a refugee who makes a living by waiting tables at a cheap eatery.

Second, when the eventual collapse and/or transformation of North Korea finally arrives, some of these refugee intellectuals will probably go back to their native land north of the DMZ. Some of them will become political and social activists, while many more will apply their technical skills in the re-emerging North Korean economy. They will play a major role as educators and instructors, teaching North Koreans how things are done in the South and, more broadly speaking, in the modern world.

Third, refugee professionals and intellectuals will become role models for the North Korean refugee community. This community is bound to grow regardless of developments north of the DMZ. Right now, a North Korean refugee tends to become part of the underclass. As is often the case with other minorities, this low social standing has become self-perpetuating. Being deprived of role models, younger refugees struggle to adjust to South Korean society—later paying a bitter price for this. It would be of great help if the mother of some unruly teenager from a refugee family can point to Uncle Kim who has succeeded in becoming a surgeon, or Aunt Park who is now a designer at LG.

CHAPTER 7

Being Ready for What We Wish For

There is little doubt that in the end, the current North Korean regime is doomed. Its innate—and incurable—economic inefficiency means the regime has lost the economic battle with South Korea. Unless North Korea successfully reforms, this will spell ruin for Pyongyang before too long.

In the end, the outside world and the vast majority of North Koreans themselves will benefit from the likely collapse of the Kim family regime. However, we should repeat the fallacies so common to freedom fighters, revolutionaries, and idealistic politicians (such politicians might be rare, but they do exist). We should not believe that the demise of this inefficient and brutal regime will herald the immediate arrival of eternal bliss and happiness. On the contrary, as every historian knows only too well, every revolution fermented, every independence declared, every liberation achieved brings a significant measure of disruption and chaos—and this is applicable even to those revolutions that with the wisdom of hindsight are seen as almost trouble-free. Unfortunately, the future North Korean revolution has little chance of being smooth, and subsequent events will most likely be painful. Regime collapse will mark the beginning of a long, difficult, and painful period of recovery for North Koreans. It will take decades to clean the mess created by the Kim family regime's long misrule, and some traces of the sorry past might be felt for generations.

Now is the time to start considering what will happen after the Kim family regime passes—and what should be done to make the recovery less tortuous. There are some simple and cheap but potentially efficient measures that can be taken now—for example, policies that aim at creating an alternative elite (discussed earlier), which will clearly help to cushion the pains and shocks of the coming transformation. In addition, it is now time to start an honest, taboo-free discussion of ways to handle the coming challenges.

A PERFECT STORM

For decades, Koreans have believed that the future unification of their country would be a major, cathartic event that would usher in an era of unprecedented happiness, harmony, and prosperity on the Korean peninsula. In the long run this is indeed likely to be the case—if judged from the perspective of a future historian living in, say, the year 2133. However, for Koreans who will live through the decades immediately following unification, it will be a time of dramatic upheaval, social disruption, and profound shock.

Alas, nobody knows when, where, or how unification will happen—and this alone makes preparing for it intrinsically difficult. It is likely to come suddenly. In all probability, unification will occur because of some crisis of political authority and collapse of state control within North Korea. Such a crisis will come more or less out of the blue, with even the presidents and prime ministers of great powers possibly learning about such a crisis from TV news reports rather than from predictions by their diplomats and reports from their spymasters.

The world has never seen a merger of two societies so different economically, technologically, and culturally. The unification of the two Germanys is clearly a precedent, but they were never as far apart as the two Koreas are. More or less every East German family watched West German TV from the late 1960s, and visits by relatives as well as letter exchanges were easy to arrange. This is very different from the North Korean situation, where the vast majority knows almost nothing about actual life in South Korea. The average North Korean has access to only two sources of information about life in the South—smuggled South Korean melodramas and the horror stories of official Pyongyang propaganda. Both sources leave much to be desired.

THE COSTS OF UNIFICATION

The last fifteen years have seen the emergence of a small cottage industry—people have begun to speculate on how much unification of the Koreas will cost.

This is a highly speculative undertaking to be sure, since nobody knows when (or, more precisely, if) unification will happen. Furthermore, reliable statistical information about the North Korean economy is absent. Moreover, comparisons with other unifications like Germany and the usually forgotten Yemen are very limited in their usefulness because these precedents are so different demographically and economically from the contemporary Koreas.

Much also depends on how one defines "costs." Does the "cost of unification" mean the cost of raising the per capita GDP of North Korea to that of South Korea? Or is it merely the cost of raising it to a respectable but lower level, like half that of South Korea? Or, rather, is it the cost of kick-starting the North Korean economy? All of these assumptions have been used and, predictably, depending on which one was used, different studies have produced wildly different cost estimates.

Another problematic issue is the question of the economic advantages of unification. Few would doubt that costs would be partially offset by, say, decreases in military spending, increases in market size, and other similar factors. However, these factors are difficult to estimate. Some researchers try to incorporate the supposed advantages into the calculations, while others ignore them.

Nonetheless, everyone agrees on one thing: unification is going to be very expensive. Estimates range from $0.2 trillion to $5 trillion. Even the lowest figure is roughly 20 percent of South Korea's annual GDP. The upper figure is, of course, nearly five times that of South Korea's annual GDP.

(continued)

In 2010 the Federation of Korean Industries (FKI) conducted a survey of twenty leading South Korean experts on the costs of unification. Estimates averaged a staggering US$3 trillion. This figure included the initial costs of stabilizing North Korea after unification, as well as bridging the economic gap between the two Koreas.[1] It is remarkable that experts were not asked how much it will cost to raise the income of the North to the level of the South, but merely to a level that will ensure that unified Korea will have a "unified and stable society." This wording is very nebulous and imprecise, but it clearly implies that even with such astronomical investment, the North will lag behind the South.

The FKI-selected expert panel was not optimistic about timing, either. One-third (35 percent) believed that it would take more than thirty years to close the gap (partially), and an additional 25 percent believed that task would require twenty to thirty years.

A few months later, in early 2011, Nam Sung-wook, director of the Institute for National Security Strategy, an influential government think tank, presented the South Korean Parliament with a report that estimated the costs at a comparable but somewhat lesser level of US$2.1 trillion.[2]

There are more optimistic opinions, of course. For example, in early 2012 the influential Korea Economic Institute, a private think tank, published a report that said the unification—assuming that unification would happen immediately—would cost merely US$0.2 trillion. This seems to be the most sanguine of the recent estimates.[3]

This optimism is not widely shared. In 2009 Credit Suisse estimated the unification cost at US$1.5 trillion. This amount was thought to be necessary to raise North Korea's per capita GDP to 60 percent of that of the South's within ten years.[4]

In 2010 Peter Beck, then at Stanford University, estimated that it would cost between US$2 trillion and US$5 trillion to raise the average income in the North to 80 percent of that of the South.[5] This might be the highest of all estimates—but, alas, may be proven accurate.

The figures thus seem to fluctuate greatly and hardly should be taken too seriously. One should not be that surprised about this, given how little data is available, the great level of uncertainty, and lack of historic precedents. Nonetheless, it seems that most estimates—or, rather, guesstimates—are between US\$1.5 trillion and US\$2.5 trillion. This is significantly larger than the entire GDP of South Korea, which is currently around US\$1 trillion.

Bearing in mind the scale of the expense, one should not be too judgmental about the increasingly cautious attitude toward the unification project among the South Korean public. At the end of the day, this project will have to be supported by South Korean taxpayers, and they are predictably wary of this.

When people talk about the costs of unification (and such talks are very common in South Korea nowadays), they usually mean the financial burden that will fall upon South Korean taxpayers. This burden is likely to be crushing, but the Koreas' unification will also produce a vast array of other social problems, many of which will have no attractive solutions. It makes sense to outline some of these likely problems—with the full understanding that many others will pop up as well, completely unexpectedly.

If we look at the experience of the anti-Communist revolutions in Eastern Europe, we can see that educated, urban, white-collar workers—the Eastern European equivalent of the middle class—played the leading role in these movements. It was schoolteachers, low-level managers, nurses, engineers, and skilled industrial workers who in the late 1980s went into the streets of Moscow, Prague, and Budapest, demanding democracy and a market economy. If a popular movement plays a role in the collapse of North Korea, the same scenario is likely to be repeated there as well. However, the North Korean "middle class" are people who—in relative terms—are likely to lose the most after unification.

This does not mean that unification will bring ruin to physicians and history teachers in North Korea. In fact, their absolute income is almost certain to increase instantly and dramatically. However, they will also discover that their skills are of little value in post-unification Korea.

North Korean professionals generally tend to have a solid background in theory, so it is quite possible that the average North Korean engineer is better at using calculus than his or her South Korean peer—not least because of a relative shortage of calculators and computers. However, their practical and applied knowledge is usually archaic and/or irrelevant. If a North Korean engineer has not worked in missile or nuclear design, he or she probably has never used a modern computer and does not know what CAD stands for (for readers without a background in engineering, it is an acronym for "Computer Aided Design"). He or she also has virtually no command of English, the major language of modern technical manuals, documentation, and reference books. A typical North Korean engineer spends his or her entire career working out how to keep in operation the rusty equipment of 1960s Soviet vintage. From the point of view of a South Korean employer, such a person has no value as an engineer.

Everyone who worked in North Korea during the famine testifies to the remarkable skills and selflessness of North Korea's doctors. They knew how to make workable IVs out of empty beer bottles and how to conduct complex heart surgery with equipment straight from the 1930s. However, after unification, North Korean physicians and surgeons will immediately discover that they have never heard of perhaps 90 percent of the drugs and procedures that are now standard in modern medicine.

Even school and college teachers will find themselves in serious trouble. Those who teach theoretical and nonpolitical subjects—like geometry or organic chemistry—will probably be able to maintain professional employment, but what about the rest, especially teachers of humanities? The average North Korean teacher of history knows a lot about events that never actually happened—like, say, the alleged leading role of Kim's family during the March 1, 1919, uprising, or Kim Jong Il's childhood allegedly spent at a nonexistent secret camp on the slopes of Mount Paekdu. He or she has little knowledge, however, about the events that defined the course of Korea's actual history—pretty much all that he or she knows of traditional Korean culture is that it is the "reactionary culture of a feudal ruling class."

It might be argued that these people should be re-educated, but this is easier said than done. Re-education will require a lot of money and time.

Some people (those with exceptional gifts and good luck) will probably master the new necessary skills, but for the vast majority of North Korea's "middle class," this will not be possible. In absolute terms, their standard of living is set to rise dramatically: they will have computers and drive cars, will eat meat and fish every day, and will have more time to enjoy sunsets or whatever else they choose to enjoy. At the same time, however, their relative social standing will decline, and many of them will perceive this as a humiliation.

Nevertheless, we should not be too elite-oriented and worry only about the fate of the relatively privileged professional strata in North Korean society. Many common North Koreans are also bound to have reason to feel disappointed by "unification by absorption." For a while, the citizens of what is now North Korea will enjoy a newfound and very welcome prosperity, since the post-unification government is likely to instantly deliver what Kim Il Sung once promised: the opportunity to enjoy a meal of meat soup with boiled rice while sitting under a tiled roof. They will appreciate individual freedoms for the first time as well—it is nice to listen to a song you like even though it has no references to the Dear Leader and his Great Family. However, they will soon inevitably start comparing themselves with their southern compatriots and thereupon discover that a significant gap continues to exist. The North Korean people will support unification (and perhaps even fight for unification) on the assumption that it will soon deliver living standards that approximate those of South Koreans. Needless to say, this cannot possibly happen.

Nearly all North Koreans will soon discover that they are not eligible for anything but low-skilled, low-paid work. Some of them will manage to retrain themselves, but a majority will have to spend the rest of their lives sweeping floors and working in sweatshops. They will view this as being born of discrimination. Indeed, as the bitter experience of North Korean refugees in the South demonstrates, some discrimination against Northerners is almost certain to occur. But to a large extent, most of this so-called discrimination will reflect the objective disadvantages that North Korean workers have because of their lack of many modern skills.

Some South Korean businesses will rejoice when they discover a reservoir of unskilled but disciplined and cheap labor in the North. However, most experts agree that cheap unskilled labor is not what the South Korean economy needs at present.

Many North Koreans will move to the alluring bright lights of the cities of the South—after all, Seoul lies within merely one day's walk of what is now North Korea. Labor migrants from the North will probably undercut unskilled South Korean workers, driving wages down and further increasing mutual distrust between the former citizens of the two Korean states. Some of them will certainly take up criminal activities, too, so after unification, South Korean cities, now remarkably safe at any time day or night, might become quite dangerous. Younger women from the North will probably contribute to the revival of the steadily declining sex industry in South Korea—with predictable consequences for the way the two Koreas perceive each other.

The mass migration of Northerners to the South is likely to produce much social friction, but on balance, it is the much smaller migration of Southerners to the North that will probably create greater problems. Rudiger Frank, an East German by birth and a perceptive observer of Korean events, recently put it nicely in a private conversation with the author: "When and if Korean unification comes, it will be necessary to protect Southerners from the Northerners, but it will be far more important to protect Northerners from Southerners—from predatory Southern businesses in particular."

Indeed, there are a number of potentially explosive problems, including North Korea's 1946 Land Reform Law, which has never been officially accepted by the South Korean government. Unlike, say, China, where former landlords were either slaughtered or, if they were lucky, cowed into permanent silence, most North Korean landlords were fortunate to escape to the South between 1946 and 1953. They seldom forgot to take their land titles, so nowadays a significant part of the best arable land in North Korea theoretically has "legal owners" who are happily living somewhere in Seoul. As the present author knows from much experience, these old land titles are carefully preserved by the second and third generations of former landowners.

The history of South Korea's economic boom was also the history of obscenely profitable land speculation. In some parts of the Apgujeong ward of southern Seoul, for example, the price of land increased some thousandfold between the years of 1963 and 1990 (this is after the adjustments to the inflation were made!). South Koreans understand the potential value of land, especially if it is located close to a future booming business or industrial center. Unless something is done, the holders of pre-1946 land titles will descend on destitute North Korean villages, using litigation in order to take from North Korean farmers the only potentially valuable asset they have. Unfortunately (for North Korean farmers), the descendants of post-1946 migrants tend to be very successful and powerful in modern South Korea and therefore, if they decide to fight for "their" property, have a chance of succeeding.

Greedy scions of long-dead landlords are not the only people who are going to create trouble in the post-unification real estate market, however. Investing in North Korean real estate is likely to be tremendously profitable in the long run. At the same time, even though a shadow real estate market is now quietly developing in North Korea, the majority of North Koreans have distorted ideas about the value of real estate. One should not be surprised about this fact—when the present author bought real estate for the first time in his life, in the still (technically) Soviet Leningrad of 1991, a one-bedroom apartment in the second-largest city in the then Soviet Union would cost less than a badly made Lada subcompact car and would be just slightly more expensive than a new IBM desktop computer (IBM PC XT with hard drive of 20 Mb, if you remember such a thing). If South Korean investors are "lucky," they might easily persuade some North Koreans to sell their derelict houses for the price of, say, a shiny new fridge or a Japanese motorbike. Needless to say, North Koreans will soon realize that they have been cheated, and this will not make them more enthusiastic about the realities of unification.

The experience of post-Socialist Eastern Europe and the USSR has shown yet another potential vulnerability the ex-Communist populations have. They are ignorant and sometimes very naïve about the workings of markets. They therefore can easily fall prey to con artists who peddle all kinds of get-rich-quick schemes. Ponzi schemes seem to be especially common. In 1994 in Russia, a Ponzi scheme run by the MMM Company wiped out the savings of five million ex-Soviet citizens. The MMM affair led to some political disturbances, but it was nothing in comparison to post-Communist Albania. In Albania, a number of Ponzi schemes succeeded in attracting the money of between a quarter and half of all Albanians—some $1.2–1.5 billion was invested (half of the annual GDP in this country with a population of three million). The collapse of these schemes in 1997 led to a short but intense civil war that left an estimated 500 to 1,500 people dead.[1] Romania—another country that resembled North Korea in many regards—also suffered from the collapse of the Caritas, an additional local Ponzi scheme, even though this collapse did not lead to much violence.

Unfortunately, similar events are also likely to happen in North Korea. North Koreans might be street-smart in their own way, but they tend to be remarkably credulous and naïve when it comes to the workings of modern capitalism. Actually, we can already see a warning sign of this: according to recent research, in South Korea one in five Northern refugees has been the victim of fraud, a rate more than forty times higher than the national average.[2] North Koreans will make easy prey for predatory outsiders, especially those from the South—and this will not promote better mutual understanding in post-unification Korea.

It is clear that the social transformation of North Korea will be difficult for everyone. There is one group, however, that seems to stand out—the military.

The North Korean military is estimated to be between 1.1 and 1.2 million strong. Most of these people can only be seen as soldiers if one stretches the definition of military service. They are essentially an unpaid labor force, whose members are also taught some basic military skills. It is also important to remember, however, that North Korea's armed forces include a significant minority (perhaps as many as 300,000 to 400,000 people) of professional warriors, who have spent their entire adult lives mastering ways of low-tech killing. They are soldiers in North Korea's Special Forces, units of the Pyongyang Defense Command, and other elite formations.

After unification, they are likely to find themselves in an unenviable situation, since these lifelong professional soldiers usually do not have even the limited skills of much of the North Korean civilian population. They are also likely to be hit especially hard by the collapse of the official value system: the sudden realization of the emptiness and lies behind the Juche ideology and the Kim family cult. Some of them will find poorly paid jobs as security guards, but many others will likely opt for more lucrative opportunities in the criminal underworld.

A PROVISIONAL CONFEDERATION AS THE LEAST UNACCEPTABLE SOLUTION

Let us now consider some ways we can mitigate the negative consequences of unification, whilst making the most of its numerous advantages.

One of the possible solutions might be the creation of a transitional confederative state where both North and South would maintain a significant measure of autonomy, keeping separate legal systems as well as, possibly, separate currencies. A major task of such a confederation would be to lay the foundations for a truly unified state and to mitigate the more disastrous effects of North Korea's future transformation.

The idea of a confederation has been suggested many times before, but in nearly all cases it was assumed that the two existing Korean governments would somehow agree to create a confederate state. One has to be very naïve to believe that the current North Korean leadership could somehow coexist with South Korea within such a confederate state. Even if they were somehow persuaded to accept such a risky scheme, very soon their own population would become dangerously restive.

In real life, a confederation will become possible only if and when the North Korean regime is overthrown or changes dramatically, to the point that a new leadership in Pyongyang will emerge that will have no reason to fear the influence of the South. In other words, only a post-Kim government can realistically be expected to agree to such a provisional confederation. It does not really matter how this government will come to power, be it through a popular revolution, a coup, or something else. As long as this government is genuinely willing to unite with the South, it might become a participant of the confederation regime. If an acute security crisis leads to a South Korean or international peacekeeping operation in the North, the emergence of a provisional confederation still remains a possible—and highly desirable—solution to the problem of Korea's reunification.

The length of the provisional confederation should be limited, and ten to fifteen years seems like an ideal interval. A longer period might alienate common North Koreans, who will probably see the entire confederation plan as a scheme to keep them from fully enjoying the South Korean lifestyle while using them as cheap labor. On the other hand, a shorter period might not be sufficient for a serious transformation—and the many things that will have to be done.

One of the tasks of such a provisional system will be to control cross-border movement. The confederation will make it relatively easy to maintain a visa system of some kind, with a clearly stated (and reasonable) schedule for a gradual relaxation. For example, it might be stated that for the first five years, all individual trips between the two parts of the new Korea will require a visa-type permit and that North Koreans will not normally be allowed to take jobs or long-term residency in the South. These restrictions should be gradually relaxed, of course.

However, we must be realistic: administrative border controls will not be particularly effective in stopping North Koreans' exodus to the South. Post-unification border guards will not machine-gun illegal crossers, and with South Korea being so rich, so attractive, and so close, fines and mild punishments will have only a marginal impact. After all, the North Korean people have spent the last two decades boldly flouting countless regulations that were supported by an exceptionally severe system of sanctions and punishments. Thus, immigration between the two countries can be reduced only if life in North Korea itself will become sufficiently attractive within a suitably short period.

To achieve this goal, North Koreans also should be protected from the less scrupulous of their newfound brethren. The provisional confederate system, while encouraging other kinds of investment, should strictly control (or even ban) the purchase of arable land and housing in the North by South Korean individuals and companies, thus reducing the risks of a massive land-grab being carried out by greedy real estate agents from the South.

It will be important that the unified confederative government accepts North Korea's 1946 land reform. The new state must declare the property claims of exiled landlord families to be null and void. To placate former owners, some partial compensation might be considered, though the present author is not certain whether grandchildren of former landlords, usually rich and successful men and women, are in dire need of such compensation (especially given that many of these families got their land by being remarkably deferential to their Japanese overlords in the colonial era).

The state-run agricultural cooperatives should be broken up. As a first step, it might be preferable to give the land of the cooperatives to the people who currently farm it—not as property, but rather on a rent-free basis. In five to ten years, families who continue to toil their plots, producing food and paying taxes, should be accorded full ownership rights. This will discourage some North Koreans from rushing to the South while also contributing to the revival of North Korean agriculture. By the end of the confederation period, land and real estate in North Korea should be safely privatized, with North Korean residents (and, perhaps, recent refugees) being major or, better still, sole participants in this process. Incidentally, it is conceivable that North Korean farmers will do what many East German farmers did after unification—re-establish agricultural cooperatives. However, these will be genuine cooperatives and not the state-run farms thinly disguised as voluntary communal farmers' organizations.

The confederation regime will also help to mitigate the problems faced by North Korea's middle class and professionals—essentially, by shielding them from competition for the most difficult initial years. During the confederation period, special efforts should be made to re-educate these people, preparing them for a new environment and helping them to master modern techniques and skills. Most North Korean doctors, teachers, and engineers will be unable to adjust, unfortunately, but at least the first ten to fifteen years will give a chance to the lucky and determined, while also providing others with time to find alternative ways to make a living. Under the confederation, people should be allowed to continue to practice their professions, even though some minimal retraining should either be strongly encouraged or even made mandatory.

The military of the two Koreas should be integrated, with large (perhaps disproportionately large) quotas reserved for former North Korean service members in the unified Korean army. If former military officers are given commissions in the post-unification forces, their remarkable skills and their sincere nationalist zeal will find a useful and safe outlet.

The confederation should also execute some policies that ensure North Koreans will not remain merely a source of "cheap labor" to be used (and abused) by the rich South. It is very important that labor activism is not suppressed and the creation of unified Korean trade unions is actively encouraged.

Naturally, the rich South will have to provide North Korea with a large and steady flow of aid. Fixed transfers plus direct investment (the more the better) and fixed-purpose aid grants will be necessary. However, it probably will make sense not to repeat the German mistake of creating a unified monetary policy and currency overnight—for a while at least, keeping two separate currency systems seems to be a better option.

It will make sense to give North Koreans a fixed admission quota to the most prestigious universities in Seoul. In South Korea, top positions in management, politics, and culture are nearly monopolized by the graduates of the top five schools, the majority of which are located in Seoul. This situation is regrettable, but it is not going to change anytime soon. Since North Korean students normally cannot be pushed through an extremely demanding system of pre-exam cramming, they are not going to be competitive in entrance exams. The only way to get them into places like Seoul

National University and KAIST is some kind of affirmative action system. Such an affirmative action system will be unpopular with South Korean parents, who are very sensitive to any hint at regional or class-based preference in admission policy. However, such sacrifices are a necessary precondition for creating a unified Korean society.

Politics in the post-unification confederation will be tricky and highly contentious. It seems that there are two possible ways to deal with the problem of how to create a unified political system in post-unification Korea.

First, it is possible that for the entire length of the transitional period, or at least the initial years, some outside government will run North Korea. Such a government might be appointed by Seoul, but some kind of UN-mandated international administration might also emerge from a future crisis. Unfortunately, such an administration is likely to be full of greedy and ignorant carpetbaggers who take every opportunity to enrich themselves before running away. Alternatively, some of the bureaucrats in a "Viceroyalty of North Korea" will be younger, idealistic officials from the South, who might be personally clean and devoted, but also very naïve.

Alternatively, immediately after the crisis, a democracy might emerge in the North. This seems to be an attractive option, but assuming that a new elite is either absent or very weak, such a democracy will most likely be dominated by lesser officials from the Kim family era—or at least their children and close relatives. These natural-born opportunists may instantly change their colors and claim themselves to have been lifelong closet democrats (as their peers in Eastern Europe and the USSR once did).

Their children will fare even better—as a matter of fact, the second generation of the current North Korean elite is bound to succeed even in the unlikely and undesirable case of their parents being ousted from the positions of power and subsequently being persecuted. It is easy enough to imagine the situation that will be faced by a South Korean company post-unification when trying to fill a position in the North. They can choose a charming girl with a degree from Kim Il Sung University, with passable English and great social skills, or they can choose a girl of the same age from the countryside with no working knowledge of the English language, a very basic understanding of the outside world, and little comprehension of how the modern economy works.

The choice seems all too simple, but one should remember that the first candidate in our thought experiment is almost certain to be the daughter of a party cadre (perhaps an efficient interrogator from the political police or a senior guard in a prison camp). This is principally because usually only well-connected people—in North Korea's case, people who have gotten their hands dirty—can give their children the opportunity to acquire the afore-mentioned education and skills. Even the good looks of the first candidate might hint that she had the rare privilege of being exempt from annual labor mobilizations (such stints of hard work in the open air are really bad for the skin, and physically age participants). Meanwhile, nearly all the children and grandchildren of the people who once were unlucky enough to fall victim to Kim Il Sung's wrath and spend their youth in camps or in exile in the countryside will look like the second girl in our example—being exiled to the countryside, she would have not the slightest chance to acquire the education and skills that could make her successful in the post-Kim world.

The present author is a historian, and this makes him immune to the idea that the good always win in the end. Most injustices of history have never been avenged, and many injustices have paid off handsomely, both for the perpetrators and their descendants. However, pushing such moral issues aside, one has to admit that there are serious problems with the Kim-era ex-elite: these people will retain their old habits, including, in all probability, a remarkable appetite for bribes. Their knowledge of modern economics and technology, while superior to that of the "lower orders," still leaves much to be desired. To complicate things further, a Northern democratic government would be prone to populist decisions, responsive to pressure from below. Ordinary North Koreans are likely to hold partic-ularly naïve views on how their society and economy can and should op-erate, and some mistakes introduced via popular vote might become ruinous and costly.

Ultimately, both solutions—a South Korean–backed viceroyalty or a North Korean–led democratic government—are very flawed. Whichever path is ultimately chosen, one must expect a great deal of mistakes, demagoguery, mutual recriminations, wild populism, and, alas, official corruption. Nonetheless, on balance we should prefer a corrupt and inefficient democracy (run by the local turncoats) over an inefficient and corrupt viceroyalty (run by the carpetbagging outsiders). It is better to give North Koreans an opportunity to sort out their problems themselves—and if they make mistakes, they will suffer the consequences and, hopefully, learn something. It is also important that they see less reason to blame outsiders for such mistakes. North Korea is their country—not a country of foreigners (even those foreigners who sincerely wish them the best) and not even the country of South Koreans—so they must be empowered as soon as possible.

One of the thorniest issues is the post-unification fate of mid-ranking and high-level bureaucrats in the current regime, as well as the small army of enforcers who have ensured the survival of the Kim family regime. It is quite possible (and indeed highly probable) that many people in both the South and the North will loudly demand justice be served to the former secret police, informers, and prison guards. The graphic exposure of the horrors of North Korean prisons and camps will greatly strengthen such demands. This is noble and understandable but, unfortunately, unrealistic.

My acquaintances from the North Korean police say that police usually have one informer for every forty to fifty adults. This claim seems plausible since it comes from a number of people who do not know one another—and do not have a particular reason to lie about the figure. If true, this means that roughly 200,000 to 300,000 North Koreans are currently active police informers—the mind boggles when trying to calculate how many North Koreans have, in the country's history, reported on their neighbors and/or co-workers. Of course, some informers will have been dropped from the secret police's roster, and therefore the total number of informers and ex-informers could easily approach a million. On top of that, out of North Koreans alive today, some quarter to half million might have been on the payroll of the secret police at some point in their lives. Unless the entire justice system of post-unification Korea is going to spend years punishing all former informers and political police personnel, no honest and fair investigation of their deeds will be possible.

In North Korea, the managerial and professional elite maintain much closer connections with the ruling bureaucracy than was once the case in the Soviet Union or countries of Eastern Europe. This closeness means that any honest and systematic attempt at "de-Kimification" (analogous to post-1945 German "de-Nazification") will amount to the removal of virtually all North Koreans with managerial and professional skills. It would of course be wonderful if efforts aimed at creating an alternative elite (as outlined earlier) produce a sufficient number of skilled and ethically untainted personnel by the time of unification. However, we should be under no illusions—even if the second elite emerges soon, it is likely to remain small.

Let us be honest: no real justice will likely be possible when the time comes to deal with the former agents of the Kim family dictatorship. There are far too many of them, and their crimes, committed over long decades, are now almost impossible to investigate thoroughly. Most of their victims became statistics long ago. Sadly enough, the rejection of the regime's henchmen and collaborators will also mean the rejection of nearly all people with useful experience and education. Thus, justice is not merely impossible: it might be very damaging.

There is also another important reason why there should be no rush to punish Kim's people. One of the major reasons why the Kim family regime has been so stubborn in rejecting reforms is the widespread perception among the regime's elite that the state's collapse (a probable outcome of such reforms) would lead to the political demise and perhaps even physical slaughter of this elite. The fear of persecution is the major reason why these people have refused to switch to more rational methods in running their country. It is also the reason why the North Korean elite and its supporters (a significant minority of the total population) are likely to fight in order to protect the system if and when the final crisis comes. A clear and unequivocal promise of a general amnesty for all former misdeeds will perhaps help to prevent a full-scale civil war. In order to be taken seriously, such an offer should be made clearly and directly, thus rendering its eventual retraction less likely. Moreover, such an offer, once made, should of course be kept.

This does not necessarily mean that the misdeeds of the Kim regime should be neglected and glossed over. A possible—and very partial—solution is a Truth and Reconciliation Commission, an approach once pioneered by South Africa, where crimes and human rights abuses under apartheid were investigated but almost no judgments passed and almost no punishments carried out.

Another possible device is lustration, akin to what was used in post-Socialist Eastern Europe. According to this system, more prominent collaborators of Communist governments—secret police officers, mid- to high-ranking party officials, and so on—were deprived of the right to occupy important administrative positions or to serve in the judiciary and/or law enforcement agencies. The same policy might be acceptable in North Korea as well, but it should not target too many members of the old elite. In a sense, for at least a few decades, every educated North Korean could be plausibly described as a Kim-era collaborator, so lustration should be applied only to those who were actively involved with the most repulsive and obvious forms of police terror—like prison camp administrators. We should leave it to investigative journalists and historians of later generations (and, perhaps, even descendants of some of the culprits) to fully investigate the crimes of the Kim era.

The Kim family itself should not become an exception. Ideally, it makes sense to let these people (and there are a few dozen of them) leave the country and proceed to comfortable exile somewhere—perhaps Macao, where they may be controlled and protected by China, which can also deny direct responsibility for sheltering the first family. Let these people do what they are rumored to be best at: devour impressive quantities of gourmet cuisine, while also enthusiastically chasing after pretty women. Perhaps some of them will also write memoirs in which they will persuasively explain how they would have brought unbelievable prosperity to their homeland had their plans not been sabotaged by corrupt officials and a "complicated" international environment (this is what overthrown politicians always do).

Even the confiscation of the Kim family's assets, now rumored to be hidden in Switzerland, Hong Kong, and Macao, might not be such a good idea. The couple of billion dollars they have managed to steal will make little difference in the mammoth task of post-Kim reconstruction and might be a price worth paying for a relatively bloodless transition. Moreover, we should not forget that if you live a billionaire's lifestyle, it is much more difficult to present yourself as a martyr and victim of unjust persecution.

The proposals discussed here are controversial and, if implemented, are bound to be described by many a future historian as "ethically dubious compromises" or even as "backroom deals between the North and South Korean elites" and thus "anti-democratic" and even "immoral." As a historian myself, I do not mind letting future historians feel self-righteous. But in real life, policy decisions tend to be choices between bad and worse. In this case, the alternative seems far worse: North Korean secret police machine-gunning civilians in the belief that by doing so they are saving their families; risky and even suicidal brinkmanship by generals who feel cornered; an alienated, bitter, but large and influential underclass of former regime collaborators who unite with common Northerners in their disgust at South Korean carpetbaggers. We should also remember that this alternative will not make future historians happy: decisive and thorough (and seriously counterproductive) cleansing of former regime collaborators will be branded as a "witch-hunt" in their writings.

SOMETHING ABOUT PAINKILLERS . . .

We have seen that neither diplomatic concessions nor military and economic pressures are likely to influence the North Korean regime. One has to wait until history takes its course while speeding up developments through persistent and patient policies. The wait might be long. It is not impossible that Kim Jong Un's succession may trigger a chain of events that will bring the regime down in the next few years. But it is at least equally possible that the Kim family regime will survive this and other challenges and will remain essentially unchanged until, say, 2020 or even 2030.

We therefore face a persistent problem whose solution will take a long time—probably decades. But what should be done in the meantime?

Due to the democratic nature of the United States, South Korea, and most of the governments involved in the region, we can be certain that at regular intervals a new group of decision-makers will pop up just to repeat the same mistakes their predecessors once made. The pendulum is likely to keep moving between overly optimistic hopes for engagement and overly bullish hopes for pressure—as has been the case for the last twenty-odd years. But even if cold-minded realists and pragmatists prevail somehow, they still have to do something about North Korea as it exists now. They need to reduce the security risks created by its nuclear program, its brinkmanship, and its risky, if cynically rational, international behavior.

The North Korean issue cannot be simply dealt with using one set of long-term policies, outlined earlier. It also requires a set of shorter-term policies aimed at preventing (or mitigating) excessive provocative behavior, reducing proliferation threats, and diminishing the sufferings of ordinary North Koreans. However, one should never forget that these short-term policies are essentially palliative, akin to a painkiller that masks the symptoms and makes life bearable until the illness itself can be treated—but does not solve the actual problem.

The first of such shorter-term policies might be a de facto acceptance of the North Korean nuclear program. Admittedly, this is exactly what North Korean strategists want. They don't talk about freezing their program for monetary rewards anymore, but they have indicated a number of times that they might be ready to stop further development of their nuclear capabilities if the rewards are sufficiently high.

The "complete, verifiable, and irreversible" denuclearization is doomed to remain unattainable as long as the Kim family regime is in control. Due to the manifold reasons outlined previously, North Korea will keep at least a part of its modest nuclear arsenal. The North Korean leaders might compromise on certain things (if they are paid handsomely enough), but this is the nonnegotiable bottom line—and after the second nuclear test, the Washington mainstream came to understand it.

Nevertheless, the North Koreans have expressed their interest in the solution recently proposed by Siegfried Hecker, the former head of the US

Department of Energy laboratories in Los Alamos, known as the "three no's": "No more nukes, No better nukes, No proliferation." This means that North Korea is expected to halt its nuclear research and production, while keeping the existent nukes—in exchange for some concessions and compensations from the outside world (which, for all practical reasons, means the United States).

This proposal might be acceptable for Pyongyang—if the fee is good, that is. After all, North Korea does not need its old rusty reactors any more. Yongbyon, the North Korean nuclear research center, cannot possibly outproduce Los Alamos in the United States or Arzamas-16 in Russia, and it does not make much political sense to increase the North Korean nuclear arsenal further. The Yongbyon laboratories have already produced enough plutonium for a few nuclear devices, and this is more than sufficient for the dual political purposes of deterrence and blackmail. If North Koreans use these facilities to increase their nuclear armory from the five to ten devices they are suspected of possessing now to, say, fifty or even a hundred devices, their ability to deter and/or blackmail will not increase five- or tenfold. As a matter of fact, it will not increase much at all. Consequently, these research and production facilities have outlived their usefulness and thus can be dismantled.

Perhaps the North Koreans will agree to accept measures that will make proliferation less likely, thus addressing another major US concern. It is open to question which types of measures will be acceptable, but perhaps surprise inspections of ships and airport facilities will be allowed (once again, North Korea's diplomats will require a high price for such a major concession, which in effect infringes their sovereignty).

Even a partial surrender of existent nukes might be negotiable. Perhaps North Korea can be bribed into giving up part of its plutonium and/or a few nuclear devices. However, this denuclearization is not going to be either "complete" or "verifiable." Actually, it has to be very partial. North Korea's leaders will need to at least maintain a high level of ambiguity about their nuclear capabilities or, ideally, receive an explicit or implicit admission that they will be allowed to keep a stockpile of weapons-grade plutonium and/or enriched uranium as well as a couple of nuclear devices. The stockpile and nuclear devices will be safely hidden somewhere in its underground facilities, to serve as a deterrent and also a potential tool for diplomatic blackmail.

Of course, the "three no" proposal is not without serious downsides. From the US point of view, such a deal would mean that North Korea is rewarded for its nuclear blackmail. Indeed, North Korea is so far the world's only state that first signed the Nuclear Non-Proliferation Treaty (NPT), then withdrew from the NPT and successfully developed a workable nuclear device. If it is not only allowed to keep its nuclear arsenal but also manages to squeeze some monetary aid from the United States, this will clearly create a dangerous precedent. Control—especially in regard to proliferation—is also a difficult issue because few would doubt that the North Korean side would use every opportunity to cheat. Last but not least, it is important to keep in mind that signed treaties have virtually no binding power in the North Korean leaders' frame of mind, so we can be sure that the North Korean side will keep its obligations only as long as they receive a steady supply of aid and other payments.

However, although these problems and concerns are real, it nonetheless might make sense to accept the "three no" approach. The alternatives are even less attractive. The North Korean government is not going to remain idle while Washington ignores it. North Korean engineers will work hard to produce more uranium and plutonium, to perfect available technologies while the North Korean diplomats quietly but persistently explore possible markets for nuclear weapons. Meanwhile, missile engineers will continue their work as well, and sooner or later they will develop a sufficiently reliable long-range delivery system that is quite capable of hitting the continental United States. In January 2011 US Secretary of Defense Robert Gates said that North Korea is "within five years of being able to strike the continental United States with an intercontinental ballistic missile."[3] As head of the US military establishment, Robert Gates might have an instinct for exaggerating threats—and some people have assumed that he exaggerated the Soviet missile threat as the CIA head in the 1980s.[4] Chances are, then, that it will probably take longer than five years—but it will happen sooner or later if the Kim family regime stays in control long enough. And there is little doubt that, while their engineers and spies are working hard, North Korean politicians will stage occasional confrontations, just to remind the world that they are capable of inflicting damage if their demands are ignored.

In order to prevent such developments, it might make sense to seriously consider the "three no" approach—in spite of its only too obvious shortcomings. But, even if such an approach is accepted, one should enter the deal without any illusions. This is merely the way to buy time—and quite an imperfect way at that.

Another possible and useful palliative is the maintenance of the six-party talks that are currently in yet another hibernation period. Ostensibly, these talks were once initiated in order to bring about the complete denuclearization of North Korea. This stated goal is unachievable (or, to be more precise, talks will not contribute much in achieving this goal). However, this does not necessarily mean that the six-party talks are of little or no value.

There are at least two important functions the six-party talks serve well. First, the very existence of negotiations contributes toward stability in and around North Korea; the six-party talks marginally reduce the likelihood of military confrontation in the region.

That said, it is the second function that is of special importance. The six-party talks create a convenient venue for diplomats of all interested countries to discuss North Korea–related problems. The six-party talks are not going to reach their stated goal of denuclearization, but they are a natural place to agree on positions and actions in case of a major crisis. When a new crisis comes (and it will come sooner or later), interested parties will have precious little time to discuss manifold challenges, so speedy and reliable interactions between all major stakeholders will be vital. Neither the unwieldy UN bureaucracy nor standard diplomatic channels are efficient and fast enough in addressing such an emergency, and the stakes in a grave crisis may be very high.

It is therefore a good idea to keep the six-party talks in place—partially as a way to mitigate tensions and handle the ongoing problems, but largely as a place where future North Korea–related issues can be dealt with quickly and decisively. Taking into account the possible political and diplomatic consequences of regime collapse in the North, this is a cheap and efficient measure. It is important, however, not to lose sight of the main goal: waiting for (and, to an extent, promoting) regime transformation inside North Korea. The measures outlined here should be seen realistically. Short-term policies are painkillers—not antibiotics.

Conclusion: No Easy Ending

What to say in concluding this book? Perhaps we should start with two pieces of bad news: first, North Korea is a problem; and second, this problem has no fast or easy solution.

Who is responsible for the North Korean tragedy? Starry-eyed Western European intellectuals who in the 1840s and 1850s, surrounded by gross injustices and inequalities, suggested an alternative to the nascent capitalist system? Young East Asian idealists who in the 1920s enthusiastically embraced Marxism (or, rather, Leninism) as the way to national salvation? Battle-hardened Soviet commanders, who in the 1940s wanted to "liberate" the Korean people, while creating a friendly government in a neighboring country? The North Koreans, who in the 1950s came to believe that the Soviet (or, rather, Stalinist) model was key to building a new Korean nation, powerful, prosperous, and proud? The sad part of the North Korean story is that most of its key players—or key culprits, should we say?—were decent human beings, often driven by noble and admirable motivation. They made decisions that seemed logical at the time. The accumulated result is, however, a complete mess, with no easy or universally acceptable solution in sight.

North Korea remains a problem for the outside world because in order to survive, its decision-makers have no choice but to live dangerously. Real or alleged proliferation attempts, nuclear and missile tests, and occasional shoot-outs do not reflect the insane bellicosity or irrationality of the North Korean leadership. Rather, these actions are manifestations of a quite rational survival strategy that might have no viable alternative if judged from the point of view of Pyongyang's tiny elite.

We should bear in mind the fact that we outsiders are not the primary victims of North Korea's situation. The greatest suffering is borne by the North Korean people. While other nations of East Asia have enjoyed an era of unprecedented improvement in living standards, educational achievement, and life expectancy, North Koreans are stuck with a system that is both politically repressive and economically grotesquely inefficient. Many of them have found ways to cope, but on balance the current situation has brought ruin to countless lives and has led to a great waste of human creative energy—and continues to do so.

So far the policies of Seoul and Washington have oscillated between a hard and a soft-line approach. Neither, however, is going to produce much impact on the behavior of the North Korean elite. These people cannot be bribed into changing their country, nor can they be blackmailed into reform.

Nonetheless, there is also good news. The North Korean regime is not sustainable in the long run. Subtle and spontaneous change is gradually eroding the ideological, political, and even economic foundations of the regime. The government understands how dangerous these spontaneous changes are, but cannot do much about the situation; the erosion cannot be stopped, let alone reversed. It is not impossible that Kim Jong Un and his future confidants will take risks and initiate reforms, hoping to create a North Korean version of a developmental dictatorship. Gradual evolution is usually better than dramatic and violent upheaval, but—perhaps unfortunately—such a reformist regime has little chance of remaining stable in the presence of an affluent South that is so very near.

So what can the outside world do? Frankly, not all that much. It can in some ways attempt to speed up the slow-motion erosion of the Kim family dictatorship, creating forces that will demand change, while also ensuring that the coming crisis will be less chaotic and painful. It makes some sense to speed things up—after all, if the inevitable happens a few years earlier, it will mean fewer people die in prison camps and more people have the chance to live, work, and raise children in a more decent society. For the outside world, it means one or two fewer major international crises. Nonetheless, one should not become too enthusiastic about these attempts to speed up the inevitable: such efforts, however admirable and useful, will have a relatively slight impact on the situation.

It is more important to prepare for the post-unification mess, because it will bring difficult and often unforeseen challenges (and the North Korean crisis is bound to be messy). Admittedly, the potential threats associated with North Korea's collapse are widely understood, but usually it makes people fantasize about a gradual transformation of the regime along Chinese lines as the way to deliver a soft landing. Unfortunately, a soft landing, while not completely impossible and indeed desirable, is not very probable. Instead, we are likely to face one of two scenarios: either a hard landing or an even harder landing. Thus, the only way to achieve the desirable soft landing is to make the hard landing as soft as possible—or, speaking less metaphorically, to find ways to mitigate the social and economic disasters that will be brought about by the likely collapse of the regime.

We must not forget, however, that the policies that might help to change North Korea eventually are not going to sell well in the countries with the largest stake in promoting such a change—the United States and South Korea. This is not because these policies are expensive or difficult to implement or might lead to unnecessary complications. On the contrary, these policies are cheap—so cheap, actually, that in some cases contributions by individuals might make a difference. However, there is a serious problem with all of these policies—they require long-term commitments to goals that are likely to be achieved well after the next election cycle. These are not the types of policies that sell well in a democracy.

Broadcasting into North Korea will cost only a few million dollars a year and potentially save hundreds of millions in the future. Similarly, providing scholarships for refugees will hardly cost more than broadcasting. Yet one cannot expect such policies to win the ringing endorsement of professional politicians once they realize that the impact is not likely to be felt until the next generation and the policy's success will, at best, find its way into a history book rather than an election campaign.

Alas, the hawkish approach sells well when the regime under consideration is a repulsive hereditary dictatorship. It is very good for both a politician's self-esteem and election results to insist that "We don't negotiate with evil; we defeat it," even when such lofty statements are nonsensical and have no impact on the world outside polling stations. Indeed, the hawkish approach is probably just as counterproductive as a dovish approach, when measured according to its aims.

Conversely, the sales pitch of the doves is powerful, too. Indeed, it is appealing to say that North Korean decision-makers are also "humans who love their families" and that therefore, sufficient kindness in dealing with them will bring with it mutual trust and a spirit of cooperation. There is no doubt that North Korean leaders are humans who love their families—actually, such noble sentiment might be the core driver behind what they are doing. After all, as we have seen, they believe that not only their futures but those of their loved ones are contingent on the continued existence of their regime and that this regime can be maintained only through skillful diplomatic brinkmanship and the generous use of terror within the country's borders.

All of this points to a sorry reality of modern democratic politics, once described by Winston Churchill as "the worst form of government." Churchill later added, however, the phrase "except all those other forms that have been tried from time to time." If government bureaucracies are not particularly interested, part of the work can and should be done by private foundations and individuals. Everything that increases the quantity and quality of interactions between North Koreans and the outside world should be welcomed and supported.

North Korean history is another sad example of how lofty ideals and good intentions can turn sour. The founding fathers of North Korea might have been brutal and shrewd, but they were neither cold-hearted killers nor power-hungry politicos. Rather, they were sincere—if ruthless—idealists who wanted to bring about a perfect world. They made the wrong choice, however, and in due course, their children and grandchildren found themselves captive to a brutal and inefficient system. This was not the result of anybody's intention, since most of the key participants in the North Korean tragedy were rational and often well-meaning human beings. Nevertheless, the result was and remains a disaster, and this disaster is likely to continue for a few more years or even decades—and its consequences are likely to haunt the Korean people for generations.

CHAPTER 1

1. For those desiring to learn about North Korean history in some depth, the best introduction is a short book by Adrian Buzo (although its main emphasis is on the 1965–95 period). Adrian Buzo, *The Guerilla Dynasty: Politics and Leadership in North Korea* (Boulder, Colo.: Westview Press, 1999).

2. Chay Jongsuk, *Unequal Partners in Peace And War: The Republic of Korea and the United States, 1948–1953* (Westport, Conn.: Praeger, 2002), 32–33.

3. On the factions in the North Korean leadership and the complicated domestic politics of the 1940s, see: Andrei Lankov, *From Stalin to Kim Il Sung: The Formation of North Korea, 1945–1960* (New Brunswick: Rutgers University Press, 2002).

4. The best biography of Kim Il Sung was written by Suh Dae-suk in the 1980s, before the Soviet archives were open and provided a wealth of additional material. However, most of what he wrote in the 1980s managed to stand the harsh test of time surprisingly well. See Dae-Sook Suh, *Kim Il Sung: The North Korean Leader* (New York: Columbia University Press, 1988).

5. For a detailed discussion of these instructions (complete with referrals to archival material and lengthy quotes), see: Andrei Lankov, *From Stalin to Kim Il Sung: The Formation of North Korea, 1945–1960* (New Brunswick: Rutgers University Press, 2002), 42–47.

6. For a detailed description of the meeting (based on the evidence of the surviving diary of Shtykov), see: Chŏn Hyŏnsu, *"Swittŭikkop'ŭ ilki"ka malhanŭn pukhan chŏngkwŏn-ŭi sŏngrip kwachŏng [Shtykov's diary and the formation of North Korea]* // yŏksapip'yŏng 1995nyŏn kaŭlho t'ongkwŏn 32 (1995).

7. In English, plentiful evidence of such support can be found in a well-researched study by Charles Armstrong, who drew on the wealth of original North Korean documents captured by the US forces during the Korean War. See Charles Armstrong, *The North Korean Revolution, 1945–1950* (Ithaca: Cornell University Press, 2003).

8. For the most up-to-date review on the emerging evidence regarding the Korean War origin, see materials (bulletins and working papers) of the Cold War International History Project. Of special importance is the working paper by Kathryn Weathersby. Kathryn Weathersby, *"Should We Fear This?" Stalin and the Danger of War with America* (Washington: Woodrow Wilson International Center for Scholars, 2004).

9. On the fate of Ho Ka-i and the factionalism in North Korean leadership, see: Andrei Lankov, *From Stalin to Kim Il Sung: The Formation of North Korea, 1945–1960* (New Brunswick, N.J.: Rutgers University Press, 2002).

10. For a detailed description of the 1956 crisis and its consequences, see Andrei Lankov, *Crisis in North Korea: The Failure of De-Stalinization, 1956* (Honolulu: University of Hawai'i Press, 2005).

    Of special importance is a well-researched work by Balázs Szalontai, who used East European documents to carefully trace the formation of Kim Il Sung's peculiar version of "national Stalinism." See Balázs Szalontai, *Kim Il Sung in the Khrushchev Era: Soviet-DPRK Relations and the Roots of North Korean Despotism, 1953–1964* (Stanford: Stanford University Press, 2005).

11. Research on the educational background of the Manchurian guerrillas was done by Wada Haruki. Wada Haruki, *Kim Il Sŏng-wa Manchu hangil chŏnchaeng [Kim Il Sung and anti-Japanese resistance in Manchuria]* (Seoul: Ch'angjak-kwa pip'yŏngsa, 1992), 303.

12. About the number of political prisoners in GULAG in 1951, see: Viktor Zemskov, "Gulag, istoriko-sotsiologicheskie aspekty," *Sotsiologicheskie issledovaniia* iss. 7 (1991), 3–16.

13. For materials on the crisis in the relations between the Soviet Union and North Korea, see: Andrei Lankov, *Crisis in North Korea: The Failure of De-Stalinization, 1956* (Honolulu: University of Hawai'i Press, 2005); James Person, *"We Need Help from Outside": The North Korean Opposition Movement of 1956* (Washington: Woodrow Wilson Center, 2006).

14. Bernd Schaefer, *North Korean "Adventurism" and China's Long Shadow, 1966–1972* (Washington: Woodrow Wilson International Center for Scholars, 2004), 9.

    This working paper by Bernd Schaefer provides a wealth of new information on the tense relations between China and North Korea in the era of China's "cultural revolution."

15. Schaefer, *North Korean "Adventurism,"* 5.

16. Schaefer, *North Korean "Adventurism,"* 2.

17. Schaefer, *North Korean "Adventurism,"* 7–9.

18. Not much is written about the debt debacle of the 1970s. For some basic information, see: Sophie Roell, "For North Korean exposure try buying its debt," *Dow Jones Newswires*, Pyongyang, May 7, 2001.

19. The "signboard incident" is reported in a book by the former Swedish ambassador to North Korea. Erik Cornell, *North Korea under Communism: Report of an Envoy to Paradise* (London, New York: Routledge Curzon/Taylor & Francis, 2002), 67.

20. For a comprehensive review of the nonclassified material in regard to North Korea's involvement with smuggling, see Sheena Chestnut, "Illicit Activity and Proliferation:

North Korean Smuggling Networks," *International Security* vol. 32, iss.1 (2007): 80–111.

21. The official report by the US Department of State in 2012 specified: "Although trafficking of methamphetamine [...] continued [in 2011], the lack of public reports of drug trafficking with an official DPRK connection suggests that high-profile state-sponsored drug trafficking may have ceased or been sharply reduced." United States Department of State Bureau for International Narcotics and Law Enforcement Affairs, *International Narcotics Control Strategy Report* (Washington, D.C.: Department of State, 2012), vol. 1, 188.

22. There is a large number of publications on the abductions of the Japanese citizens. For example, see Patricia Steinhoff, "Kidnapped Japanese in North Korea: The New Left Connection," *Journal of Japanese Studies*, vol. 30 (Winter, 2004), 123–42. A great wealth of up-to-date information on the issue can be found on the special website maintained by the Japanese Foreign Ministry.

23. See Charles Armstrong's excellent review of North Korea's foreign policy: Charles Armstrong, *Tyranny of the Weak: North Korea and the World, 1950–1992* (Ithaca: Cornell University Press, 2013), 238.

24. For a detailed study of the politics behind the transfer of the ethnic Koreans to the DPRK, see Tessa Morris-Suzuki, *Exodus to North Korea: Shadows from Japan's Cold War* (Lanham: Rowman & Littlefield Publishers, 2007).

25. In 1969 Chad and Central African Republic became the first two states to maintain full diplomatic relations with both Koreas. See Barry Gills, *Korea Versus Korea: A Case of Contested Legitimacy* (London and New York: Routledge, 1996), 132.

26. For new data about North Korea's attitude toward the Vietnamese War, see Charles Armstrong's excellent review of North Korea's foreign policy: Charles Armstrong, *Tyranny of the Weak: North Korea and the World, 1950–1992* (Ithaca: Cornell University Press, 2013), 146–49.

27. Mitchell Lerner, *Kim Il Sung, the Juche Ideology, and the Second Korean War* (Washington, D.C.: Woodrow Wilson International Center for Scholars, 2011).

28. For a general history of the South Korean student movement in English, see Namhee Lee, *The Making of Minjung: Democracy and the Politics of Representation in South Korea* (Ithaca: Cornell University Press, 2007).

29. For a comprehensive overview of the PDS since its inception and until its collapse in the 1990s, see No Yong Hwan and Yŏn Ha Chŏng, *Pukhan-ŭi chumin saenghwal pochang chŏngch'aek p'yŏngka [Evaluation of the welfare policies in North Korea]* (Seoul: Hankuk pokŏnsahoeyŏnkuwŏn, 1997), 47–62.

30. According to a 1998 law, the maximum size of the kitchen gardens is limited to 30 pyŏng (100 sq. meters) for farmers and 10 pyŏng (33 square meters) for industrial workers. See the law cited in: Pak Il-su, *Konan-ŭi haeggun ihu kaein soyugwon pyŏnhwa-e kwanhan yŏngu [A study of relational changes in individual ownership system after the "ardous march"]* (Seoul: Kyŏngnam Taehakkyo Pukhan Taehagwon, 2006), 57.

31. For more information, see Viola Lynne (ed.), *Contending with Stalinism: Soviet Power and Popular Resistance in the 1930s* (Ithaca, N.Y.: Cornell University Press, 2002), 173; Alex Dowlah, and John Elliot, *The Life and Times of Soviet Socialism* (Westport, Conn.: Praeger Publishers, 1997), 168.

32. Chad Raymond, "No Responsibility and No Rice: The Rise and Fall of Agricultural Collectivization in Vietnam," *Agricultural History* 1, iss. 1 (2008): 49.

33. Michael Nelson, *War of the Black Heavens: The Battles of Western Broadcasting in the Cold War* (Syracuse, N.Y.: Syracuse University Press, 1997), 163.

34. For the most detailed description of the North Korean prison system in English, see David Hawk, *Hidden Gulag, Second Edition* (Washington, D.C.: U.S. Committee for Human Rights in North Korea, 2012).

35. See David Hawk, *North Korea's Hidden Gulag: Interpreting Reports of Changes in the Prison Camps* (Washington: The Committee for Human Rights in North Korea, 2013), 33–34.

36. Hawk, *North Korea's Hidden Gulag*, 30.

37. See prison memoirs by Kang Chŏl-hwan: Kang Chol-hwan, and Pierre Rigoulot, *The Aquariums of Pyongyang: Ten Years in a North Korean Gulag* (New York: Basic Books, 2001).

38. Benjamin R. Young, "Our Common Struggle Against Our Common Enemy": North Korea and the American Radical Left. NKIDP e-Dossier no. 14 (Washington: Woodrow Wilson Center, 2013).

39. Kang Chŏl-hwan, "Pukhan kyogwasŏ sok-ŭi Namhan" [South Korea in North Korean textbooks], *Chosŏn ilbo*, December 7, 2001, 54.

40. Yi Hyo-bŏm and Ch' oe Hyŏn-ho, "Pukhan kyokwasŏ-rŭl t'onghan chŏngsonyŏn kach'igwan yŏngu: Kodŭng chunghakkyo kongsanjujŭi todok 3,4 haknyŏn chungsim-ŭro. Pukhan yŏngu hakhoebo" [A study of the youth value system through North Korean textbooks: centered around the textbooks for "Communist Morality" for years 3 and 4 in high school], *Pukhan yŏngu hakhoebo*, 2000, iss. 2, 250.

41. This dualistic (neither-pro-nor-anti) attitude is described in a brilliant book by Alexei Yurchak, which should be recommended to all interested in popular attitudes toward the official ideology in the later-stage Leninist regimes: Alexei Yurchak, *Everything Was Forever, until It Was No More: The Last Soviet Generation* (Princeton, NJ: Princeton University Press, 2006.)

42. See Joan Robinson, Review of "Socialist Korea" by Ellen Brun, Jacques Hersh.//*The Monthly Review*, October 1977, 61.

43. *DPR Korea 2008 Population Census. National Report* (Pyongyang: Central Bureau of Statistics, 2009).

44. For the per capita GDP data, see: CIA Factbook, 2013, available at https://www.cia.gov/library/publications/the-world-factbook/index.html.
    For the WHO infant mortality data, see the WHO database, available at http://apps.who.int/gho/data/node.main.

45. *World Health Statistics 2011* (Geneva: World Health Organization, 2011), 116–22.

46. Brian Myers, "The Watershed That Wasn't: Re-evaluating Kim Il Sung's 'Juche speech' of 1955," *Acta Koreana*, 2006, iss. 9: 89–115.

47. Kim Jong Il, *On the Juche Idea of Our Party* (Pyongyang: Foreign Languages Publishing House, 1985), 7.

48. The life story of Kim Jong Il has been a topic of many works, but due to the nature of his regime it is often difficult to distinguish between facts and unsubstantiated rumors. So far, the most comprehensive Kim Jong Il biography in English is

Michael Breen, *Kim Jong-il: North Korea's Dear Leader* (Singapore and Hoboken, N.J.: Wiley, 2004).

49. George McCune, *Korea* (Cambridge, Mass.: Harvard University Press, 1950), 56–57.
50. Historical statistics compiled by Angus Maddison and his research team. Available for download at: www.ggdc.net/maddison/Historical_Statistics/horizontal-file_02-2010 .xls.
51. On the scale of the North Korean military, see Nicholas Eberstadt, *Korea Approaches Reunification* (Armonk, N.Y.: M. E. Sharpe, 1995), 51–72.

CHAPTER 2

1. For trade statistics, see Kongdan Oh and Ralph Hassig, *North Korea Through the Looking Glass* (Washington, D.C.: Brookings Institution Press, 2000), 44–45.
2. Bank of Korea, *Pukhan chuyo kyŏngjae chipyo pigyo* [North Korea, a comparison of the main economic indicators], can be found on: www.bok.or.kr.
3. Im Kang-taek, *Pukhan kyŏngjae kaebal kyaehwaek surip pangan yŏngu: Paet'ŭnam saryae-rŭl* [Taking the example of Vietnam: Research on North Korea's economic development planning] (Chungsim-ŭro, Seoul: T'ongil Yŏnguwon, 2010), 164.
4. Stephan Haggard and Marcus Noland, *Famine in North Korea: Markets, Aid and Reform* (New York: Columbia University Press, 2007), 35.
5. Daniel Goodkind and Loraine West, "The North Korean Famine and Its Demographic Impact," *Population and Development Review* vol. 27, iss. 2 (2001): 219–38.
6. Pak Keong-Suk, "Economic Hardship and Famines since the 1990s and Their Impact on Population Dynamics in North Korea," Presentation at the 51 Asia Seminar at Waseda University, Tokyo, Japan, December 2010.
7. Daniel Goodkind, Loraine West, and Peter Johnson, "A Reassessment of Mortality in North Korea, 1993–2008," Paper presented at the annual meeting of the Population Association of America, March 31–April 2, 2011, Washington, D.C.
8. Kim Byung-Yeon and Song Dongho, "The Participation of North Korean Households in the Informal Economy: Size, Determinants, and Effect," *Seoul Journal of Economics* vol. 21, iss. 2 (2008): 373.
9. Kim Pyŏn Yŏn and Yang Mun Su, *Pukhan kyŏngche-esŏŭi sichangkwa chŏngpu [The government and market in North Korean economy]* (Seoul: Sŏul taehakkyo ch'ulp'anmunhwawŏn, 2012), 124.
10. Pyŏn Yŏn and Mun Su, *Pukhan kyŏngche-esŏŭi sichangkwa chŏngpu*, 124.
11. The decrease in official-sponsored drug production was reported by the AFP (Agence France-Presse), which cited the US State Department. See "US says N. Korea's State Drug Trafficking on Wane," *Asiaone News*, March 4, 2011, accessed at news.asiaone.com. This agrees quite well with the observations of the present author.
12. Yi Yŏng-guk told his own story in a recently published book: Yi Yŏng-guk, *Na-nŭn Kim Chŏng-il kyŏnghowon iŏssta [I was the bodyguard of Kim Jong I]* (Seoul: Sidae chŏngsin, 2004).
13. P *Tumankang-ŭl kŏnnŏon saramtŭl [People who have crossed the Tumen River]* (Seoul: Chŏngdo ch'ulp'an, 1999), 27.

14. For a review of the existent research on the number of North Korean refugees in China, see Stephan Haggard and Marcus Noland, *Witness to Transformation: Refugee Insights into North Korea* (Washington, D.C.: Peterson Institute for International Economics, 2011), 2.

15. For a description of such VIP defection (arranged for an aged woman by her daughter), see Barbara Demick, *Nothing to Envy: Ordinary Lives in North Korea* (New York: Spiegel & Grau, 2010), 239–47. In her informative and highly recommended book, Demick also provides detailed descriptions of far more common, cheap defections.

16. Some rough estimates of the scale of remittances have been made in 2009–11 by a number of people, including the present author. These estimates are in the $5–20 million range.

17. International Crisis Group, *Strangers at Home: North Koreans in the South Report N°208* (Brussels: International Crisis Group, 2011), 14–15. This report is the latest (and arguably the best) of a small number of English-language materials dealing with the refugee problem in South Korea. There is a large quantity of Korean-language material, however.

18. The spread of videos was widely reported by refugees and the media. For a detailed account of the North Korean "video revolution," see Yi Chu-chol, "Pukhan chuminui oepu chongpo suyong taeto pyonhwa" [The Research of Changes in North Koreans' Attitudes Toward the Outside World Information], *Hankuk tongpuka nonchong* vol. 46 (2008): 245–48.

19. InterMedia, "International Broadcasting in North Korea: North Korean Refugee/ Traveler Survey Report," April–August 2009.

20. Remarks about the role of the computer as a status symbol: Kim Po-kŏn, "The 5 Storages and 6 Contraptions Which Serve as Symbols of Prosperity in North Korea," *T'ongil Hankuk [Unified Korea]* vol. 27, iss. 1 (2009): 80. I would add that in my own talks with defectors, this new symbolic significance of the computer was mentioned frequently.

CHAPTER 3

1. Surjit Bhalla, *Imagine There's No Country: Poverty, Inequality, and Growth in the Era of Globalization* (Washington, D.C.: Institute for International Economics, 2002), 16.

2. According to the calculations of Angus Maddison, the most respected economic historian of our days, in 1960 the per capita GDP was: $1,226 for South Korea, $1,277 for Somalia, $1,353 for Taiwan, and $1,445 for Senegal (measured in 1990 International Geary-Khamis dollars).

3. Chad Raymond, "No Responsibility and No Rice: The Rise and Fall of Agricultural Collectivization in Vietnam," *Agricultural History* vol. 82, iss. 1 (2008): 54–55.

4. Sang T. Choe, "North Korea Moving from Isolation to an Open Market Economy: Is It Time to Invest or to Continue Observing?" *Competitiveness Review* vol. 13, iss. 2 (2003): 60–69.

5. Terence Roehrig, "Creating the Conditions for Peace in Korea: Promoting Incremental Change in North Korea," *Korea Observer* vol. 40, iss. 1 (2009): 222.

6. For details on the ongoing argument over the actual size of the North Korean GDP, see I Chong-sok, "Pukhan kukmin sotuk chaepyongka" [Reassessment of the National Income of North Korea], *Chongsewa chongchaek* 3 (2008): 1–4.

   For the most recent estimates of the North Korean GDP, see: 2011 *Pukhan-ŭi chuyo t'onggye chip'yo* [*Major Statistical Indicators for North Korea, 2011*] (Seoul: National Statistics Office, 2012).

7. Richard Vinen, *History in Fragments: Europe in the Twentieth Century* (London: Abacus, 2002), 513.

8. There is, actually, an ongoing debate on the reasons behind this relative success of the former nomenklatura and, more broadly speaking, Communist Party members in the post-Communist societies. Majority opinion is that it was brought about by the survival of institutions and networks, while the minority believes it is due to their personal qualities—opportunism, ambitions, organizational skills. There is no need, however, to go into excessive details: the continuing domination of the former elite is an undisputable and widely recognized fact. See Akos Rona-Tas and Alya Guseva, "The Privileges of Past Communist Party Membership in Russia and Endogenous Switching Regression," *Social Science Research* 30 (2001): 641–52.

9. *Tokyo Shimbun*, February 2, 2011.

10. Nicholas Eberstadt once aptly described North Korean diplomacy as a "chain of aid-seeking stratagems."

11. For a detailed study of the "food diversion problem," see Stephan Haggard and Marcus Noland, *Famine in North Korea: Markets, Aid and Reform* (New York: Columbia University Press, 2007), 108–25.

12. Seen as the beginning of a long-awaited Chinese-style reform program, the 7.1 measures have been treated at great length by numerous scholars. For the best summary in English, see Young Chul Chung, "North Korean Reform and Opening: Dual Strategy and 'Silli (Practical) Socialism,'" *Pacific Affairs* vol. 77, iss. 2 (2004): 283–305. For Korean, see Kang Il-chon and Kong Son-yong, "7.1 kyongche kwanri kaeson chochi 1 nyonui pyongkawa chaehaesok" [The First Anniversary of the 7.1 Economy Management Improvement Measures: The Analysis and Appraisal], *Tongil munche yonku* vol. 15 (2003): 131–46.

13. See, respectively, *Wall Street Journal*, June 20, 2004; Victor Cha and Chris Hoffmeister, "North Korea's Drug Habit," *The New York Times*, June 3, 2004; Howard W. French, "North Korea Experiments, with China as Its Model," *The New York Times*, March 28, 2005.

14. Yim Kyong-hun, "Pukhansik kyongche kaehyok-e taehan pyongka-wa chonmang: 7.1 kyongche kwanri kaeson chochirul chungsim-uro" [The Appraisal and Prospects of an Economic Reform, North Korean Style; Centered around 7.1 Economy Management Improvement Measures], *Hankuk chongchi yonku* vol. 16 (2007): 290, 295–391.

15. Nam Song-uk, "Nongop punyaui kaehyok tanhaengkwa paekupche chaekae" [Execution of Reforms in Agriculture and Revival of the Rationing System], *Pukhan* iss. 12 (2005): 81.

16. Between May and June of 2005 rice at Hamhung market cost 950 won per kilo. See Kim Yong-chin, "Hampuk Musan chiyok ssalkaps sopok harak" [Rice Prices in Dramatic Decline in Musan and North Hamgyong], *Daily NK*, July 17, 2007.

17. Kim Yong-chin, "Paekŭp 700g taesangŭn motu chikchang chulkŭnhara" [Those Who Are Eligible for 700 g Rations Must Go to the Workplace], *Daily NK*, December 7, 2006.

18. The coming of this ban was reported in October when rumors began to spread. The ban went into effect on December 1, 2007. See *Onŭl-ŭi Pukhan sosik*, December 6, 2007, 2.

19. *Onŭl-ŭi Pukhan sosik*, March 12, 2008, 2–3.

20. *Onŭl-ŭi Pukhan sosik*, November 6, 2008, 1–2.

21. There is no comprehensive description of the 2009 currency reform in English. For the best available review of the events in Korea, see: Yang Mun-su, "Pukhan-ŭihwapyaekaeyŏk: Silt'aewa pyŏngga," *T'ongil munjaeyŏngu*, 22(1), 2010, 59–91.

22. "North Korea: 6 Million Are Hungry," *Reuters*, March 26, 2011; Charles Clover, "Catastrophe in North Korea; China must pressure Pyongyang to allow food aid to millions threatened by famine," *The Times*, March 22, 2010. 2; Blaine Harden, "At the Heart of North Korea's Troubles, an Intractable Hunger Crisis," *Washington Post*, March 6, 2009, A.1; Reuters, "Food Shortage Looms in North Korea," *International Herald Tribune*, April 17, 2008, 3.

23. 2009 *nyŏn pukhan kyŏngchesŏngchangryul ch'uchŏng kyŏlkwa* [Results from estimates of North Korea's 2009 growth rates] (Seoul: Hankuk ŭnhaeng, 2010), 1.

CHAPTER 4

1. Choe Sang-Hun, "Web Postings Stir Interest in Teenager's Relation to North Korean Leader," *The New York Times*, October 6, 2011.

2. The interview was widely reported in the media. For example, see: "Kim Jong Il's Son Talks Succession." *CNN World*, October 12, 2010.

3. As quoted by *Yonhap Agency Report*, January 28, 2011.

4. "Rodman: Kim Jong-un's island is the Ibiza of North Korea," *The Sun*, October 17, 2013.

5. Peter Ward, "'Money-masters' hold lifeline for North Korea," *Asia Times*, October 19, 2012, retrieved at http://www.atimes.com/atimes/Korea/NJ19Dg01.html.

6. Lim Chang-Won, "North Korea confirms end of war armistice," *AFP*, March 13, 2013.

7. Choe Sang-hun, "North Korea Cuts Off the Remaining Military Hot Lines with South Korea," *The New York Times*, March 28, 2013.

8. "North-South Relations Have Been Put at State of War: Special Statement of DPRK," *Korean Central News Agency*, March 30, 2013.

9. Ellen Barry, "Embassy Warning Joins Drumbeat of North Korea Threats," *The New York Times*, April 5, 2013.

10. "KAPPC Urges Foreigners in S. Korea to Take Measures for Evacuation," *Korean Central News Agency*, April 9, 2013.

11. Jeremi Suri, "Bomb North Korea, Before It's Too Late," *The New York Times*, April 12, 2013.

CHAPTER 5

1. Gregory Schulte, "Stopping Proliferation Before It Starts," *Foreign Affairs* (July/August 2010): 83.

2. On Syria–North Korea nuclear cooperation, see, for example: Gregory Schulte, *Uncovering Syria's Covert Reactor* (Washington, D.C.: Carnegie Endowment for International Peace, 2010).

3. For a description of South Korea's short-lived nuclear weapons program, see Don Oberdorfer, *The Two Koreas: A Contemporary History* (New York: Basic Books, 2001), 68–74.

4. Walter Clemens, "North Korea's Quest for Nuclear Weapons: New Historical Evidence," *Journal of East Asian Studies* vol. 10, iss. 1 (2010): 127.

5. The United States' near obsession with the nuclear program produced an impressive volume of literature dealing with the topic—dozens of books, hundreds of research papers. For a short and document-based introduction into the early history of the North Korean nuclear project, see a collection of articles edited by James Clay Moltz and Alexandre Y. Mansourov, *The North Korean Nuclear Program: Security, Strategy, and New Perspectives from Russia* (New York: Routledge, 2000). For more up-to-date information, a report by the Congressional Research Service might be of great help: Larry Niksch, *North Korea's Nuclear Weapons Development and Diplomacy* (Washington, D.C.: Congressional Research Service, 2010). For a short and highly professional review of the North Korean nuclear program, see an article by Siegfried Hecker, the former director of the Los Alamos Laboratories: Siegfried Hecker, "Lessons Learned from the North Korean Nuclear Crises," *Daedalus* 139 (2010): 44–56.

6. Korean Peninsula Energy Development Organization, *2005 Annual Report* (New York: KEDO, 2005), 13.

7. For a short but comprehensive review of KEDO's history, see Yoshinori Takeda, "KEDO Adrift," *Georgetown Journal of International Affairs*, vol. 6, iss. 2 (2005): 123–31. The article might be seen as an unintended obituary for the KEDO, which ceased operations soon after it was published.

8. Jeffrey Smith, "U.S. Accord with North Korea May Open Country to Change," *Washington Post*, October 23, 1994, A36. Expectations of imminent collapse were widely—albeit privately—shared with the journalists at the time. See, for example, Jim Hoagland, "The Trojan Horse at North Korea's Gate," *Washington Post*, August 2, 1995, A25.

9. The World Food Program INTERFAIS database. Available at www.wfp.org/fais.

10. For a detailed description of the monitoring regime, see Stephan Haggard and Marcus Noland, *Famine in North Korea: Markets, Aid and Reform* (New York: Columbia University Press, 2007), 92–102.

11. Siegfried Hecker, "Lessons Learned from the North Korean Nuclear Crises," *Daedalus* 139 (Winter 2010): 47.

12. The Kosis, the database of the National Statistics Office, is available at nso.go.kr.

13. *2010 T'ongil ŭisik chosa [2010 Survey of unification opinion]* (Seoul: Sŏultaehakkyo t'ongilp'yŏnghwayŏnkuso, 2010), 22–23.

14. Aidan Foster-Carter, "Towards the Korean Endgame," *The Observer*, December 1, 2002.

15. The World Food Program INTERFAIS database. Available at www.wfp.org/fais.

16. T'ongkyechŏng, *Pukhanŭi chuyot'ongkyechip'yoo [North Korea's main statistical indicators]* (Seoul: National Statistical Office, 2010), 35, 87.

17. Statistics for the Kŭmgang project can be found at "Kŭmkangsan kwankwang 10 chunyŏn kwanlyŏn charyo," *Pukhan kyŏngche ripyu* iss. 11 (2008): 78–95.

18. For the best available summary on the KIZ situation in English, see Dick Nanto and Mark Manyin, *The Kaesŏng North-South Korean Industrial Complex*. RL 34903 (Washington, D.C.: Congressional Research Service, 2011).

19. Hahm Chaibong, "South Korea's Miraculous Democracy," *Journal of Democracy* 19 (2008): 138.

20. Kando, known in Chinese as Jiandao, is an area located on the western bank of the Tuman River. The exact borders of the area are disputed, but more radical Korean nationalists include a large part of Manchuria in Kando.

21. Hangyore, September 4, 2004.

22. For a detailed treatment of the history of wars between China and the Koreas, see Terence Roehrig, "History as a Strategic Weapon: The Korean and Chinese Struggle over Koguryo," in *Korean Studies in the World: Democracy, Peace, Prosperity, and Culture*, ed. Seung Ham Yang, Yeon Sik Choi, and Jong Kun Choi (Seoul: Jimoondang, 2008); Peter Hays Gries, "The Koguryo Controversy, National Identity, and Sino-Korean Relations Today," *East Asia* vol. 22, iss. 4 (2005): 3–17; Andrei Lankov, "The Legacy of Long-Gone States: China, Korea and the Koguryo Wars," *Japan Focus*, September 2, 2006.

23. For 2010 data, see Chungang Ilbo, May 27, 2011; for other data, see Dick Nanto and Mark E. Manyin, *China-North Korea Relations* (Washington, D.C.: Congressional Research Service, 2010), 15. For 2011 data, see: *2011 nyŏnto Pukhan-ŭi taeoe kyŏngche silchŏk punsŏk-kwa 2012 nyŏnto chŏnmang [2011 North Korea's domestic and international economic performance and 2012 outlook]* (Seoul: Taeoe kyŏngche chŏngch'aek yŏnkuwŏn, 2012), 4.

24. "Trade between N. Korea, China hits record $6.45 bln in 2013," Yonhap New Agency, February 1, 2014.

25. For a detailed review of the current state of Chinese economic advances into North Korea, see Jaewoo Choo, "Mirroring North Korea's Growing Economic Dependence on China: Political Ramifications," *Asian Survey* 48 (2008): 343–72.

CHAPTER 6

1. Wade L. Huntley, "Sit Down and Talk," *Bulletin of the Atomic Scientists* 59 (2003): 28.

2. Wade L. Huntley, "Threats All the Way Down: U.S. Nuclear Initiatives in a Unipolar World," *Review of International Studies* 32 (2006): 49–67.

3. Lee Edwards, *Mediapolitik: How the Mass Media Have Transformed World Politics* (Washington, D.C.: Catholic University of America Press, 2001), 126.

4. InterMedia, *International Broadcasting in North Korea: North Korean Refugee/ Traveler Survey Report April–August 2009* (Washington, D.C.: InterMedia, 2009).

5. Peter Beck, "North Korea's Radio Waves of Resistance," *Wall Street Journal*, April 16, 2010.

CHAPTER 7

1. On the MMM scheme in Russia, see William Rosenberg, "The Democratic Experience in the Transitional Russia." In *Extending the Borders of Russian History: Essays in Honor of Alfred Rieber* (Budapest and New York: Central European University Press, 2003), 525–26. On the Albanian civil war of 1997, see Dirk

Bezemer (ed.), *On Eagle's Wings: The Albanian Economy in Transition* (New York: Nova Science, 2008), 22–24.

2. International Crisis Group, *Strangers at Home: North Koreans in the South Report N°208* (Brussels: International Crisis Group, 2011), 17.

3. Elisabeth Bumiller and David Sanger, "Gates Warns of North Korea Missile Threat to U.S.," *New York Times*, January 11, 2011.

4. Doug Waller, "The Second Time Around for Bob Gates," *Time*, December 4, 2006.

THE COSTS OF UNIFICATION (BOX)

1. "Korean Unification Will Cost Over US$3 Trln, Experts Say," *Asia Pulse*, September 14, 2010. Original report available at the website of the FKI, www.fki.or.kr.

2. "Think-Tank Estimates Unification Cost for Koreas at $2.14 tln," *Korea Herald*, February 27, 2011.

3. Kim Hee-jin, "Post-Kim Unification Cost Estimates Keep Rising," *Korea Joongang Daily*, January 12, 2012.

4. The report is not publicly available, but Credit Suisse funding was reported at the time. See, for example, "Peace Worries Some Korea Watchers More Than War," *China Post*, October 28, 2009.

5. Peter Beck, "Contemplating Korean Reunification," *Wall Street Journal*, January 4, 2010.